Batting 10th for the Yankees

Recollections of 30 Yankees You May Not Remember

Kenneth Hogan

authorHOUSE®

AuthorHouse™
1663 Liberty Drive
Bloomington, IN 47403
www.authorhouse.com
Phone: 1-800-839-8640

First published by AuthorHouse   7/30/2010

ISBN: 978-1-4490-7190-5 (e)
ISBN: 978-1-4490-7188-2 (sc)

Library of Congress Control Number: 2010910017

Printed in the United States of America
Bloomington, Indiana

This book is printed on acid-free paper.

I would like to take this opportunity to thank the thirty former players who agreed to be interviewed for this book. As a Yankee fan speaking to them was exciting but also made me a bit nervous. To a man they were kind and generous to me and I will never forget our conversations.

I would also like to thank my editor, Margaret Copeley for her extraordinary work and Francis Kaiven for his graphic design assistance.

*10% of the proceeds of this book will be donated to **Winning Beyond Winning.** This organization comprised of former major league baseball players and other concerned adults, promotes participation in sports and athletics in youths beyond merely winning a competition. They present programs to children in order to educate them about wellness and the dangers of drugs and alcohol.*

Contents

1980s

1990s

Foreword

The major league baseball season is the longest of any major sport—a total of 162 games, and if you are fortunate enough, as many as 19 more. From spring training to October, injuries and other situations will occur, inevitably necessitating players' absences. When your roster is set in spring training you must be prepared and have contingencies in place. It is an absolute certainty that some of the regulars will be lost for parts of the season—no team is injury free.

A team's success often falls upon its ability to overcome challenges. How well a team can adapt to short and long periods without its core players can determine how far that team can go. The ability of a manager to send in a bench player or a GM to recall capable AAA players is crucial to his organization's success. A team with a weak bench is one injury away from disaster. Depth is a team's strength. The manager of a team that has depth in reserve players can look down his bench and feel comfortable knowing that he has the flexibility to maneuver. These often little-known players allow a manager to give a regular a day off without putting his team at a big disadvantage.

A player who makes it to the majors for just a single game is nonetheless a major leaguer, and should be counted on to perform. The players in this book may not be household names, but they share a love for the game and the unique privilege of having worn the Yankee uniform.

Buck Showalter

Preface

I have been a die-hard Yankee fan since 1973. Not many followers of the Bronx Bombers can trace their roots back to that specific year, but I can. It was in the third grade when I was eight years old that I became fed up with the gloating, bragging, and Yankee bashing of Mets fans. The Mets had just won the National League pennant—barely. They went on to the World Series with the worst record (83–79) of any fall classic participant in history. I traded all of my Topps Mets baseball cards for Yankees. My schoolyard mates could not believe their good fortune. To this day I have a couple of hundred 1974 Yankee cards.

When I began researching this book I had no idea how much I would learn about the Yankees and their minor league system. In fact, I doubted that I, an unknown blue-collar worker, could even get enough former team members to speak with me to make this project work. The most amazing part of this two-year process was how helpful and generous these players were to me. There was nothing in it for them except one copy of a book from an unknown author. These guys were great and I will never forget how they treated me.

This book will show you just how incredibly hard it is to make it to the major leagues, much less the New York Yankees. You will see how many great and versatile athletes, how many gifted baseball players just don't make it in the big leagues. The players in this book realized their dream—albeit briefly or from the bench.

I hope you have as much fun reading this book as I had writing it.

Introduction

Ruth, Gehrig, Dickey, DiMaggio, Ford, Berra, Mantle, Maris, Howard, Murcer, Jackson, Guidry, Gossage, Munson, Mattingly, Winfield, Jeter, Rivera, Williams, Pettitte, Posada. The mention of these names means only one thing: Yankees. The pride, the tradition, the winning: 40 American League pennants and 27 World Championships. The New York Yankees are the most successful professional sports team in history, in any sport.

We know the stories of these legends and we know their histories. What true Yankee fan doesn't know Babe Ruth's 714, Roger Maris's 61, Ron Guidry's 25–3, and Mattingly's eight consecutive games with a home run? We have all watched Reggie smashing three home runs on three consecutive pitches in Game 6 of the 1977 World Series. And we have all viewed Maris being pushed out of the dugout after breaking the Babe's record, Berra leaping into the arms of Don Larson after his World Series perfect game, and Derek Jeter diving into the stands face first during a Red Sox game. These Yankee legends have many stories to tell; indeed they have been written many times, hundreds of times.

However, they did not go it alone. There have been 1,473 men who have worn pinstripes as of the conclusion of the 2008 season. They all have stories. Taken in the big picture, 1,473 is a miniscule number, well under 10% of all major league players. It is said that the chances of a high school or college baseball player making it to the major leagues is about 16,000 to 1. Multiply that by about 10 to be a New York Yankee and you see what you're up against. Every player who has worn a Yankee uniform has beaten the odds and made it to the top of baseball's Mount Everest. Even if you played just one game in the majors and wore the pinstripes on that day, no one will ever be able to take away from you the fact that you were a member of baseball's most elite family.

Kraly, Tepedino, Klimkowski, Buddie, Bladt, Kaufman, Tillotson, Wiesler, Burbach . . . These are their stories.

1940s

Photofest

RALPH HOUK
1947–54

You attended Lawrence High School in Kansas, where you were both a quarterback and linebacker along with discus thrower and track member. Were you a starter on their baseball team as well?

Well, we didn't play baseball in high school in Kansas at that time. I was in what was like Little League and I was a standout player.

Despite not having a team at your high school, the Yankees signed you as an amateur free agent as an 18-year-old. Had you wanted to be a professional baseball player?

Well I didn't even give that much thought in those days. When I signed of course I did, but up to that time I wasn't thinking about it. I wasn't a Yankees fan, I was a Kansas City Blues fan—which was a AAA club at that time—and a Cardinals fan.

Did they sign you as a catcher?

I think so, yes.

When you signed did you think that you had a chance of making it to the big leagues?

I never really gave that a thought.

Did the Yankees regard you as a big prospect?

[Laughs] Well, I don't know. Bill Essex signed me. He was one of the main scouts in the Midwest.

The Yankees assigned you to Neosho of the Arkansas-Missouri League your rookie season, when you hit .286. The following year they brought you up to the American Association at Joplin and you hit .313. After playing well for Augusta in 1941 your career was interrupted due to WWII. On February 22, 1942, you enlisted in the army and wound up a Ranger assigned to the Ninth Armored Division. You worked your way up to the rank of major and received a Silver Star, Bronze Star, and a Purple Heart. You were also listed as MIA for a short while. That must have been some experience.

Yeah, I had quite a few experiences during the war. I was captured for a little bit and got away. I was listed as missing in action just for a very few days. I jumped off of a truck that was carrying prisoners back and then managed to get back to my unit.

Did being an army major help you in any way to become a leader in major league baseball?

3

I don't think so, no. I actually became a major when I was discharged. Usually what they would do if you had no problems or anything like that, when they'd release you they would give you one more rank. Then my teammates started calling me "Major" and I sort of went with that name. It just stuck.

After returning from the war you reached the majors in 1947 as a 27-year-old rookie. How did it feel to finally put on pinstripes and be in Yankee Stadium?

Well, it was naturally a real thrill. But the funny part was that my first time I was with the Yankees was when they went to Cuba in spring training. I met Aaron Robinson, who was the first-string catcher then, at the hotel [in New York] and the next thing I know we're on our way to Cuba.

It's interesting that you bring his name up. 1947 was your rookie year in the majors, along with Yogi Berra. The Yanks had an All-Star catcher in '47 but Yankee fans today may be surprised that it was neither Berra nor Bill Dickey, but Aaron Robinson. Was he helpful to you and Yogi in any way?

No, no, back in those days the regulars didn't much go for the rookies. [Laughs]

In 1947 the Yankees also had another catcher who would go on to play for the White Sox and appear in seven All-Star games.

Sherm Lollar. Sherm was a good hitter and had good power.

The Yankees had some glut of catching talent then. Was this typical of the depth of the Yankee system?

They had a big farm system at that time, yes.

Another name Yankee fans may not be familiar with is that of your Hall of Fame manager in '47, Bucky Harris.

Yeah, I liked Bucky. The only thing I got a little perturbed about was he didn't play me in the World Series.

Obviously you went on to a long, successful career as a manager. Bucky Harris was different from Casey Stengel. Did you learn anything from these men?

I never really learned that much from managers that I played for. You have to manage in your own way. The one thing I did learn from Casey—the writers all liked Casey—was he told me,

"The one thing you ought to remember is, you know more than the writers do so you can lie to them and they won't know the difference." [Laughs] And that's a true story.

By the end of your first year you find yourself in a World Series against Brooklyn. You pinch-hit in Game 6 and single off Joe Hatten in your only at bat. The following day the Yankees won Game 7 and the Series. That's a great way to end your first season after waiting so long to get to the majors.

That was a powerful drive to left field . . . not really. [Laughs] it was a high hopper to third base and I beat it out. It really was unbelievable—I made more money then; my World Series check was bigger than my salary checks for the whole year.

Was Yogi Berra the heir apparent to take over the starting catcher's job, or was it still open for competition?

No, Yogi played right field part of that year. But you know, he was such a good hitter that he finally became the catcher. In fact, earlier that year I was probably rated a better catcher than Yogi. But not a better hitter. [Laughs]

Bill Dickey's final season as a catcher was 1946, just before you were brought up. As a coach on the team, did he help you as a catcher in any way?

No, not really. They all have their own way of catching and Dickey had a different way of throwing altogether than I did.

In 1948 the Yankee starting catcher was actually Gus Niarhos, before Berra took over in '49. There was actually a lot of change behind the plate for the Yankees for several years.

He was a good all-around catcher; he was pretty good. I liked Gus. He didn't hit like Yogi—well, nobody hit like Yogi.

You caught an amazing staff of pitchers on the Yanks. Did any one of them stand out as the best they had?

Well, Reynolds had the best fastball but they were all good pitchers. Rachi and Lopat.

Two pitchers on your staff agreed with you—Art Schallock and Bob Kuzava both said Reynolds was the best.

I hit my only home run off Schallock, by the way. That was before he came to us. I think it might have been an exhibition game back when we toured the West Coast and he was with California.[1]

During Yogi Berra's career he basically had three backup catchers: yourself, Charlie Silvera, and Elston Howard. You and Charlie worked the pitching staff together for many years. Did the two of you have things set up in any particular way? Was he the primary bullpen catcher and you the bullpen coach?

I think it just happened that way—we were just bullpen catchers and that's just the way it was. I think he's still in baseball, still a scout. Charlie was a real good catcher. Elston was a good catcher but also a real good hitter.

Tommy Byrne is an overlooked pitcher from the Yankees' great teams. I remember hearing that Casey Stengel was upset when they traded him to the Browns in '51 and pushed for the team to get him back, which they did in '54. How important was he? You never hear his name mentioned when people talk about the Yankees' glory days.

Well, he had real good stuff. He was a little wild, but he was a pretty good pitcher.

When Whitey Ford came up in 1950 could you tell that he was going to be something special?

It didn't take very long to see that. He had good control of all his pitches and he had all of them—a good fastball, a good changeup—and also he was a smart pitcher.

Jim Turner was the Yankees' pitching coach for decades. How valuable was "the Milkman," and did he help you transition into a bullpen coach?

He was probably the best pitching coach that they had. I think he helped me [become a coach]; I think so. I played for him at Beaumont in the Texas League, where he was the manager at AA.

During your last several years playing for the Yankees you served as the unofficial bullpen coach. Did management come to you and ask you to do that?

No, they didn't. There really isn't much to being a bullpen coach. You just get up and catch all the different pitchers when needed.

Did you see this as a way to become a coach or manager when your playing career was over?

---

1. The Hollywood Stars minor-league team.

No, I never gave that a thought at that time.

Do you think that you might have had a longer playing career or been a starter if you had been with a major league team other than the Yankees?

Well, I really don't know. There were several clubs that were following me with the Yankees. There were two or three clubs that would have signed me. One of the reasons that I was glad I stayed was those World Series checks looked pretty good. Word got back to the GM [Roy Hamey] and he came to me several times and told me, "Don't get any big ideas about leaving."

After your playing career ended the Yankees made you the manager of Denver, their AAA club. That's a pretty high-up job for a rookie manager. Did they tell you what their future plans were for you?

They came to me and told me that I was going to manage the AAA club at Kansas City. Lee MacPhail told me that. That's when Kansas City went to the big leagues and our AAA club moved out to Denver.

After a long career as a player, coach, manager, and GM of the Yankees, your final game in a Yankee uniform came on Sunday, September 30, 1973, which was the final game at the old Yankee Stadium.

It was a terrible day for me, no question. It was a very sad day. I wanted to get back and see the game at the stadium that last day [in 2008] but I haven't been feeling well enough.

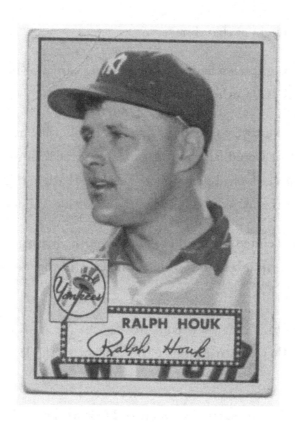

Topps

HOUK, RALPH GEORGE
Born: August 9, 1919 Lawrence, Kansas
Bats: Right Throws: Right
Height: 5' 11" Weight: 193 lbs.

Year	Team	G	AB	H	2B	3B	HR	AVG	RBI	R
1947	YANKEES	41	92	25	3	1	0	.272	12	7
1948	YANKEES	14	29	8	2	0	0	.276	3	3
1949	YANKEES	5	7	4	0	0	0	.571	1	0
1950	YANKEES	10	9	1	1	0	0	.111	1	0
1951	YANKEES	3	5	1	0	0	0	.200	1	0
1952	YANKEES	9	6	2	0	0	0	.333	0	0
1953	YANKEES	8	9	2	0	0	0	.222	1	2
1954	YANKEES	1	1	0	0	0	0	.000	0	0
	Total 8 Yrs	91	158	43	6	1	0	.272	20	12

Getty Images

JACK PHILLIPS
1947–49

During your playing career you had the unfortunate knack of playing behind some pretty good first basemen. When you were called up with the Yankees in 1947 George McQuinn was their regular first baseman, and he represented the team at the All-Star game that year.

Yes, it was my first time with the team except for '44 in spring training, just before I went into the service. Joe McCarthy was the manager and you couldn't go below the Mason-Dixon Line for spring training. Bear Mountain was the Dodgers and the Giants and we went to Atlantic City for spring training.

They sent me out because of the first basemen. [Tommy] Henrich moved into first base in '48 and then Joe Collins took over for me the following year in '49. And then Mantle came along—his first year was '50, I believe.

I just wanted to be on the Yankee ball club and I felt like I could play there, but evidently George Weiss had some other ideas. In fact, Joe Trimble—I don't know if that name strikes you or not; he wrote about the Yankees in a little short New York paper, I forget which one, the *Mirror* or the *News*—he said that if the Yankees don't win it in '48 it's because they sent me out to Kansas City [AAA]. I told George Weiss I'd go but not until he gave me the money he'd promised me for playing shortstop in Kansas City [AAA]. The Yankees had 13 farm clubs back then. I wound up playing shortstop there with Cliff Mapes in left field and Hank Bauer in right field, Dick Haas at first base, Ralph Houk catching. We also had Eli Culberson of the '46 Red Sox as our center fielder. Dick Bartell was our manager and that was the ball club that we had. We finished 23 ½ *out* of first place with that ball club! [Laughs]

Wow, that doesn't seem to make sense.

[Laughs] It sure doesn't, does it? We were out by July 3. We were in third place by one game.

I was traded from the Yankees [to the Pirates] in August of '49, when I was hitting .308! There's a book, *The Summer of '49*, and I'm not even in it; the only place I'm mentioned is in the statistics. The year before in 1948 it was Casey Stengel's first season with the Yankees and he went full boat into the platoon system with Johnny Lindel and Gene Woodling.

What was it like to finally be called up to the New York Yankees in 1947?

Well, my manager was Bucky Harris, the Wonder Boy. He had come from Washington. When they sent me to Newark after spring training in '47 he called me in his office and said, "Don't worry, you'll be back, Jack." They recalled me in September of that year and put me on the World Series roster.

In 1951 the Pirates moved Ralph Kiner from the outfield to first base, his only season not in the outfield. Why did they do that?

That's right, I taught him how to play first base. Branch Rickey had just come over to the club from Brooklyn. Rickey came over with his son Twig and the entire scouting staff. He thought by moving he'd get more home runs. He did a lot of things: he moved Dick Hall from outfield to pitching, he hired the O'Brien twins from Seattle to play too, but that's why you heard the "Shot heard 'round the world,"[2] because of our club. We went in there and beat the Dodgers two games late.

 Then Dale Long came along and played first base too. He came out of the Yankee chain. We had originally played together in 1953 in Hollywood in the PCL.[3] He hit those eight straight home runs[4] in 1956. That's how I wound up back in the minors; they sent me down to Hollywood. In 1952 I only had one at bat with the Pirates and it was a pinch-hit appearance against the longest tenured left-handed pitcher in baseball, Warren Spahn. I wound up playing shortstop mostly and the outfield occasionally for[Hollywood]. I actually didn't play that much first base there. That's how I wound up winning the MVP of the Pacific Coast League in '54 for the Hollywood Stars. Bobby Bragan was our manager and he wound up with the Pirates as their manager.

The Pacific Coast League was actually considered by many to be a major league at that time [1940s and '50s].

Well, it was. That's when Rickey made his move with the Dodgers to Los Angeles, and so did the Giants. Now that old Pacific Coast League was littered with young guys and older guys who had left the majors. Some of those younger guys were tied up there for a year or two because they were that important to the ball club. Most of them didn't want to go to the big leagues, except the younger guys. The older guys retired to the West Coast and just wanted to play out there. Hollywood and Los Angeles were side by side and had a big rivalry. O'Malley[5] took the center of the Pacific Coast League and he convinced Stoneham[6] to bring the Giants and they affected Portland and Seattle up there at the northern end. The Los Angeles Angels and San Francisco Seals were gone. Next thing you know Seattle is in the big leagues, and San Diego, which was down at the southern end with Sacramento. He destroyed the Coast League.

You had some nice old stadiums in the PCL.

---

2. Bobby Thomson's October 3, 1951, home run in the bottom of the 9th inning against Ralph Branca in the final game of the National League playoffs to win it for the New York Giants over the Brooklyn Dodgers.
3. Pacific Coast League
4. Eight consecutive games with a home run.
5. Walter O'Malley, owner of the Brooklyn/Los Angeles Dodgers.
6. New York Giants owner Horace Stoneham.

Yeah, Wrigley Field in Los Angeles and Gilmore in Hollywood were nice ballparks. You see, back then they built the ballparks according to Sportsman's Park in St. Louis. They built these minor league parks in the cities. They had a measurement of short distances; the field was right there.

Were you disappointed when the Pirates sent you out there in 1952?

Oh, I definitely was, because I had just come off the injured list.

After a great run in the PCL you were brought back to the American League with the Tigers in 1955 & 1956. Why did they let you go shortly into the '57 season?

Same thing, because they had had Greenberg[7] over there. All of these ball clubs now wanted a home-run hitter at first base. They wanted first basemen in the big leagues that were hitting 15–20 home runs.[8] The Tigers sent me to Boston in '57, but they sent me out to AAA, which was the San Francisco Seals. We won the pennant there. Then I stayed at AAA in Buffalo and retired after the 1959 season. It was just eighteen miles from my hometown where I finished up. I hit a grand-slam home run against Toronto, who we beat out of the pennant that year, and then two days later I was out in the bullpen as a pitcher. Big Luke Easter was there—you ran into all these guys that were being sent in and out.

The Yankees signed you as an amateur free agent in 1943. You were 22 years old already. That's older than most young ballplayers being signed back then.

In 1941 I signed an option that I would sign with the Yankees when I graduated from Clarkson College. The Cardinals had signed Joe Garagiola in '43, who had played with Yogi as a kid. The Yankees signed Yogi because he wanted as much money as Garagiola, and that's how come he didn't sign with the Cardinals.[9]

After the Yankees signed you did you play in the minors before you went into the service?

Yeah, '43 was my senior year at Clarkson. I had just enough time to go to spring training with the Yankees in Atlantic City in '44. Nobody went south because of the gas rationing. All of the colored teams like the Kansas City Monarchs and the Philadelphia team were barnstorming to keep their money up and the great white team that you had to have a beard to play on—the House of David[10]—were out

7. Hall of Fame first baseman Hank Greenberg.
8. Earl Torgeson was the Tigers' primary first baseman in 1956 and '57. Both he and Phillips were let go early in the 1957 season with the emergence of Ray Boone at first base.
9. Yogi Berra and Joe Garagiola were both from St. Louis.
10. The House of David was a religious commune founded in Michigan in 1903 that believed Jesus would return in the year 2000. Members were required to wear long hair and beards. The group's founder, Benjamin Purcell, was fond of baseball. He started a team in 1913 and turned it into a barnstorming team to raise money for the commune and preach to crowds across the country. Eventually the team began hiring professional players, including Satchel Paige, and competed against teams from the major and minor leagues. They played through 1955.

there too. They were out of Detroit. They were the original House of David and they traveled with their own lights.

But I went into the navy in April of 1944. I played *one* game at Newark! They opened ahead of the New York Yankees. I played one game at Newark and went right up to Sampson [New York] and went into the navy the first day after having been with the Yankees in spring training.

I wound up over in Japan in Sasebo, which was supposed to be the first place where the atom bomb was to have been dropped. It was overcast, though, and they went right on through and hit Nagasaki. After I landed in Nagasaki they put us in a camp that had been an internment camp. I was an enlisted man but they wanted me to be an officer if I could have passed the physical—I had been hurt. Maybe they would have sent me to Colgate or Cornell, where they had the officer program where they came out lieutenants. Yogi went into the navy about the same time as I did and went through quite a bit. He was on the barges taking the men in and out of Normandy, and he said he thought it was like the Fourth of July.

After you came back from World War II you made it up to the majors with the Yankees at the end of 1947 and you played in the World Series. That must have been some experience.

I got out of the navy in '46 and was discharged at Needle Beach, Long Island, and went right across to Yankee Stadium and saw Bob Feller pitch a no-hit, no-run game against Bill Bevens, who did the same thing against the Dodgers in the '47 Series. He lost his ball game and the no-hitter, but it was a one-runner.

It was a tremendous experience. I got my World Series ring the following year [1948]. The only thing I have that might have been greater than that was when I hit the ultimate grand-slam home run for Pittsburgh. That was only the third ultimate home run hit in the entire history of baseball. The first time I came up in the Series was as a pinch-hitter in the third game and I flied out to left field in Brooklyn. The second time I grounded out.

One thing about the Yankees is Joe DiMaggio—he's the greatest baseball player I ever saw. I sat in the background a little after I just came up but Frankie Shea and I were always pulling something or other. Joe Collins and I played together in 1947 in Newark before I came up. He was a good first baseman but he'd been in the Yankee chain two or three years longer than I. First base was the only position he could play so they kept him. I played third base too. Yogi and I played together in Norfolk in '43 and Bobby Brown was the shortstop in Newark, when I played third, so these were guys I knew also. Rizzuto was a character too. I played shortstop behind him. Phil would stand behind me and run through my legs to field ground balls in practice. Bill Dickey used to be the infield hitter, and that's what Rizzuto used to do.

You mentioned the famous home run you hit with the Pirates. That was July 8, 1950.

Yes it was, that was the ultimate grad-slam home run I hit. That was in the ninth inning, when we beat St. Louis 7–6. An ultimate home run is a game-ending, grand-slam home run in which you win the game by one run. You had to be behind by three. Mine was the third one of only 16 that were hit.[11] The pitcher was Harry Brecheen. He was a hell of a pitcher. That's what made it so good! [Laughs] The *New York Times* wrote it up and that's how it got so much notoriety. The last one to hit one was Giambi in the 14th inning.[12]

Did you like playing at Forbes Field?

Forbes Field is a nice big ballpark. I liked Yankee Stadium too. It was a big ballpark, a nice ballpark to hit in. My long balls were to center field and right center, and I was a right-handed hitter. Similar to the shortstop, Jeter: he hits a lot of home runs to right field.

You grew up in Marilla, New York, and stayed there your entire life.

Yes, yes. I was born in 1921 in Clarence and we moved to Marilla in 1923. It was a town of four square miles and 356 people! I went to Lancaster High School. There were three buses that left Marilla each day for different high schools and I chose Lancaster.

My father ran a boys' team in Marilla, New York, and my uncle pitched, but he was a little hardheaded and he hit an umpire in a ball game, and that barred him from going into the big leagues or minor league ball. He's the one that helped me an awful lot.

After I retired I coached at Clarkson College. It's now Clarkson University after they got the disciplines to issue doctorates and master's degrees. Hockey and baseball were the big sports up there. I coached all together 34 years up here. We only had two baseball coaches in 60-something years! I coached golf and cross-country too.

I'm holding on now. [Laughs]. They're going to name the ballpark after me up here at Clarkson, sometime in May [2008]. I watch the program *YES*—I don't know if you know it or watch it. They have a show called *Yankeeography* and they go through all the stars that they've retired and things like that. They just had Jackie Robinson and Larry Doby—he came in three months after Robinson. They also had the third baseman Alex Rodriguez—he's some ballplayer!

They just resigned him for ten years—not too bad.

Yeah. [Laughs] I was lucky to get a half a year contract.

11. As of this writing there have now been 23 ultimate home runs.
12. May 17, 2002 against the Minnesota Twins. The Yankees won 13–12.

Brace Photo

PHILLIPS, JACK DORN
Born: September 6, 1921 Clarence, New York
Bats: Right Throws: Right
Height: 6' 4" Weight: 193

Year	Team	G	AB	H	2B	3B	HR	AVG	RBI	R
1947	YANKEES	16	36	10	0	1	1	.278	2	5
1948	YANKEES	1	2	0	0	0	0	.000	0	0
1949	YANKEES	45	91	28	4	1	1	.308	10	16
1949	Pirates	18	56	13	3	1	0	.232	3	6
1950	Pirates	69	208	61	7	6	5	.293	34	25
1951	Pirates	70	156	37	7	3	0	.237	12	12
1952	Pirates	1	1	0	0	0	0	.000	0	0
1955	Tigers	55	117	37	8	2	1	.316	20	15
1956	Tigers	67	224	66	13	2	1	.295	20	31
1957	Tigers	1	1	0	0	0	0	.000	0	0
	Total 9 Years	343	892	252	42	16	9	.283	101	111

Photofest

CHARLIE SILVERA
1948–56

You grew up in San Francisco when baseball was at its pinnacle of popularity. Were you a Seals fan?[13]

Oh yeah, I lived eight blocks from the ballpark. I saw them quite a bit. They let us in and we'd drag the infield, take the batting cage away. Before the game we'd go over the fence and wait for balls to be hit during practice and get the balls and use them. If we got a good one we'd use it for our game ball on Sunday. They didn't pay us. We were all 14, 15, 16 years old and playing semipro ball.

The San Francisco area turned out many Yankee players and other major league players during the '30s, '40s, and '50s. Was that a way of life for boys and young men at that time in the Bay area, constantly playing ball?

Well, you've got to go back to Ping Bodie,[14] number one, then Lazarri, Crosetti, DiMaggio. We always played. There were always semipro games. There were four games on each diamond. There was a nine o'clock, eleven, one, and three and it was full, and you played constantly. They had a night league, [American] Legion ball, there was a Saturday league, and of course high school. The owner of the Seals, Mr. Charlie Graham, let us use his field so we were playing all the time.

You played for St. Ignatius High School. Were you considered a standout player?

Yeah, I guess so. I led the league in hitting my senior year at .640. We only played eight games, though. Jerry Coleman and Bobby Brown and I are all going to be 84 years old this year. We played in the high school league against each other, but we played for a semipro team on Sundays, the Kenneally Yanks. We had Yankee uniforms and we played together on that team.

Were you always a catcher?

Primarily, yes. I played shortstop in high school when we didn't have a shortstop.

You were signed by the famous Yankee scout Joe Devine as an amateur free agent at 17 in 1942 for $2500.[15] How influential was Joe Devine to your development as a player?

13. San Francisco Seals, Pacific Coast League.
14. Center fielder Frank Bodie.
15. Devine signed Yankees Joe Coleman, Gil McDougald, Bobby Brown, and Gene Woodling. He also told the Yankees that the high price the Seals were asking for Joe DiMaggio was well worth it.

He's the one who signed us all—Coleman, Brown, and myself. He was outstanding, number one. He was the right-hand man to George Weiss, who started out as the scouting director and then became the general manager. He relied a lot on Joe Devine. Devine ended up with Gil McDougald, who's from here, Billy Martin, Jackie Jensen, Andy Carey, who's from Alameda, Gus Triandos, Lew Barbarette, Bill Renna, and Duane Pilette.

I had read somewhere that your parents would send you to 7:00 a.m. mass and then you'd go off and play ball.

Oh yeah, that was it. Generally when we started we had a 9:00 a.m. game because the young kids would play the first game, and many a time we'd hang around and try to catch on with another team—maybe they didn't have enough players so you'd play at another position.

Your first season was at Wellsville, New York, class D of the PONY League, and you had hand-me-down uniforms from the big club.

I wore Gehrig's traveling pants, and Crosetti's upper home uniform, and Red Rolfe's and I think Charlie Keller—they were all hand-me-downs. Gehrig's pants now would probably get you a few hundred thousand! [Laughs] But you never thought of taking something like that home. With the Yankees we always took our uniform home with us because you would play exhibition games here, like the Elks game in Alameda, every year and then we would go to Stockton and we'd play two or three after the season. But we had to put a hundred dollars up, and when you brought your uniform back you got your hundred dollars back. I never got a Yankees uniform or a jacket.

After just one season in the minors you joined the Army Air Force in April of 1943. Where did you wind up?

Jerry Coleman and I broke into ball together in Wellsville, New York, but that was it, two and a half months of D ball. Jerry had talked about being a marine flyer and asked me if I would come along. I said, "I don't know," because flying really didn't appeal to me then. So I went into the Air Corps.[16] During that war most air force bases had baseball and football and basketball teams, depending on the size, and I ended up in McClellan Field in Sacramento. Eventually we went overseas and [Red] Ruffing and Joe Gordon and DiMaggio joined us, so we had a pretty good baseball team. We went to Hawaii first with the Seventh Air Force and we went to Saipan and we played games in Iwo Jima and Kwajalein. I was fortunate to more or less have my low minor league experiences during the war.

---

16. Enlisted Air Corps members were overwhelmingly ground personnel.

I got to play with DiMaggio. I'm 19 years old and here he is my idol. He's playing center field and I'm catching.

After the war you came back and progressed rapidly through the Yankee system, eventually hitting .301 at AAA Portland in 1948. Late in that season you got called up. What was it like putting on a Yankee uniform and walking out onto the field at Yankee Stadium?

Well, I had gotten called up in '47. You see, in those days they kept about three or four extra pitchers and a catcher to pitch batting practice. Your roster could be 30 in those days. So they kept me around to catch batting practice and I never got an at bat. After the first two weeks of the season they took me on the road with them back East, and then when they went out to St. Louis I caught a plane and joined the Portland club in San Francisco. In fact, the first day I went to Yankee Stadium in '47 I never went into the locker room—I went right into the dugout to look at Yankee Stadium and it was like the Eighth Wonder of the World to me.

Bill Dickey retired as a player after the 1946 season.

Yeah, but he came back in '49 as a coach when Stengel took over the team.

The Yankees also had an All-Star catcher in '47, Aaron Robinson.

That's right. They also had another one in '48 and I wound up with his number—Sherman Lollar. They recalled me and Sherman Lollar was on the bench. I got his number the next year when he went to the Browns.

The Yankees may have had the best group of catching talent ever back in the late '40s.

[Laughs] We were Yogi rejects. I mean, not really rejects, but players who didn't play with the Yankees but were owned by the Yankees at one time or played a little for the Yankees at one time. Just like the Dodgers at shortstop, the Yankees had catchers.

When you came up it was at a time when veteran players really didn't embrace rookies.

Oh, yes they did; they did on the Yankees. They had guys that were great. You see, I went to spring training with the Yankees in '46 and during the war I played with DiMaggio and Joe Gordon and Red Ruffing. Here I was after the war with just two and a half months of D ball, and I got to go to spring training with Joe McCarthy, who was my first manager. So I was no stranger and [my war teammates] told the Yankees that I had some ability, so they took me to spring training.

You knew your idol Joe DiMaggio from the war. He had a reputation of being standoffish. Did you get to know him at all, or did he embrace you as a fellow San Franciscan?

He was a bit of a loner but if he knew you he was good to you. He was always good to me and my wife Rose. When they had the fiftieth anniversary of being a Yankee he invited us back and we were part of his entourage, so to speak. He treated me very well— he'd get me tickets to plays on Broadway. Joe and I were very good friends and we played a lot of golf out here [in San Francisco].

Hank Bauer's wife and my wife were having babies [at the same time]. Billy Martin's first year was 1950, and we were roommates up at the Concourse Plaza. We would stay after the game together along with DiMaggio, who would stay and have a beer and talk for sometimes maybe two hours, and we'd go across the street to Goldman's Restaurant and have dinner. Sometimes Joe would invite us down to Toots Shor's Restaurant and we would have dinner with him there. Yeah, Joe was great to us. He loved to talk baseball.

You know, Joe couldn't go anyplace. You could put Joe in a field with 50,000 people and they'd say, "There's Joe!" He stood out. He was a little standoffish because he had no peace; he couldn't go anyplace in New York. He had to eat in his hotel room and Billy would more or less stay with him, because he liked Billy. People would just mob him. But he was great to me and great to his teammates. He would come down once in a while I was sneaking a smoke in back of the dugout and he'd say, "Hey Charlie, get those guys going, pump 'em up a little bit." I'd say, "OK, Joe." He was a leader but he didn't go around with a C on his jersey.

You mentioned the Concourse Plaza Hotel. That was on the Grand Concourse in the Bronx.

Yeah, right up River Avenue up to the top on the Grand Concourse. I went by there two weeks ago after the Old-Timers' Game and things have changed a bit around there. It's a little sloppy, shall we say. When I came up everybody who was on the bubble stayed there until you made the club, and then you could look for an apartment.

Jim Turner was the Yankees' pitching coach for decades. How helpful was he to you as a catcher and trying to learn the staff?

He was also my manager at Portland. I learned baseball from a catching standpoint from Dickey, and from Turner from a pitching standpoint. Jim Turner was very instrumental in my making it to the major leagues because during batting practice—he's a former pitcher—he wouldn't let me hit the fastball. He'd throw me breaking balls and told me to go to right field with it. That's how I went from .247 to .301 in one year in the same league, against the same pitchers. So he had a great impact on me.

You caught one of the most impressive pitching staffs in major league history. Does any one of those pitchers stand out in your opinion as the best?

Well, there was Whitey Ford, who came up in '50 and then went into the service. Then there was Raschi, Reynolds, and Lopat—that was the three that were there for the five consecutive pennants. I always said that they should all go into the Hall of Fame as a single entry, the three of them together. Allie Reynolds would start and relieve. He was like a Smoltz but he was either a starter or a reliever. Allie did both [at the same time]. Vic [Raschi] and Ed [Lopat] didn't relieve except in the World Series—every pitcher is on call during the World Series.

In fact, I warmed up Larson before his perfect game in Game 5 [of the 1956 World Series] and then I warmed up Whitey Ford during the last two innings. We had to win that, and then we won the Series the next day.

When you were warming Larson up prior to that game, could you tell anything was different?

No, he warmed up the same. He was very lackadaisical. Larson had great control, but he went out there and he never shook Yogi off. He went to three balls on only one hitter, Pee Wee Reese. But he had good control and enough stuff. Well, that was one game—what are you going to say? Perfect.

Most major leaguers never get to play in a World Series, and you were in seven in ten years.

Yeah, caught one game!

Do you think that you would have had a longer playing career or been a starter with another organization?

No, because I never hit any home runs. The Yankees never traded anybody to a first-division ball club in the American League, ever, with one exception: they let Charlie Keller go over to Detroit because Charlie's career was at an end. Tommy Byrne went over to the Browns and they brought him back later on. Once you left they never brought you back. But those were the two exceptions, Keller and Byrne.

I would never have survived with somebody else. I was making too much money to go to a second-division club, and I wouldn't have survived because I didn't hit home runs. I was the perfect backup guy.

You hit one home run: July 4, 1951.

Off Fred Sanford on July 4 at Yankee Stadium. I got the ball, I got the picture. Gene Woodling is on deck and I'm saying to him, "Hey, Gene, go get that ball." I went in and got a new ball and he went and took it and got it from the guy. In fact I got on it, "First Home Run," and then I put a little note on it: "Onlyest Home Run"!

You mentioned Tommy Byrne. He was on the Yankees for many of their championship seasons, and yet he seems to have been forgotten today. After trading him away the team got him back three years later.

Tommy was a little wild but a great competitor, a great arm. He'd make twice as many pitches as some of these guys today and he'd still be out there throwing. He went from the Yanks to the Browns, and then to the White Sox and then to Seattle of the [Pacific] Coast League. He learned how to pitch and then came back. I was his designated catcher, with all his pitches in the dirt. They didn't want Yogi to get hurt so I caught him quite a bit.

The Yankees were the only team to win five consecutive championships, and only eight players were there for all five. Those teams were so good and had so much talent. Did you think that after the fifth World Series Championship that it was just going to keep going?

Yeah, I think so. When you think about the best year we ever had, in '54, it was the only time Casey Stengel ever won a hundred games and we got beaten by eight. Cleveland won 111 and we won 103. And then we won the next two in '55 and '56. But there were only eight guys who were there for every inning of every game those five years: Raschi, Reynolds, Coleman, Woodling, Bauer, Rizzuto, Yogi, and myself. Now there's only four of us left: Yogi, Gerry [Coleman], Bobby [Brown],[17] and myself. That will never be done again because you have to win two series before you get into the World Series. No way.

Most fans assume that players automatically received World Series rings going back to the early part of the century, but you actually got a World Series cigarette case one year.

---

17. Brown was on the roster but missed the entire 1953 season while serving in the military during the Korean War.

That's correct. That was in 1953. You could choose what you wanted and I chose that. My wife got mad at me over that because that was the fifth straight World Series win and she said, "Why didn't you get a ring?" and she still does to this day. I said, "Look, the only game that I caught was in '49 and that ring means more to me than the '53 one." So I got the silver cigarette case, and I got a belt buckle for '55, when we lost to Brooklyn. The other ones I got a ring for my mother and father and for my daughters. I'm with the Cubs now, you know.[18] We are hopefully going to go to the World Series— wouldn't that be something? I have one more ring, too, from the Florida Marlins, when I was a scout for them in '97.

You received a standing ovation just once in your career.

I got hit in the groin from a foul ball from Dom DiMaggio. They packed me off the field and that's when they gave me the ovation! I was hurtin'. That was up in Boston.

After nine seasons in New York the Yankees sent you to the Cubs on December 11, 1956. How did you feel when they told you about the trade?

The Yankees didn't tell me about it, I read it in the newspaper. My second daughter was being born and it was the last day of the winter meetings. A guy I knew who ran one of those Coney Island shops down on 42nd Street that sold trinkets and watches called me up and said that I had just been traded to the Cubs. I said, "What are you talking about?" He told me that it was in the afternoon papers, and it was. The Yankees didn't even have the courtesy to call me or have somebody call me—and I grew up with the Yankees. That really shook me.

Anyway, I went to the Cubs and I was doing alright. I was starting to play and on Memorial Day in Milwaukee I sprained my ankle going back to first base when the pitcher tried to bunt. I jammed my ankle against the base and that was it. The doctor said I would have been better off if I had broken it because we could have reset it. But I had lost my skills because I hadn't played in so long.

Did you continue to play after that?

In 1958 I came back to the Yankees and was a player-manager at New Orleans, and then I was a player-manager at Binghamton in '59 and after that I was let go. In 1960 I went to Salt Lake City as a player-coach because the GM and part owner of that club was Eddie Leesman, who played on the Kenneally Yankees with me as a kid in high school.

---

18. As a scout.

Is it true that Billy Martin and you agreed to hire each other if either of you got managing jobs in the PCL?

That's right. He was from Oakland and I was from San Francisco. We were rooming together in '50 and we made a pact that if I ever got the Seals he'd be my coach and if he ever got the Oaks, I'd be his coach. He ended up in the major leagues and by God, from 1950 when we roomed together until 1969 when he got the job managing Minnesota, I got the call. I worked for him with the Tigers [1971–73] and the Rangers [1973–75].

Was 1975 your last year in uniform on the field?

Yeah, with the Rangers. Then I went to scouting with Atlanta, where Eddie Mathews was the GM.

You've mentioned that you've gotten back to Yankee Stadium.

Oh yeah, I've been back to about ten Old-Timers' games, including this last one [2008].

You know, I want to mention one fellow—Gary Hughes. He's with the Cubs as an assistant to the general manager, and I also worked for him with the Marlins. He's been instrumental in my staying in baseball. Like a lot of people, when you get old they get rid of you because they have to pay your Social Security. This has kept me in the game. I'm only eight miles from the ballpark here in San Francisco, and it keeps me going. He's one of the scouts that has kept a lot of the older guys working.

TOPPS

SILVERA, CHARLES ANTHONY RYAN
Born: October 13, 1924 San Francisco, California
Bats: Right Throws: Right
Height: 5' 10" Weight: 175

Year	Team	G	AB	H	2B	3B	HR	AVG	RBI	R
1948	YANKEES	4	14	8	0	1	0	.571	1	1
1949	YANKEES	58	130	41	2	0	0	.315	13	8
1950	YANKEES	18	25	4	0	0	0	.160	1	2
1951	YANKEES	18	51	14	3	0	1	.275	7	5
1952	YANKEES	20	55	18	3	0	0	.327	11	4
1953	YANKEES	42	82	23	3	1	0	.280	12	11
1954	YANKEES	20	37	10	1	0	0	.270	4	1
1955	YANKEES	14	26	5	0	0	0	.192	1	1
1956	YANKEES	7	9	2	0	0	0	.222	0	0
1957	Cubs	26	53	11	3	0	0	.208	2	1
	Total 10 Years	227	482	136	15	2	1	.282	52	34

1950s

Photofest

Bob Kuzava
1951–54

You were born Wyandotte, Michigan, and still live there.

Named after an Indian chief. I was born here and I'm still here.

You were probably not a Yankee fan then?

We lived just outside of Detroit and I was a great fan of the Detroit Tigers. Tiger Stadium was called Navin Field and we used to go to the bleachers for 55 cents. It's where I saw my first major league game.

You were signed by the Indians at 18 as an amateur free agent.

Well, they didn't have free agents then and you weren't drafted. If they thought you looked pretty good some scout would ask you if you wanted to play baseball professionally. I was playing American Legion baseball and a scout asked me if I wanted to play baseball. I said yes and I went away and played in D ball for $65 a month and I was still in high school.

You must have been pretty good already. Were you always a pitcher?

Yeah, I was pretty good at that age. But when you're a kid you do everything. I played first and pitched, but I started pitching seriously in high school. In 1941 I went to Mansfield, Ohio, for D ball. I think it was called the Ohio State League.

The following year in 1942 at Charleston you were 21–6 with a 1.72 ERA.

I had a great year and then everybody got drafted. They let you graduate from high school, but once you graduated you were fair game for the military. The war was going on and I came home and got drafted into the army. I was in the military police in the Burma-China theater. I was also in India but never got to China.

The army discharged you in January of 1946 and you actually made it up to the Indians for two games by the end of September. You must have been happy with that.

Oh, yeah. You were always happy to go up to the big leagues, because that's what you set out to do. They had to call you up in those days because a major league team had three options on you, and after the third option you could go to another club.

September 21, 1946, was your major league debut for the Indians in Cleveland. You played that game at League Park, which just so happened to be the final game at that ballpark, which was built in 1891. Do you remember that game or anything about League Park?

At that time they played all their weekend games at Municipal Stadium, which was a football stadium, but their day games in League Park. I don't think they played night games there. Certainly I was nervous. Even when you're a veteran in the big leagues and you're in Yankee Stadium or wherever, if you're not nervous there's something wrong with you.

The following year in '47 you played in four games for Cleveland, including a shutout, but then you spent '48 in the minors before being traded to the White Sox.

What happened was, I was in AAA Baltimore and I didn't think I would ever get back to the Indians because they had pretty good older starting pitchers. So I asked Bill Veeck if he had a chance to trade me I'd appreciate it, and he did during the wintertime and I went over to the White Sox. I knew Bill real well. He was very friendly with all the players. When I retired I managed for him in Charleston, South Carolina, in 1960 and he got me a scouting job. He was a great guy. He was in the Marine Corps and I think he lost a leg.

The White Sox trade you to the Senators, who then trade you to the Yankees on June, 15, 1951. How did you feel about becoming a Yankee?

Well, you know, you're going to laugh, but when they traded me I was on crutches. I had been spiked a couple of weeks earlier by Nellie Fox of the White Sox. I got a compound sprain and they cut my Achilles tendon. So I'm going to the ballpark with my wife to get my check on the 15th of June and I'm on crutches. Mr. Griffith[19] called me up into the office and he said, "We traded you to the Yankees for three pitchers and a hundred thousand dollars." I said, "You gotta be kidding me. You traded me and I'm on crutches?" He told me to call Mr. Weiss so I called George Weiss[20] and I said, "My wife is pregnant and I am taking her home to Wyandotte and I'll join the ball club when I get her settled." This was a Friday and he said to me, "Well, no. Come over here and pitch the second game Sunday. We have a doubleheader." I said, "I can't pitch." He says, "What do you mean, you can't pitch?" I told him, "I'm on crutches!" He didn't know it; the organization didn't know it. [Laughs] So he told me, "I didn't know that! Take your wife home and get here when you can." Do you believe that? It's the truth. They traded Bob Porterfield, Freddie Sanford, and Tom Ferrick for me and a hundred grand, and I couldn't pitch. I was sure the deal wouldn't be consummated, but it was.

I got over there about a week later. I had never relieved in my life. I was always a starter. So the pitching coach told me, "Go in the outfield and strengthen your legs and pitch some batting practice, and when you're ready we'll build up your arm."

19..Senators owner Calvin Griffith.
20. Yankee General Manager.

That's how that happened. I couldn't even run fast at that point.

The pitching coach was Jim Turner when you arrived, I believe? He was still there in the '70s.

Yeah, Jim Turner. When he died he was about 90-something years old. He was there with [Frank] Crosetti for years.

The Yankees were your fourth AL team that you played for. Was there anything that set them apart from the other organizations in the American League?

Well, we had good players and the Yankees used to trade a lot for pitchers. Allie Reynolds and I came from Cleveland, and so did Gene Woodling. Cliff Mapes came from Cleveland too. We had about four or five guys that came from the Cleveland organization. The Yankees would trade if they needed a certain pitcher. I used to work against the Yankees a lot, and their hitters probably liked what they saw and said if they get a chance to trade for a guy, get him. That's the best benchmark in the world, having hitters like the type of stuff you got and they recommend that you should be in a trade.

You made it to the World Series your first year with the Yankees in '51. The Yankees won in six games and you were on the mound for the final out after relieving Johnny Sain. Do you recall how you pitched to preserve the lead for a 4–3 win against the Giants?

Yeah, the bases were loaded and nobody out. I got a save; I flied three guys out. The Giants had just had that great run where Thompson hit the home run. That was great, you bet, being in Yankee Stadium and a full house.

In 1952 you returned to the Yankees and had a fine year splitting between starting and relieving. Did you mind being used like that, or would you have preferred to stay a starter?

Well, naturally you'd rather start as starter, but that's how I got started as a reliever, with the injury to my leg. Jim Turner would use me to relieve in games where we were either way ahead or way behind, in order to strengthen my arm. Then I got to be a closer along with Allie Reynolds. We were the left- and right-hand closers in the bullpen, to be used in the eighth and ninth innings. Reynolds was the right-hander. And I would spot start also.

The following year the 1952 World Series was a classic Subway Series that went seven games, with Game 7 being held at Ebbets Field. You weren't used for the first six games,

but in what must have seemed like déjà vu you were called into the game and recorded the final eight outs for another save.

Yes, it was never done before. The only time a closer saved the World Series [final game] back-to-back. Yeah, that was nice. Eddie Lopat had started.

Lopat only went four innings. Do you remember what happened to him that day?

Eddie had a little age on the rest of us—I think Eddie was about eight years older than me. Brooklyn had a pretty good ball club that could run pretty good. They had Gilliam, Robinson, Snider. They started laying down bunts and they got on base a couple of times with bunt hits. [Lopat] might have been tired too—it's a long year; people have got to realize it's the seventh game of the World Series and you started in April. Being a little bit older may have gotten to him.

When you got back to Wyandotte after the '51 and '52 World Series was there any fanfare or reception for you?

Oh yeah, they gave me a dinner in '52, a testimonial dinner in Wyandotte. They had about 400–500 people there and the mayor. We had some ballplayers invited down from the Detroit Tigers and the White Sox, and that was very nice.

In 1953 the Yankees won the World Series for the fifth year in a row and you were there for the past three. Do you think these may have been the greatest baseball teams in the history of the game?

Well, I'll tell you, I don't know how many Hall of Famers Brooklyn had, but they had some great clubs over there, but we had a few Hall of Famers too. But, honestly, I think our '52 club was a pretty good club. Mantle was coming into his own and we had Skrowon, and Woodling, McDougald, Rizzuto, and Martin. Our pitching was pretty good. But you know, I saw a lot of those Cincinnati clubs, and they had some pretty good clubs later on. But I'd say maybe the '61 Yankee club was better than we were. They had some great clubs in the '60s .

You had an incredible pitching staff with Ford, Raschi, Lopat, Reynolds, and Sain. Did any of them stand out in your mind as the best pitcher on the staff?

Oh, I'd say Reynolds was the best we had because he could throw real hard and he wanted it real bad; he was tough. He was an Indian from Oklahoma and he was a tough guy. One year I was there he pitched two no-hitters. A beautiful guy, a nice guy. Raschi was tough, but Vic hurt his knee and I think he left us in '53. I think we only had about eight pitchers. Lopat would pitch his spots; he didn't throw real hard. Ford got educated by Lopat—he taught Ford a lot. Whitey was tough, he was tough, but I'd still say Reynolds was the best we had at that time.

You played with Feller when you first came up with Cleveland. Was he the best you ever saw?

He was a true Hall of Famer. He could really throw. But no, the best I ever saw was Bob Gipson. I played with Bob in the minor leagues in '58. Gipson was the best I ever saw, but I never saw Koufax and I never saw Drysdale either. I saw Gipson later on too, but when we were in Rochester in '58 I didn't know what he was doing there. He should have been in the big leagues a year or two earlier. Bob was a competitor and he had all the pitches. If you gave him one or two runs you were home free. The best left-hander I ever saw was Steve Carlton. But again, I never saw Koufax. Friends I talked to claimed Koufax was the best left-hander. Well, how could you argue about Carlton?

Who did you room with on the Yankees?

I roomed with a fellow named Irv Noren who was from Pasadena, California. A real quiet guy and good ballplayer who played with me over in Washington. He started out in the Brooklyn organization and the Senators paid at that time a lot of money for him— $75,000. Then the next year he came and joined me over in New York. He was with us all that time. He and Bauer would take turns playing, depending on who pitched.

Did your wife and family come to live with you in New York?

Yes. I lived in Ridgewood, New Jersey, about forty minutes from the stadium. Mickey Mantle and I and Gene Woodling all lived out there, and I had the whole family out there during the summer. I paid $500 for the house for all summer. [Laughs] The three of us would carpool to the stadium and then the wife would come to the ballpark later on. I loved New York. The people are great and they tell you what they think! I was lucky enough to go there for years when I was visiting with other clubs. I had a couple of friends in New York. One of them owned a jewelry store down on 43rd Street. New Yorkers were great people.

The Yankees let you go by waiving you in August of '54. Did that surprise you?

Yeah, because I was hurt. I had pulled my rib cage and instead of putting me on the disabled list, which I thought that they would do, they released me and they told me they wanted me to go to Toronto in the minor leagues. They couldn't do that[21] so I went over to Baltimore. There were about nine of us that went over there: Lopat, Bauer, Bill Miller, Jim McDonald, and Harry Byrd. They cleaned house at the end of the year. When we all went over to Baltimore, Turley, Larson, and Duren came over to the Yankees. That was 1954, the original year for the Orioles, but I had played there in the minor leagues.

That was some change, going from a team that won a hundred games to a team that lost a hundred games.

[Laughs] Well, I left Washington to go to New York, too.

After the 1954 season you played around the majors with the Orioles, Phillies, Pirates, and Cardinals. When did you retire as a player?

I was hoping to get a pitching coach's job somewhere and I was kind of promised that but it didn't materialize. But I felt I could still pitch in the big leagues. In '56 I pitched in Columbus. I had a real good year there and I thought I was going to get a shot, but I went to spring training with Pittsburgh. I got cut after a month, and I went back to Columbus and that was it. I got into managing and scouting. My last year as a player was actually '59 with Indianapolis. Then I managed Charleston, South Carolina, for the White Sox.

When you came to the Yankees in 1951 it was Joe DiMaggio's final season. He had the reputation of keeping to himself. Did you ever get to know him?

Yep, great guy. I pitched against Joe for years and when I went over he was just about a shell of himself. He had a lot of problems with his heel before that. I think what the Yankees did was, they knew Joe would draw people anyplace he went so he stayed around a year later than he wanted to. When I first met Joe I asked Gene Woodling if I could get a couple of tickets for a play called *South Pacific*. He said, "Go ask the Dago." So I went over and I asked, "Do you have any influence in getting tickets to Broadway?" Well, he lived with a guy named George Solitaire who was a ticket agent in New York. He got me two tickets to the play.

---

21. The Yankees had a working agreement with Toronto that would allow them to bring Kusava back up from the minors and resign him if they needed a pitcher. But they couldn't force Kusava to go to the minors after releasing him. He chose to stay in the majors by signing with Baltimore.

He was very private. One night we were in Chicago and I was in the lobby of the hotel and I got paged. It was Joe. He said, "Come on up to the room. I'm lonely and I want to talk to somebody." I went up and I spent about two and a half hours with him. It was great. We ordered up a couple of drinks and we just shot the breeze. He was very lonely because he couldn't go anywhere to eat or anything. How could he? As soon as people spotted him they'd walk over to his table. I guess that's the penalty you pay for being an immortal. He was a super guy. To me he was great, but there were a lot of people he didn't bother with.

Billy Martin was close to him. Billy was a character. He never won a fight but he got us into about five of them. [Laughs] [Jimmy] Piersall[22] beat the hell out of him. Matt Batts[23] beat the hell out of him. Then he had another player that broke his arm and beat him up.[24]

What did you think of Casey Stengel as the Yankees manager?

You know, we didn't have too much to do with the manager as pitchers. He more or less let Turner work with the pitchers. I don't know how much Casey knew about pitching. I got along with him but I never had too much to do with him because I spent most of my time in the bullpen.

Obviously you spent most of your time throwing to Berra. How was he to work with?

Great, he was great. I never shook him off. If I shook him off two or three times in a game that was a lot. He's a Hall of Famer.

Because of Berra, mostly forgotten is a man named Charlie Silvera.

Charlie Silvera was in the bullpen for ten years, I guess. He was there for all of those championship years. Charlie and Ralph Houk, all they did was warm up the pitchers and answer the phone. Yogi caught every game except maybe ten or twelve a year. Ralph Houk or Charlie, that was the only time that they would get in. Then later on we got Gus Triandos and Elston Howard. When Elston was catching they put Yogi in left field.

I read that you sold appliances in the off-season.

No, I delivered them. You had to get a job in the winter when I played ball, because we didn't make any money. I had to put food on the table. All the ballplayers were like me—you got a job in the winter doing whatever you could.

---

22. Center fielder for the Boston Red Sox.
23. Catcher for the Detroit Tigers.
24. Martin had a penchant for fights. The altercation with Yankees pitcher Ed Whitson occurred in a Baltimore hotel in 1985.

I worked for this friend of mine who owned an appliance store and I would deliver washers, dryers, and whatever else. I think I got $50 a week.

What do you think of today's salaries?

Today's salaries . . . they're all millionaires! I'm happy for them! [Laughs] When we played there was no draft, no free agency, and no multiyear contracts. You had a one-year contract and you got paid for what you did, not what you might do. I can't believe these club owners are doing what they're doing—signing guys to $20 million for two or three years, and they get hurt and can't produce and you're stuck with them. But that's the way it is. Look at Schilling over at Boston—he'll never pitch again and they have to pay him $11 million!

We were the pioneers. In '47 the pension plan came in. If you played before that you could have played 20 years and you got nothing. So the pension plan started in '47. Before that, in the old days, a lot of players died broke. We try to take care of the old baseball players who are destitute—B.A.T., the Baseball Assistance Team. We help more guys out than people know about.

TOPPS

KUZAVA, ROBERT LEROY
Born: May 28, 1923 Wyandotte, Michigan
Bats: Both Throws: Left
Height: 6' 2" Weight: 204

Year	Team	G	W-L	SV	GS	CG	IP	SO	W	ERA
1946	Indians	2	1-0	0	2	0	12.0	4	11	3.00
1947	Indians	4	1-1	0	4	1	21.7	9	9	4.15
1949	White Sox	29	10-6	0	18	9	156.7	83	91	4.02
1950	White Sox	10	1-3	0	7	1	44.3	21	27	5.68
1950	Senators	22	8-7	0	22	8	155.0	84	75	3.95
1951	Senators	8	3-3	0	8	3	52.3	22	28	5.50
1951	YANKEES	23	8-4	5	8	4	82.3	50	27	2.40
1952	YANKEES	28	8-8	3	12	6	133.0	67	63	3.45
1953	YANKEES	33	6-5	4	6	2	92.3	48	34	3.31
1954	YANKEES	20	1-3	1	3	0	39.7	22	18	5.45
1954	Orioles	4	1-3	0	4	0	23.7	15	11	4.18
1955	Orioles	6	0-1	0	1	0	12.3	5	4	3.65
1955	Phillies	17	1-0	0	4	0	32.3	13	12	7.24
1957	Pirates	4	0-0	0	0	0	2.0	1	2	9.00
1957	Cardinals	3	0-0	0	0	0	2.3	2	2	3.86
	Total 10 Years	213	49-44	13	99	34	862.0	446	415	4.05

Brace Photo

ART SCHALLOCK
1951–55

You grew up in Mill Valley, California, and still live nearby in Sonoma. I suppose you weren't a Yankee fan?

No, no, I was a San Francisco Seals fan—the old Pacific Coast League. I went over and saw quite a few Seals games. I made a name for myself in high school in baseball and I wanted to sign up with the Seals. Lefty O'Doul, who was the manager there, said, "He's too small." [Laughs] So years later I wound up with the Hollywood Stars in the Pacific Coast League, and every time I threw my glove out on the mound at Seals Stadium I'd beat the Seals. Eleven or twelve times I beat them, and every time I'd get through with an inning on my way to the dugout I'd cross Lefty and he'd say, "You little son-of-a-gun, I should have bought you back a couple of years ago!" [Laughs] He was a unique man.

Was it a big deal in that area when Joe DiMaggio started playing for the Yankees?

You know, I didn't even know there was major league baseball—it was all the Coast League. They'd broadcast games and in the paper and such, but there wasn't too much about major league baseball until they moved out here.

You graduated from Tamalpias High School in 1943 and you were on the baseball team there. Were you scouted by professional teams?

I guess so, my junior and senior year, yeah, I was. And then I played semipro baseball over in San Francisco. That was a big thing in those days fifty years ago, semipro baseball. I played against Charlie Silvera, and Jerry Coleman, and Bobby Brown and a whole bunch of other guys.

Two weeks out of high school they drafted my fanny into the navy. I never did see a baseball for three years! [Laughs] I was aboard the aircraft carrier Coral Sea then, but then they took the name away from us in '45 and made it the USS Anzio, because they were building a great big USS Coral Sea. This was a liberty ship that was converted into an aircraft carrier—they called them the "Kaiser's Coffins." I was a radar operator aboard that ship.

In 1989 you were inducted into your high school's hall of fame, where former Yankee Joe DeMaestri is also a member.

Yes, and another fellow, Sam Chapman—does that name ring a bell? He was an All-American football player for the University of California. When he graduated he went right straight to the Philadelphia Athletics, where he played center field for about ten or twelve years.

You were actually signed by the Brooklyn Dodgers in '47 as an amateur free agent and then played for the Hollywood Stars from 1949 to 1951.

Actually, the first year with the Dodgers I signed up with the Montreal Royals and went to spring training down in Havana, Cuba, where Leo Durocher was the manager of the Dodgers—he had just married [actress] Lorraine Day. Then I went to Montreal and they optioned me out to Pueblo, Colorado, of the Class A league. Walt Alston was my manager there—he wound up as the Dodger manager for twenty-five years. Then I went back to Montreal and they kept me there for the year and the following year. In '49, I was out here on the coast and I was going to travel back to Vero Beach, Florida, with my family. I talked Buzzy Bavasi, who was the general manager of Montreal then, to sell me to Hollywood, because they had a working agreement with Hollywood back then. So they sold me for a buck from Montreal to Hollywood! I won the pennant with Montreal in '48 with Duke Snider in right field and Chuck Conners, the Rifleman, was the first baseman, Don Newcome was a pitcher. We had a hell of a ball club up there.

Back when you were with Hollywood people referred to the Pacific Coast League as the "third major league." In fact some players preferred to stay there and didn't want to go to the AL or NL. Did you want to remain out on the coast, or were you happy about the trade to New York?

I was pitching with the Hollywood Stars in '51 when the Yankees bought me. I was pitching a game against Portland and I didn't know one of the Yankee scouts, Joe Devine, had scouted me. Fred Haney, who was our manager, called my wife out of the stands and said, "I just sold Art to the New York Yankees." She said to Fred, "Who the hell are the New York Yankees?" [Laughs] She loved the Hollywood Stars because she got to rub elbows with Groucho Marx and all the rest of the movie stars. I went straight to the Yankees on July 12. They won it in '49 and '50 and I get up there in '51 and they win it again. Then they win it again in '52 and '53. Five years in a row! [Laughs] Most guys are up there 20 years in the major leagues and they never see a World Series. I got into three of them.

I met the ball club in Detroit. My claim to fame is they had to get rid of somebody on the roster to make room for me and they sent Mantle down to Kansas City. That's a trivia question.

You made the majors as a 27-year-old rookie in '51 and went 3-1 for the Yankees in 11 games. After the season how did you feel about your future on a club that had Raschi, Lopat, Reynolds, Sain, Tom Morgan, and Whitey Ford, who was coming back from military leave?

Well, I knew that when I got up there because they started me a few times and then they threw me into the bullpen. My roommate was actually Yogi Berra that first year. The reason why they put me with him was so he could teach me about all the hitters with the different clubs. He was damn good at that—he knew every hitter and what their weaknesses were, and you'd try to pitch to those weaknesses.

You would pitch four more years for the Yankees, but never appeared in as many as ten games in a season for the big club. Did you spend a lot of time at Kansas City [AAA]?

Yeah, they optioned me down to Kansas City a few times and I'd win 12 and lose 4 and then they'd call me right back again. "Have suitcase will travel."

Obviously it was a daunting task for a pitcher to crack the Yankees pitching staff in the 1950s. Do you feel you would have had a longer major league career if you had been with a different organization?

Well, that's hard to answer, awful hard to answer. You just don't know. But I was pitching in Washington one night—I guess it was about my third year up there—and we won the ballgame 7–5. We go back to New York and I wake up the next morning and I can't even raise my arm off the pillow. I couldn't even comb my hair. Evidently I pulled or tore a muscle in my left arm up above in the shoulder. I had a hell of a time coming back and they had to stretch the heck out of my arm. They didn't know about the Tommy John operation then.[25] So I'd had a little hop on my fastball and it slowed down quite a bit. I had to come up with some junk pitches and I wound up pitching about every eighth day. I couldn't come back every forth or fifth day—my arm just wouldn't stand it. I lasted another couple of years like that. I bounced back to the Coast League for a year in '56 and then I said, "That's it, I have to go to work for a living now."

This might be a hard question but with all the great pitchers you played with on the Yankees staff, do you think any one of them stood out as the best?

I thought Allie Reynolds was. He was something else. They called him "the Chief"—he was part Indian. He was a hell of a pitcher. He'd not only start games, but toward the end of the season he'd come into important games in between and relieve for a couple of innings and shut them out. He was something else.

Did any particular pitcher take you under his wing or help your career in any way?

All of them helped me as far as learning the hitters on the other clubs. We'd sit out in the bullpen and talk about the different hitters. We'd do that before a ball game—go over the hitters that you would be facing that particular day. They helped in that way.

---

25. A surgical technique in which a damaged ligament in the elbow is replaced with a tendon taken from somewhere else in the body. It is commonly performed on athletes.

Your first year with the Yankees was Joe DiMaggio's final year with the club. You were both from the San Francisco area but he was about ten years older than you. He had a reputation of being standoffish. Did you get to know him during your time in New York in 1951?

He was a very quiet guy; he was very reserved. He wouldn't say boo to hardly anybody when he would walk into the clubhouse. He'd say, "Hi Art, how are ya?" and that would be the end of the conversation. He was quiet and shy more than anything else, I think. But he was a wonderful ballplayer. Gosh he was so good out there in the field. I didn't get to associate too much with him.

The Yankee catcher, of course, was Yogi Berra and his primary backup was Charlie Silvera, with Ralph Houk being the third catcher. Houk eventually became the Yankees GM and manager. Could you see anything that would have led you to believe that he was heading for that career?

When I got up there Ralph was already there in the bullpen. He didn't catch much. Neither did Charlie—Yogi did almost all of the catching. They warmed up the pitchers. He was a good guy, a wonderful man. I got along real well with Ralph and his wife. We used to commute back and forth to the ballpark together. We lived out in Ridgewood, New Jersey.

Your first game was on July 16, 1951, at Tiger Stadium. You gave up 4 runs on 7 hits in 2 ⅔ innings. New York eventually won 8–6.

Yeah, but that was probably nerves more than anything else. I don't remember that far back! [Laughs] It was a thrill though when we got off the road trip and went back to Yankee Stadium. Probably my biggest thrill in baseball was just walking into that stadium and looking at it.

In 1951 the Yankees were the American League Champs and then beat the Giants in the World Series. You did not appear in a game during that World Series. Were you on the roster?

Oh yeah, I had a great seat in the bullpen.

In the 1953 World Series, Game 4 at Ebbets Field, you came on in the seventh and pitched two innings. In this classic Subway Series you got out Jackie Robinson, Gil Hodges, Carl Furillo, Jim Gilliam, and Pee Wee Reese. Can you describe that day and how it felt?

Oh yeah, I sure remember it. After Campanella walked, Snider hit a double off me right down the left-field line—and he's strictly a pull hitter! They scored one run off me. But I didn't have any trouble with the other guys—Hodges and Reese and those guys. Ford came out after one inning. I think they hit him pretty hard—in fact they did. It was just one of those days, you know. The Dodgers beat us by 11–2 or something like that, but it was a great thrill just playing against those guys.

After pitching in just two games for the Yankees in 1955, you were traded to the Baltimore Orioles on May 11. Did the trade disappoint you, or did you view it as perhaps a chance to pitch more?

Oh, I was a little upset, but then, I would be going from a first-place ball club to a last-place ball club. One of the best games I pitched was while I was there against the Yankees, and they beat me 1–0.

After pitching for the Yankees at the beginning of the season you were pitching against the Yankees on August 15 at Memorial Stadium. Mickey Mantle had hit a home run against Oriole starter Ray Moore batting from the right side of the plate earlier in the game. He came to bat against you left-handed and hit another home run—one of ten times he hit home runs from both sides of the plate in the same game.

Oh yeah, I remember that. I get little postcards with Mantle's picture on them with "Home Run #113 hit off Art Schallock at Baltimore Memorial Stadium," and a note to please sign this card! [Laughs] I never had any contact with Mantle though. In fact, after I left the Yankees the only players I ever had any contact with were Charlie Silvera and Bill Renna, guys from the San Francisco area.

After pitching in 30 games for Baltimore in 1955 you concluded your major league career. Did you stay in the game after that?

I did. They sold me down to Seattle, the Seattle Rainiers of the Pacific Coast League. I pitched the year [1956] and won 11 and lost 9, but my arm just wasn't the same. I couldn't throw a baseball—I had to wait at least eight days before I could pitch again. And it bothered me, my arm hurt after I pitched, and I said, I'm not going to do this anymore. I had a chance to become a pitching coach for Sacramento, but they were over in Honolulu at that time so I refused and I had to go to work for a living! I worked in the title-insurance business.

Have you ever been back to New York City since your days with the Yankees?

I've been back to a couple of card shows, yes. I've seen Yogi Berra, and Phil Rizzuto, and Ralph Houk, and Bob Kuzava. I went back one year and they had the 1951 Giants and the '51 Dodgers and '51 Yankees at a banquet there. Larry King was the master of ceremonies and they had Giuliani there. It was quite a gathering.

Are you going to make it back to Yankee Stadium this year [2008]?

[Laughs] I don't know—they haven't asked me yet! They only ask the big stars to go back there to those things.

National Baseball Hall of Fame

SCHALLOCK, ARTHUR LAWRENCE
Born: April 25, 1924 Mill Valley, California
Bats: Left Throws: Left
Height: 5' 9" Weight: 160

Year	Team	G	W-L	SV	GS	CG	IP	SO	W	ERA
1951	YANKEES	11	3–1	0	6	1	46.3	19	20	3.88
1952	YANKEES	2	0–0	0	0	0	2.0	1	2	9.00
1953	YANKEES	7	0–0	1	1	0	21.3	13	15	2.95
1954	YANKEES	6	0–1	0	1	1	17.3	9	11	4.15
1955	YANKEES	2	0–0	0	0	0	3.0	2	1	6.00
1955	Orioles	30	3–5	0	6	1	80.3	33	42	4.15
	Total 5 Years	58	6–7	1	14	3	170.3	77	91	4.02

Bob Wiesler (L), Casey Stengel, Bob Cerv   *Corbis*

BOB WIESLER
1951, 1954–55

You were born and raised in St. Louis. Were you a Browns or Cardinals fan?

I read the book *Pride of the Yankees*[26] and from that point Lou Gehrig was my idol. . . . When I got out of high school I could have signed with the Cardinals, or the Dodgers, or the Yankees. I had the same kind of deal with each so I picked the Yankees.

Did you play a lot of baseball growing up in St. Louis?

We played a lot of sandlot and pickup teams. I played American Legion and in '47 we won the state championship and lost in the Central Division in Iowa.

You attended Beaumont High School in St. Louis, a school that was known for producing ballplayers. No less than 17 former major leaguers came out of that school.

Yeah, Roy Sievers, Bobby Hoffman, Earl Weaver—my first year with Beaumont he was a senior. Neal Hertweck was our first baseman at Beaumont. Lloyd Merritt came after I graduated and Jim Goodwin, a left-hander, was before me.

Were you a pitcher in high school?

Yes.

Your coach, Mr. Elliot, was credited by some of those major leaguers for their development.

Ray Elliot. He had quite a few graduates that went to pro ball.

The Yankees signed you as an amateur free agent in 1949 at 18. Did they scout you in high school?

Oh yeah, Luke McWallis. They signed me right out of high school. I graduated in January and I signed right after that.

By 1951 you were on the Yankees' top farm club at Kansas City, where you went 10–9 with a 2.92. ERA. You also led the American Association with 162 strikeouts and led your team in shutouts. Were you surprised at how quickly you progressed through the Yankee system?

Well, I had a pretty good year at Joplin [C ball]. The first year I was pretty wild at Independence [D ball]. Then the next year at Joplin I got better control and had a good year—well, we all had

---

26. *Lou Gehrig: Pride of the Yankees*, by Paul Gallico, published in 1942 and made into a movie that same year.

pretty good years. That's when Mantle hit about .380 or .390. We had a hell of a team. We had four guys from there hit the big leagues: Mantle, Kraly, Skizas, and myself. [Kraly] had a hell of a year that one year in Binghamton.[27] When we were in the minors in the Yankee system we had our own bus driver, like a Greyhound bus and driver. A lot of these teams had school buses. We had pretty good conditions on the bus. We had a licensed driver, whereas a lot of those teams had a player or manager drive the bus.

The Yankees called you up to the majors in early August 1951. Do you remember how that came about?

Yes, they called me and [outfielder Bob] Cerv up together and sent Mantle and Morgan down to Kansas City.

This was a little over two years after you had signed. That was very fast, especially considering that the Yankees were in the middle of winning five straight world championships.

[Laughs] Well, there were only 16 teams back then and now there are what—30. It's a lot easier now.

Were you surprised how quickly you made it up to the New York Yankees?

Well, they told me that I had pretty good stuff. The thing was, I couldn't control it. In 1951 I was in a [National] Guard outfit. I had to go to meetings once a month, so they would fly me into and out of St. Louis and I'd report to the club wherever they were.

Had you ever been to New York before?

No. Right when I got there Pete Sheehy—he was some clubhouse man—he showed me underneath the stands the old-time uniforms. I couldn't believe what those guys used to wear in those days—100% wool uniforms!

What was it like walking out onto the field at Yankee Stadium that first time wearing a Yankee uniform?

Unbelievable! I used to go and walk out to center field and see the monuments out there. I couldn't believe Mantle hit a couple of home runs out there that one year I was there—it was unbelievable the distance that ball traveled.

Did Casey Stengel or pitching coach Jim Turner say anything to you when you got called up?

27. Steve Kraly pitched 18–2 in 1953.

Oh, they both congratulated me. He was a good manager. I didn't know him that well until later, but he knew his baseball.

Your first game was on August 3 at Yankee Stadium against the Browns.

I lost 8–0.

Were you nervous going out there for the first time?

Oh yeah—in front of all those people? We used to have about 1,000 in the minors. In Kansas City we'd usually have about 4,000. In Yankee Stadium they used to almost have full houses.[28]

You played in a total of four games and the Yankees became the eventual 1951 world champions. Did they send you back down after you joined the team during the summer?

They sent me back down in August, but they did send me a little check at the end of the year after they split the World Series money.

Did they give you a ring?

No, the ring was strictly for the guys that stayed up there.

You spent all of 1952 in the military.

We got called up in the Guard at the end of '51, in November, and then we got activated and went to Burlington, Vermont.

In 1953 and '54 you were back in Kansas City (AAA) until being recalled to New York again for six games in '54. Did anyone from the organization tell you what their plans were for you?

Well, in '54 I went back up there and I started. We had a ten-game winning streak. I was supposed to pitch against Baltimore Sunday, and then Saturday night there was a note in my box in the hotel.[29] It said that Skowron and Cerv wanted to see me. I went up to their room and they told me I was getting sent down to Kansas City, and I said, "What?!" They signed Branca up. Branca was released[30] and he was traveling around with us throwing batting practice.

I go out to the ballpark and Casey said, "I had nothing to do with it." So I was very— pardon the expression—pissed off. I didn't finish those games but we won and I was the winning pitcher,

---

28. The capacity of Yankee Stadium in the 1950s was about 67,000.
29. The Concourse Hotel in the Bronx, where many Yankee players stayed.
30. By the Detroit Tigers on July 16, 1954.

and they sent me down. I went back down to Kansas City. We weren't doing much there so they sent me up to Toronto. They were fighting for the championship. Elston Howard was the catcher. When I played with him in '53 he was an outfielder. In '54 they made a catcher out of him.

Toronto was in the Yankee organization?

No, no. We were lend-lease. They usually lend-leased players to different clubs. We were in sixth place in Kansas City and we were in first place in Toronto.

That surprises me about Ralph Branca. He was really at the end of his career.

[Laughs] Don't tell me. That was the general manager, George Weiss..

The Yankees at that time had one of the best pitching staffs of all time.

That was Raschi, Reynolds, Lopat, and Ford.

Do you think any one of them was the best on the staff?

Well, Raschi and Reynolds—to me they were great. Raschi and Reynolds could throw hard. Lopat would get in there and throw the screwball and different speeds. He was great. Ford had great control.

You were known for having a fastball that moved, and a curveball.

That's right.

Did Jim Turner help you in anyway?

Nah, they tried to do different things with me. They tried to move me from one side of the mound to the other and slow my motion down. It just was the wildness, I guess. I just couldn't control it when I got up there.

How was Yogi Berra to throw to?

He was good. [Laughs] I crossed him up a few times. You had to see the gloves they used in those days—did you ever see them? If you get a chance, they have them in the Hall of Fame. There was so much padding in them there was just enough room in them for a ball. Now they look like first-baseman's mitts.

Ralph Houk was the third-string catcher. Did he run the bullpen?

Yeah, he and Charlie [Silvera]. They were both out there.

Did it surprise you when he became the Yankees manager and then GM?

Oh, he knew a lot. He was very educated with the pitchers. They sent him to Denver to manage there, and then they brought him back to manage the Yankees.

1951 was Joe DiMaggio's final season. Did you get to meet him or talk to him?

Oh yeah, I was up there for a while with him. We would go on the road. Joe never ate with us. Joe was hounded too much. Joe would be eating and people would come up and say, "Would you sign my autograph?" and that, so he ate mostly in the room. He'd just order room service. When you're eating you don't want anybody disturbing you and he would draw too many people to him.

Did you get to know Mickey Mantle at all?

Well, I played with him those first two years. Well, I'll tell you, he came out of high school in '49 and he joined us in Independence and he was alright, but the next year in Joplin he was unbelievable the way he hit the ball. He would hit the ball to the opposite field—right-handed he hit to right center and left-handed he'd hit to left center. It was unbelievable the power he had, and he could run.

What hitter gave you the most trouble?

To me when I was up there, Ted Williams was the best hitter I ever faced. With the Senators I used to throw him a curveball and he would punch it out to left field. He was unbelievable.

On February 8, 1956, the Yankees traded you to Washington. How did you feel about the trade?

That was the year after we went barnstorming to Japan. Heck, Dick Tettelbach was in that trade, and Whitey Herzog, Herb Plews, and Lou Berberet. I think there were five of us in that trade for Mickey McDermott. I went from a first-place club to a last-place club. It was kind of disappointing. I got to pitch more at Washington—I got to start every fourth day.

When did you retire as a player?

In '61. I was at Dallas-Ft. Worth [AAA].

You had a very long AAA career.

I had four years at Richmond, three years at Kansas City, and then Dallas-Ft. Worth. I only had a couple of years at D and C ball and the rest was AAA or the big leagues.

In 1964 I started pitching batting practice for the Cardinals, and that's when the Yankees came in and played the Cardinals for the World Series. I did that all the way to '68, and then I had knee trouble. I pitched Sportsman's Park and Busch Stadium, and they won two World Series and one pennant while I was throwing batting practice.

Obviously you went to Sportsman's Park[31] as a kid a lot. How did you feel when they closed it down and moved into Busch Stadium during the '66 season?

Oh, at the old one people who had backyards charged for parking. People used to park their cars in there—there was no parking. There was one little area where you could park a car. When they built that new stadium they had a number of parking garages.

Have you been back to Yankee Stadium since you retired?

No. I've been up to New York signing autographs a couple of times but not to Yankee Stadium.

So are you going to come to the new stadium?

[Laughs] I don't know. If they ask me I will. I don't get around too much anymore.

Any other Yankee memories?

Well you know, this is a funny story. Yogi used to like reading comic books, and I'll never forget this one time we were taking a train up to Boston or Philadelphia. The first time I got to go with the Yankees on a road trip I got to room with Bobby Brown, who was studying to be a doctor. We got on a train and Yogi was sitting across from Bobby Brown, who was reading his medical book, and Yogi was reading a comic book. Yogi said, "How'd your book turn out, Bobby?" [Laughs] He was something else, Yog. I see him once in a while when he comes to St. Louis. He married his wife, Carmen, here. When he comes in and does autographs I go out there and see him.

You know, that stadium, I still think that's a beautiful stadium. It's a shame that they're going to tear it down. There's a lot of memories in that place. I watched it, most of the last game. The House that Ruth Built. Now it's "the House that Steinbrenner Built." I don't know how the average fan will be able to afford the ticket price at the new stadium.

---

31. Home of the Cardinals until 1966 and St. Louis Browns until 1953. .

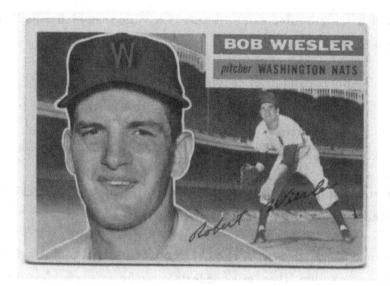

TOPPS

WIESLER, ROBERT GEORGE
Born: August 13, 1930 St. Louis, Missouri
Bats: Both Throws: Left
Height: 6' 2" Weight: 195

Year	Team	G	W-L	SV	GS	CG	IP	SO	W	ERA
1951	YANKEES	4	0-2	0	3	0	9.3	3	11	13.50
1954	YANKEES	6	3-2	0	5	0	30.3	25	30	4.15
1955	YANKEES	16	0-2	0	7	0	53.0	22	49	3.91
1956	Senators	37	3-12	0	21	3	123.0	49	112	6.44
1957	Senators	3	1-1	0	2	1	16.3	9	11	4.41
1958	Senators	4	0-0	0	0	0	9.3	5	5	6.75
	Total 6 Years	70	7-19	0	38	4	241.3	113	218	5.74

National Baseball Hall of Fame

STEVE KRALY
1953

This interview is dedicated to the memory of Irene Kraly, Steve's wonderful wife of 49 years.

You were born in Whiting, Indiana, where you graduated from Whiting High School in 1947. I believe you were a star pitcher for them.

Correct. I pitched, but played the outfield also. Mainly in my last couple of years I had a better shot at going to college if I stayed with pitching. I was a good basketball player too. I led my team in scoring in high school.

I went to college [Indiana University] in '48 but there was a difference of opinion with the coach. We were freshmen and we wanted to go out for the fall program and he wouldn't let us go out. Well, I decided the hell with this, you gave me a four-year scholarship and I can't even get a uniform to try to make the team. He asked me what I did, and I said I pitched. He told me that his pitching staff was already picked and that's it. So I told him, "Why did you give me a four-year scholarship? You only won 30 games and lost like 50. Something's wrong here." So I challenged the varsity to a game with all my fellow freshmen and we beat them. I think I struck out 21. I called my scout up and I left college. . . . All [my college teammates] came to me to try to get me to stay, but I told them that it was too late and that I couldn't play for him anyway with that attitude.

If you want to know the ending of the story, that was my first year, 1948 to 1949. When I made the Yankees in 1953 we came and played Detroit and there was a message from . . . the coach at Indiana University. He came to apologize. I told him, "What you did by not letting us put on a uniform prevented every one of us from [getting] a college education." He became the athletic director and he changed the program.

I guess growing up in Indiana you were not a Yankees fan?

Ah, no. In fact my mother got mad at me. My parents were from Yugoslavia and she wanted to know, speaking in broken English, "Why you go with Yankees when I like Cubs?" I said, "Ma, you'll understand!" Back then we were Cubs fans and White Sox, mostly.

How big of a deal was it with your family and circle of friends to be going off to play in the New York Yankees system?

Well, the way I could put it to you is, it was a challenge, number one. Number two, I knew how great they were, and three, I thought the odds were against me because I wasn't big—I was small framed. But I had a live arm and my [repertoire] of all my pitches I had learned when I was like 14. We had a semipro team at home so I had the experience. But when I saw all these guys 6' 4" and 6' 5" it gave me more determination that size means nothing, and the only way to show it is when you get a chance to perform.

How did your minor league career go? I know you lost two years to the army.

My first year I made the All-Star team at Independence, Kansas. My record was 17–10 and my ERA was two point something. That was class D ball. Mickey Mantle and I and a couple of others all started out there. From there I went to Joplin, where I had an 18–6 record with a 2.86 ERA, I think. Then we were called up just to see what major league baseball was like. There was Mickey, myself, Bob Wiesler, and Lou Skeesas. We couldn't play, but we joined them in Chicago. We got to watch and shag fly balls and all that, but we couldn't perform. At that time you could bring up potential prospects and you could practice, but then [you had to] take a shower and sit in the stands.

You came out of the army and went to the Binghamton Triplets, Class A, where you had a season that they still talk about.

That was a good league; it was strong. There were only eight teams in the Eastern League but you would see ex–major leaguers there. When I came here I went to spring training while I was in the army. They wanted to see what I could do, and I think I struck out five out of the six that I faced. Stengel used to call me "Sergeant" and I'd tell him, "I'm only a corporal, but thanks for the promotion."

Then he told me , "We'll see you pretty soon." Then they gave me a contract to come to Binghamton, but I held out because I wanted to go to Kansas City [AAA]. He wouldn't let me. The manager I had played for my first two years was Harry Kraft. He wanted me at K.C., but the Yankees told me that they wanted me [in Binghamton] because it's closer to New York and I said, "I can't buy that." The difference was in money, and they wouldn't let me work out until I signed a contract. So I said, "Let's put a clause in my contract for 30 days, and if I stay with [Binghamton] I want what I figure I'm losing, a $2500 bonus. Lee McPhail was our minor league farm director at that time and he said that they normally don't do that with minor leaguers. I told him, "Look, if you don't, I'm not going to play." He asked me, "Well, what are you going to do?" I told him, "A lot of things. I could make a lot of money just playing semipro." He said, "Well, if that's what it takes, we'll do it." I was the most serious pitcher out there and I worked hard—well, you've got the stats.

Yes, 19–2; 2.08 ERA. The most amazing thing—something that you will never see again— you started 22 games and you completed 19!

Correct. I pitched opening night and I was throwing 92 or 93 and it was a cold night here. I was going to show them how hard I could throw. I went seven innings and struck out 11. We had a catcher here named Robinson who was going to AAA. He had just stopped to see the game because they were traveling through. He just said to me that if I came up with a great changeup, you could just throw a glove out on the mound.[32]

I went to Phil Page, who was my manager. He was a left-handed pitcher for the Philadelphia Phillies and I knew he threw a screwball. I said to him, "Can you teach me to throw the screwball? I'd like to use it when I run the count 3–2, when they usually look for a fastball. That way I can take something off and throw that screwball that would dive down." He was good and he worked with me almost every morning. So when I would run a count 3 and 2 you would never see a fastball.

The Yankees called you up on July 31, 1953.[33] How did you find out that you were going to New York?

I had a roommate named Jim Finnigan. Later he was traded and played for Philadelphia and Kansas City. The call-up deadline was midnight. I was 18–2. I was scheduled to pitch the next day and they had all the tickets just about sold out to see me pitch. Well, I wake up in the morning and my roommate was gone and I go downstairs where we were staying and said, "Where is everybody?" Someone said, "Well evidently they're at the ballpark. I guess you're late." I thought, I can't be late, I'm pitching. The owner of this restaurant already knew but was told to keep quiet if I showed up to eat.

When I got to the ballpark my trainer comes in and said to not suit up right away, Phil[34] wanted to talk to me. I said, "Why is everybody here so early?" So he comes in and takes me in the office and says, "Stephen, you're leaving. You're not going to be pitching tonight." I thought I was going to Kansas City [AAA] and asked him if I was going [there]. He said, "No." Well, I didn't want to go to Beaumont, Texas—that was our AA team. I asked, "Well, am I traded?" He said, "No, you're going to New York." I just looked at him and said, "Come on, you're joking." He told me no, that I was going to pitch on Sunday and then I was leaving. I cried and he cried. I couldn't believe that in that short span I would go from A ball to the New York Yankees. Actually, I was the first one to be called up from A ball to the Yankees.

I'm surprised they let you pitch that one last game.

---

32. Old baseball saying meaning the pitcher would not have to wear a glove because nobody was going to hit the ball.
33. Kraly actually went 19–2 for Binghamton before July ended.
34. Manager Phil Page.

Well, they did because it was a farewell. They brought four of us up: Gus Triandos, Bob Wiesler, and another left-hander, Bill Miller. I was pitching every fourth day, but when they brought me up I didn't get into a game for two weeks, when I came in to relieve Vic Raschi against the White Sox.

Had you ever been to New York City before?

No.

Were the Yankees home when they called you up?

Yes. I went from here to the Hoboken train station. The cab drivers were fighting over who was going to take me across to the Bronx. One guy pointed at me and said, "I think that's him!" They knew I was coming—I guess it was in the news.

What was it like, a 24-year-old from Indiana, walking out onto that field at Yankee Stadium for that first time wearing a Yankees uniform?

We're talking the original Yankee Stadium, which seated 65,000 people. You're really starry eyed and you can't believe that you're there. When I put the uniform on I was 5' 10" and I think I grew to be six-foot-something. It's really hard for me to even explain. It was a reality shock that hits you as a rookie. You know the history of the New York Yankees and that stadium and all the great ballplayers that played there before any one of us. You're just in awe.

I think Mickey might have been instrumental in me coming up. We had played together in Joplin and he said, "Why don't you bring him up? He could help the ball club." In fact when he visited here he always wanted to see the wife and kids, and they called him Uncle Mick.

Your first game was on August 9 in New York.

That's a funny story. Stengel told me to go and get 15 minutes of throwing in, because when we go to Washington I'm going to pitch. When you go out to the bullpen in the old stadium you go underneath the stands to get to right field. So I'm getting my throwing in, and I think Tom Gorman was throwing with me—a left-hander and a right-hander—and we're playing the White Sox. Raschi was pitching and I got my throwing in. Then the phone was ringing and Ralph Houk answered the phone. Stengel was on the mound—you see, we didn't have a pitching coach come out; when Stengel came out you were done. So he's signaling for a left-hander and Houk says, "Kraly, you're in." I said, "No, I'm just getting my throwing in. He said I'm going to pitch in Washington." Houk said, "No, no, no. Take a look—he's signaling for you." I thought, oh my God, I can't believe this.

I wasn't ready for it so I get my jacket and I've got it over my shoulder and I'm starting to go from the pitcher's rubber to go out. Bob Kuzava and Johnny Sain stop me and they told me that they had a code of ethics in the bullpen. They said, "We don't let them open the gate[35] when you go out—we hurdle it." I thought, oh hell, I know what track is like; I can hurdle a four-foot fence. I got over with my front foot but my back one caught and I went down and my jacket came off. I was so starry eyed—there were about 55,000 people at this game and I didn't see one, to be honest with you. I'm now walking in and I tripped in a drain in right field. I could see Stengel scratching his head thinking, "What the hell is this coming in?"

I got out to the mound and the conversation went like this:

Kraly: Mr. Stengel.

Stengel: Well, ya know, ya had me a little worried there. Are you alright? I

know I told ya just to warm up, but I didn't want to tell ya what I'm gonna do.

Kraly: Thanks a lot.

Stengel: You have runners on first and third and nobody out. You and Yogi go over the signs.

To this day I don't know what the hell Yogi said. One was a fastball, two was a curveball, three was a changeup, or whatever. So the first batter comes up and I throw the first pitch and hit Yogi on the inside of his thigh. So he came walking out to the mound and our conversation went like this:

Yogi: What did you throw?

Kraly: Well, what did you call?

Yogi: Well, what did you throw?

Kraly: Well . . . I think I threw a fastball.

He turned around and went back. Rizzuto comes to me and says, "Look, Steve, sometimes he forgets what he puts down." I said that wasn't the problem with me because I had a tough time seeing his fingers, because Yogi had short, stubby fingers. Then I said to him, "I'm not really nervous." He told me, "Don't be nervous. Just pitch like you did in Binghamton.

---

35. In the four-foot chicken-wire fence.

There's no difference up here." I said to him, "Before you go, where's the rosin bag"? He said, "I think you're standing on it." So I get it and I say to myself, oh my God, I worked really hard to get here and now I'm in a jam. So with my next pitch I bean Chico Carrasqual and I load the bases. Stengel was going berserk in the dugout. Nellie Fox was the next batter and I struck him out. Then I struck out Rocco Krsnich. The next guy popped up and I got out of it. That was my experience coming in for the first time in the major leagues.

When you came up did Casey Stengel say anything to you or tell you what he expected?

Oh yeah. As a matter of fact I stood at attention when I went into his office. When it came time for me to go sign my contract with George Weiss he asked me if I wanted to read it and I said, "No, just tell me where to sign." I didn't even know what I was getting paid. The minimum at that time was $6000. [Stengel] came to watch me pitch a game one time and I pitched a shutout, so he knew what I was capable of doing.

Did the longtime pitching coach Jim Turner help you in any way?

No, not really. Everybody used to tell me to shy away from him because he'll try to change [your pitching] philosophy. Turner did—he would tell you that maybe you shouldn't grip the ball that way, you should try to grip it this way for your curveball, and this and that. Johnny Sain tutored me quite a bit.

What was it like sitting in the bullpen with Whitey Ford, Vic Raschi, Allie Reynolds, Ed Lopat, and Johnny Sain?

Yes, it was a little intimidating, but what they would do is, you would sit out there between them and they would go over the hitters, so you studied the hitters. The trick of it was . . . to throw strikes, because if you don't you're going to get into deep trouble. You make one bad pitch and you're going to get hit hard and lose. They were very helpful. The guy I replaced was Joe Ostrowski.

Did any of these pitchers stand out in your mind as the best on the team?

Oh yeah. I would say the one I admired was Whitey. [The press] even wrote it up that I threw harder than Whitey Ford, but Whitey had deception—he had a curveball that he could throw on any count. He could take something off the curveball. That's what we would talk about, "Lefty and Lefty." The ball we used was a Reach ball[36] with high seams.

---

36. The Reach Sporting Goods Company manufactured baseballs and gloves until bought out by the Spaulding Company in 1892.

When you have high seams and you have humidity the ball really breaks. If it's cool to colder it won't break as much, so what you try to do is make it spin slower and then it breaks. Whitey could do that—he had good control. Well, all the Yankees back then had good control. If you look at the time element of the ball games, they are like an hour and 58 minutes.

When I got shut out by Cleveland I outpitched Bob Lemon and I lost 1–0. I threw a four- hitter and I got beat. They scored a run in the first inning and then I shut them down. That was in Yankee Stadium. Then I pitched what was called the "Game of the Week" back then. It was in Cleveland and Lemon beat me again. When Whitey came here [Binghamton] to be inducted into our Hall of Fame he said to my wife, "We threw him to the wolves!" [Laughs] I didn't mind, but I think what happened was, when I got called up and didn't pitch right away, when you get taken off your normal four days, you get too strong and that's no good.

You probably only threw to Yogi Berra in live games. How was he to throw to?

In our day Yogi called all the pitches. Nobody from the bench called the pitches—he called every one of them. With the Yankees at that time, when runners got on second base we would look at the scoreboard. If the count is even then it's a fastball; if the count is odd then it's a breaking ball. What you can do is change speeds on either one of them. [The catcher] may just wiggle those fingers behind the plate, and that means "slow curve" or "take something off the fastball." That's the way we did it.

In the five games that you played you started three and relieved in two. The Yankees seemed to just plug you in where needed.

The thing was, the starters were Raschi, Lopat, Reynolds, and Ford—that was the mainstay. The other ones were myself and Bob Kuzava. Johnny Sain was what we called the long reliever.[37] There was no such thing as closers.

After the season ended did you think you would be back in 1954?

Yes I did. I think even all my ex-managers were a little dismayed because they were sending me down to Kansas City. Stengel said it was only temporarily, but I stayed there all year.

You wound up going 5–14.

Even though [the statitistics] show that a lot of us were doing well, we weren't winning. I think that ball club lost 17 in a row. Actually, records sometimes are misleading—you have to see the

---

37. A relief pitcher who enters in the early part of the game, from the first to the fourth inning.

facts of the game and how it went. In '55 in spring training I was going real good, and against the Cardinals my arm tightened up. I didn't think anything of it at that time.

Were you on the '53 World Series roster?

Yes, actually I was scheduled to pitch the fifth game. It was at Ebbetts Field. I got a phone call at about midnight, and I thought it was some fella pulling my leg. He said, "I got bad news for you," and I just hung up. They used to tell us to never answer the phone because it could be a gambler or whatever. I got up in the morning and my hotel manager said, "Gee, I'm sorry to hear about your parents." I said, "What are you talking about?" and he asked me if I had seen the paper. Some guy set their house on fire. Stengel talked to me and took me out of the rotation and told me to come on down to his office and we'd try to reach my parents. We did and they were OK. But anyway, I was there and it was a thrill of a lifetime. I don't think anybody realizes when you're on a team and you're in the World Series what a thrill it is even if you're not participating. Fortunately I have the ring that's got number 5 on it.

When did you retire as a player?

In 1961. When they had expansion and Casey went over and became the general manager and manager of the Mets, he bought my contract and wanted me to pitch for the Mets. I had just taken a job with the IBM Corporation and I came home from work—I had worked one day— and my wife said, "You're not going to believe who called." I told her not to keep me in suspense and she told me Casey Stengel.

He called back in a few hours and we talked. He told me that he knew he didn't use me like he should have, but I said that it was alright. I told him that I had a problem, that I had just taken a job with the IBM Corporation. He asked me if I wanted more money and I told him no. He was offering me $26,000. That was 1961 and that was a lot of money. I told him to give me a couple of weeks and I'd get back to him. I went to work the next day and went to the personnel office and asked if I could take a leave of absence. I think they all froze. They said, "Well, let's see." It took them about three seconds and they said, "Wait a minute—you only worked one day!" They told me I needed a year to take a leave of absence.

I came home and my beloved wife said to me, "Are we leaving?" I said no and told her that I had spoken to lawyer friends of mine, and "You and the kids are more important to me and this is for our welfare and longevity. I can go and play and I don't know if my arm will hold out." My wife cried and said, "You did that for me. That was your life, baseball." I told her that I think I accomplished everything that I set out to do. I would make the same decision if I had to do it again.

You are still in the game, though, as the official scorer back at Binghamton for the Mets' AA team. As a matter of fact you have a big day coming up.

Yes, bobble head![38] [Laughs] Seventeen years here [as Binghamton's official scorer)].

When the Yankees signed you in 1949 did you ever think that you would have a bobble head doll of yourself?

No, no. As a matter of fact I didn't even know that I was up for this thing with six other people. I came back from bowling in Albuquerque and my teammates were calling me "bobble head." I thought, what are they talking about? They had a vote on the internet and I won overwhelmingly. Actually it's neat and I think it's great that the fans thought that much of me. There's a lot of good company—David Wright got it one year, Pizza got it one year, so I'm honored.

The 1953 World Series was not the only championship that you have been involved in. You've had a number of 300 bowling games to your credit and you've participated in many United States Bowling Congress championships.

200-plus average. What I'm doing this spring is I'm taking all my boys to Las Vegas, where the USB championship is being held, and they're going to be on my team. We bowl on the 16th and 17th of April and on the 18th I'm going to be 80 years old. I have four 300 games. Once you shoot the first one, that's the one you're proud of. I actually didn't start bowling until later because when you're playing baseball they didn't want you bowling.

---

38. Steve Kraly bobble head night was held August 23, 2008.

TOPPS

Kraly, Steve Charles
Born: April 18, 1929 Whiting, Indiana
Bats: Left Throws: Left
Height: 5' 10" Weight: 152 lbs.

Year	Team	G	W-L	SV	GS	CG	IP	SO	W	ERA
1953	YANKEES	5	0-2	1	3	0	25.0	8	16	3.24
	Total 1 Year	5	0-2	1	3	0	25.0	8	16	3.24

Photofest

ZEKE BELLA
1957

You were born and raised in Greenwich, Connecticut. That's either Yankee or Red Sox territory.

I was actually a Giant fan, the New York Giants.

The Yankees signed you in 1951 when you were 20 years old as an amateur free agent. At that time you were already playing semipro. You must have had an excellent high school career.

Well, not really. I was average, I guess. I did play all four years at Greenwich High, where I was an outfielder and played first base. I threw left and hit right. The reason for that was that I broke my right arm and they set it wrong, so I had some trouble there.

You played for the Dartmouth Arrows of the District League in 1949 and 1950, your first two years in organized ball. Was that an independent league?

That's in Nova Scotia. [The Arrows] weren't associated with anybody. It was just mostly college players that hadn't signed yet or weren't going to sign.

You had some great years up there?

Oh yeah. Then I went to Amsterdam Class C the following year in 1950, when I signed with the Yankees. I hit .370, something like that. Then they moved me up to Binghamton.

I read that you never hit below .300 in you entire minor league career.

No, no. I never did.

Your career was well on its way when it got interrupted by the army.

I got called up during the Korean War. Well, that's the way it goes, back in those days anyway. I went to Germany, thank God.

When you returned from the service you wound up going back to the District League, I believe. Why did you return there?

Well, I was supposed to go to Binghamton and then they wanted to send me to Norfolk but I wasn't ready, so I went back to Halifax for a year. I got suspended. [Laughs]

In 1955, back in the Yankee system, you won the Eastern League Batting Title.

That was Class A at Binghamton—.372 I hit.

You seemed to have no problem hitting minor league pitching.

No, I didn't. I think I could have hit major league too if I had the chance, but I didn't get much of a chance.

The Yankees moved you up to Denver [AAA] for the next three seasons [1956–58], where you hit .320, .317, and .339. Did you ever get discouraged being an outfielder in the Yankee organization back then, with so little opportunity to get to the big club?

Well, yeah, but you know, I made the choice. I could have signed with the Red Sox and I could have signed with Philly. I don't know, I just thought that being from Greenwich and near New York it would help, but it didn't. There were too many outfielders.

Do you feel that you would have had a longer major league career had you been with a different organization?

Oh yeah, I think I would have—although the reason I dropped out was I had two operations on my left eye. I couldn't pick up the ball like I used to so I had to get out. Yeah, I could have done it. I think the biggest thing today is there are 30 teams, and back then there were only 16. That's a big difference. But that's the way it goes.

In September of 1957 the Yankees finally called you up to the big club. Do you remember how you found out that you were going?

Ralph Houk was the manager in Denver and he called me into his office and said, "Pack your bags. You're going to the Yankees." The Yankees were home and I met them in New York.

How did it feel after putting in your dues in the minors to finally put on that pinstripe uniform and walk out onto the field at Yankee Stadium?

Oh, it was tremendous. I can't describe it. Just being out there is amazing. It was a real thrill. The first time I went out to right field I looked up and said to myself, "This is really something."

Your first game came on September 11, 1957, during the second game of a doubleheader. Do you remember that game?

It was against Detroit and I'll never forget it because we had a day-night doubleheader. It rained most of the time and they finally got the game in with no batting practice.

They called me up in the ninth inning to pinch-hit and I struck out against Ray Nareski.[39] Casey said, "You with the funny first name, get up and hit." [Laughs]

You were a 27-year-old rookie. How did your teammates treat you?

Oh, fine. I got along with all of them, Mantle and the rest. They were a bunch of good guys. Bobby Richardson, Kubek—they were all great.

Was Mantle the greatest hitter that you ever saw?

No—Ted Williams.

After the '57 season did you think that you would be back with the Yankees in '58?

Yes, but then I got traded.

Late in the 1958 season the Yankees almost had the pennant clinched when they traded you from Denver to the Kansas City A's for reliever Murray Dickson. It was said that the Yankees wanted a veteran in the bullpen. How did you feel about the trade?

Well, I thought it would be an opportunity. It never worked out that way for some reason.

You made it back to the major leagues for the 1959 season with the A's out of spring training. In fact, you had a two-out, pinch-hit double off Herb Score that cleared the bases and beat the Indians in April. What happened to the rest of your season?

Our manager was Harry Craft and it was his birthday, so we had a party after that game. From [Cleveland] we flew to Detroit and the clubhouse guy said to me, "Harry wants to see you." I thought he wanted to congratulate me for the hit I got. Instead he told me that they were sending me down to Shreveport because they just bought Tommy Carol! That's the way it went in those days. That's when I had the eye surgery [after the season] and I called it quits.

Since you retired have you gotten back to Yankee Stadium?

Oh yeah, sure. Not lately but I go once in a while. I'm going to try to get to the new stadium.

---

39. Two-time All Star.

TOPPS

BELLA, JOHN
Born: August 23, 1930 Greenwich, Connecticut
Bats: Right Throws: Left
Height: 5' 11" Weight: 185

Year	Team	G	AB	H	2B	3B	HR	AVG	RBI	R
1957	YANKEES	5	10	1	0	0	0	.100	0	0
1959	A's	47	82	17	2	1	1	.207	9	10
	Total 2 years	52	92	18	2	1	1	.196	9	10

BRACE Photo

JOHNNY JAMES
1958, 1960–61

You were born in Bonners Ferry, Idaho. Is that where you grew up?

Well, my father worked for the government so we moved around quite a bit, but in 1947 we settled in Hollywood, California.

You were probably a Hollywood Stars fan.

Well, actually my sister was a Stars fan and I was a Los Angeles Angels [PCL] fan, which was the other AAA club here in town.

Did you play a lot of Little League or American Legion ball, or on your high school team?

Well, they really didn't have Little League ball back in my day, but I did play American Legion and high school ball. I also played a lot of what we called semipro ball around Los Angeles back in the early and late '50s. It was a fast league. As you may expect, there were a lot of professional ballplayers that lived in southern California that came home and played in the wintertime. I was in high school and pitched against some major leaguers that were on these semipro teams, so it was a fast league.

Were you always a pitcher?

Yes.

Did you play any other sports?

Not really, but I played university football one year because the coach made me go out for it, but I didn't like it. Next year come football season I broke my leg so I lucked out and didn't have to play football anymore.

You went on to pitch at the University of Southern California.

Right, just for one year. Actually, I didn't pitch much at USC. It was at the height of the Korean War and the freshmen had to go out for the varsity, and the varsity was pretty much loaded. As a result I didn't pitch much. I pitched in some what you'd call junior varsity games; I pitched a little bit.

At the time the USC coach was Rod Dedeaux, who was a famous baseball coach—in fact he was the coach of the first Olympic baseball team. At that time Rod was working with the Yankees and I told him that I wasn't made for school, and so he sent the Yankee scout over to sign me. I'm not sure if the Yankees were interested in signing me [Laughs] or if it was just Rod's recommending me. Rod is about the most famous college baseball coach ever. He won a lot of college World Series, five or six.

The Yankees sign you in 1953 and you go and have a very successful minor league career in their system. In your first four years you went 14–9 [Boise, 1953], 11–8 [Modesto, 1954], 10–6 [Binghamton, 1955], and 11–2 [Binghamton, 1956)]. Did the Yankee organization consider you a big prospect with those numbers?

Not a big prospect, but I think they thought highly of me. In my first year at Binghamton word came down to me that Casey wanted to raise his own relief pitcher within the system and they kind of anointed me to try and do that. So starting in '55 at Binghamton I pitched nothing but relief from then on. I can't really say that the Yankees thought I was a great prospect. I played then at 5' 10" and 145–150 pounds. Casey always had that against me, the fact that I was so small.

In 1958 you were pitching for Richmond AAA when New York called you up. How did you find out that you were going to the major leagues?

I remember like it was yesterday. It was at the end of our season. We had two or three games left. I was always kind of a nut for staying in shape and I was out running in the outfield before the ball game. The clubhouse man came out and told me to go back, that Eddie Lopat, the manager, wanted to see me. I went into Eddie's office and he told me that the Yankees had called me the night before and that I was going up.

Eddie Lopat was not only a fabulous man, he was a good coach for pitchers. He was the only one during the whole time I played baseball that I learned anything from. Believe it or not, back then the Yankee organization was probably the best around and they didn't have pitching coaches or hitting coaches in the minor league system. So wherever you were you pretty much learned on your own or from a veteran pitcher who may be on the team, or someone like Eddie. Eddie really worked with me and taught me the value of the changeup and pitching to spots—pitching more than throwing. I was always a thrower until I got Eddie's guidance and I became a pitcher.

Had you ever been to New York before?

No, I hadn't.

What was it like finally putting on those pinstripes and walking out onto the field at Yankee Stadium?

Whew, about like it would be if you envision if it had happened to you. The difficult thing for me was when I got to New York I went straight to the Concourse Plaza Hotel, where I was told to stay. The stadium was in walking distance. I couldn't figure out how to get into the stadium, into the locker room. I was walking around the outside of the ballpark trying to figure out how to get in. The New York street urchins, who can be wise guys and could spot a ballplayer a mile away, were following me around kind of harassing me. There was a group of six or eight of them, but they finally showed me where the door was. Then I couldn't get by the guy at the door. I was wearing a white T-shirt and Levi's and weighed 145 pounds, so I'm sure I didn't look like a ballplayer to him, so he had to call down to have someone come up and get me. But walking into that fabled dressing room, that locker room that had carpeting on the floor and those great lockers that you weren't used to anything that big, and putting on that uniform for the first time and walking out onto that field was a real thrill.

Did Casey Stengel say anything to you when you arrived?

No, I don't recall him saying anything. You were under the guidance of the coaches. I remember Jim Turner, who was the pitching coach, welcoming me. I had been in spring training a couple of times so I knew some of the guys a little bit and my roommate from the year before, Zach Monroe, was on the team so Zach took care of me too.

The mistake I made was at my first game. Before the game I went out to sit on the bench and I apparently sat in the one spot that Casey sat in. Some of the guys kind of snickered at me as they walked by. Casey finally came out and stood in front of me and looked at me, and Bobby Richardson said, "John, that's where Casey sits." [Laughs] How does that make you feel?

Your first game was on September 6, 1958, in relief of Art Ditmar at Yankee Stadium against the Senators, and you pitched three scoreless innings.

Yes, actually a very famous thing happened in that game. I think it was the third inning that I pitched. I walked Albie Pearson, who was very walkable at five-foot-whatever he was, and the next guy got a line drive single to left field. The next hitter was Clint Courtney, and he hit a screaming line drive right at Gil McDougald, the second baseman. Gil threw the glove in front of his face and caught it, and then threw to Tony Kubek, forcing the guy at second, and then over to first for a triple play. That was on a Saturday Game of the Day and the announcers were Dizzy Dean and Buddy Blattner, so a lot of people saw that game across the country. I was told that Casey was extolling the virtues of a rookie pitcher in his very first game, forcing the hitter to hit into a triple play. [Laughs] In fact that story has been written up several times in the years since. It was in a Yankee program that they sold at the stands in the late '70s. Someone sent it to me.

In 1959 you spent the entire year at Richmond [International League] again and posted a 2.06 ERA. You pitched in 70 games and went 9–6. Were you surprised that they never called you up?

Actually 78 if you count the eight games I pitched in the play-offs. I was [surprised], but there were reasons for those things. I didn't have a particularly good spring training, but in '58 I had a good spring. Casey saw me on the Yankee B team that year. In '59 I was told to put on some weight and I went home and drank milkshakes all winter. Put on about 15 flabby pounds and consequently I had a lousy spring. There were two of us on that '59 Richmond team that had good first parts of the season, me and Eli Grba. We both pitched in relief and had very similar records and we were both pitching very well. Eli was a big strapping guy at 6' 2" and 190 pounds or whatever. He had really good stuff, and so they called Eli up. I always felt that I was the one that should have gotten called up. I may have had a better record but Eli was a lot better prospect than I was.

In 1960 did you start the year with the big club?

I did. I had one of those springs that you have in your dreams. The Yankees have this award called the James P. Dawson Award. It's given to the rookie that has the most outstanding spring and I won the award that year. I think I pitched 18 innings and gave up one run. I got a lot of good press and made the team from spring training.

You wound up having a great year, going 5–1 with two saves for the eventual AL Champions.

The first month of the season Casey didn't pitch me. Eddie Lopat, who had moved up as the Yankee pitching coach, told me that Casey didn't want anyone to see me, so they wouldn't want me in a trade. Eventually I ended up pitching a little bit and wound up 5–1 with two saves. At that time I had pitched in more games than any other pitcher. I had just finished a game against the White Sox and I got a save in that game. It was a couple of weeks after the All Star break, as I recall. Casey called me into his office and I'll never forget, he was sitting on the edge of his desk clad in only his shorts and he started talking to me in Stengelese. I really had no idea what he was saying until he leaped out in the middle of the floor on his stomach—now this is a guy who's 65 or 66 years old—and held his hands out in front of him and said, "When you get down to Richmond make 'em give you a low target." And that's how I knew I was being sent back to Richmond. Up until that moment I had no idea what he was talking about.

So I kind of didn't handle it in a very mature way. I went back to the hotel where I was rooming with Tony Kubek, and I wouldn't go down to Richmond. In the next room was Joe Demastri and Bobby Shantz. We all hung out together but Tony was my roommate. Tony kept coming back and saying, "John, they're telling me to tell you to get back to Richmond." I said, "Tell them I'm not going." I figured that if I did something like that they'd trade me. So one day Tony came in and told me that if I didn't get down to Richmond that they were going to stop paying me. I was making a grand total of $10,000 at the time. That was big money, so I went down to Richmond and I didn't do well there either. I had a bad attitude and it was my fault. I figured that my dream was burst and that I wouldn't get another shot.

That year [1960] Whitey Ford actually had an off year, going 12–9. Art Ditmar led the staff with a 16–9 record. What type of pitcher was he?

Sure, Art was a good pitcher. He didn't have overpowering stuff but he was a true pitcher. He worked the corners and he had a slider that he could throw for a strike most anytime he wanted to. Art pitched some good ball. He didn't smoke the ball by you like Bob Turley did.

Did any member of the pitching staff help you in any way when you got up?

No, not really. I was a little on the shy side and didn't go around asking questions and talking to people and doing the things that you should do. I don't remember who it was but I read it just the other day . . . about the awe factor when you get to the big leagues and that's true. It took me a long time to get over the awe of being where I was. You read about the Yankees and Yankee Stadium all your life and when you finally get there, you're in awe.

Despite how your '60 season ended, you were back in 1961.

I made the team out of spring training and in retrospect, I now know why: because I was trade bait. Sure enough, before the trading deadline I got traded to the Angels. That's just my opinion; nobody would admit that. Hell, ballplayers know what's going on. I made the team and the first month of the year I pitched once for an inning and a third. It's funny, our first trip into L.A.—it was the Angels' first year as an expansion team—we played a three-game series and every time our pitcher got into trouble they would warm me up, and when it came time to take the starter out they would put in somebody else. I wasn't smart enough to know that they were showcasing me to the Angels.

Was there any difference between pitching to either Yogi Berra or Elston Howard?

Well, that's a fair question. I enjoyed pitching to Yogi but I didn't really pitch to Howard much at all because he really didn't catch that much. Blanchard was there too and John was a good catcher, but Yogi did most of the catching. There was a comfort having him back behind the plate because of his reputation, and because he'd been there so long and knew the hitters. As far as a catcher, Howard was probably a better catcher but that's not really a big issue. They called their own pitches and I could shake them off, a pitcher could shake them off. I'm not so sure a pitcher can do that so much anymore.

Did you get to know Mickey Mantle at all?

Not really. The only time I ever spent any time with Mickey was in 1990. I went into the shopping center business in management and we opened a fancy new shopping center in Scottsdale, where I live. We had a lot of money in the budget for a grand opening promotion, and I had seven of the Yankees come out for an autograph show in the mall. Of course Mickey was a key Yankee to get and I paid his fee, which was $20,000 a day. I got him and Larson, Richardson, Whitey, Ryan Duren, Hank Bauer, and Bill Skowron, so it was a good mix. I got to spend a couple of days driving Mickey and his agent, who was this gal Greer Johnson, around town, you remember her. I'd pick them up at the hotel and drive them to the mall and take them here and there. It was the only time I got to know him.

I had kind of a funny incident happen when I was pitching for the Angels in '61 at the stadium. This was when he and Maris were in that home run hitting contest. I was pitching in relief. I went in in the fourth inning. The first time around Roger popped up and Mickey struck out. The next time around Roger hit home run number 20 off me. It really kind of ticked me off because I grooved a pitch—Mickey was hitting next and I didn't want to have Roger on base with Mantle coming up when I had struck out the first two hitters. So I grooved one to Roger and he hit it out. So I struck out Mantle again for the third out. You know Mantle had that funny way of taking off his helmet—he'd lift it off the back of his head—and as he did that we kind of made eye contact as I was walking off the mound and he said, "If you'd pitched that way when you were a Yankee you'd still be here." [Laughs] I had a chance to tell him that story when he was here for the grand opening of the shopping center and he got a kick out of it.

You started the 1961 season with New York but pitched in only one game. On May 8 you were traded along with Lee Thomas and Ryan Duren to the expansion Los Angeles Angels for Bob Cerv and Tex Clevenger. Did you view the trade as an opportunity to play more?

Oh, I certainly did. I could see that I was never going to be a star or whatever with the Yankees. I could see the handwriting on the wall; I wasn't that naive. At the end of that three-game series in Los Angeles I asked Ralph Houk, who was our manager by then, if I could stay over in L.A., where my family was. The team had a day off the next day. They were going to play in Kansas City and I asked if I could catch up to them in Kansas City. He said, "Sure!" [Laughs] If I had been smart about it I'd have realized that they were going to trade me to the Angels. The next day I happened to be down at a department store where I worked during the off-season with my friends. I got a call and I went up to the office. It was Ralph telling me to stay there, that I'd been traded.

I felt good about it, though. I knew some of the guys—I had played with Fritz Brikell and Kenny Hunt and Eli Grba, so I felt comfortable there. Gene Autry was a great owner—you couldn't ask for better ownership. It was a great place except for the ballpark, old Wrigley Field,[40] but I went to the ballpark for games when I was a kid so it was kind of neat to be playing there. It felt like this room I'm sitting in talking to you, it was so small. I was supposed to be a sinker-ball pitcher so I never worried about the size of the ballpark,[41] but I was happy to be in my hometown. In a way I hated to be gone from the New York Yankees because that was my dream team from the time I was 11 or 12 years old. That's who I wanted to pitch for.

Roger Maris broke Babe Ruth's record by hitting 61 home runs in 1961. He hit number 20 off you at Yankee Stadium on June 11. He had hit number 19 off Eli Grba earlier in the game. Do you still get any fan mail about that?

You know, that's the only reason I ever do get any fan mail. I'll get a couple of things to autograph a week, maybe three in a good week. Most of it's because I threw Roger a home run. I'm looking at a picture right now of Roger hitting a home run and it's signed by all the pitchers that threw him a home-run ball. A fan in Connecticut had sent this around and I asked him to send me a copy of it and he did. I get a lot of requests for autographs for that, and for being on that '61 team. They tell me that the '61 team has become known as the best team of all time. I'm not sure, but a lot of people think that.

In nine minor league stops prior to 1960 you only had one losing record [8–9 in 1958]. Do you think that you would have had a longer major league career if you had been with another organization than the Yankees?

Oh yes, definitely. There were three clubs that made me offers—the Yankees, the old St. Louis Browns, and the Dodgers. I think that if I had signed with the St. Louis Browns I would have

---

40. In 1961, the Angels' first year of existence, they played in a former Pacific Coast League stadium in Los Angeles named Wrigley Field. This should not be confused with the Wrigley Field in Chicago that was originally owned by the same family.

41. A sinker ball breaks downward at the plate, often resulting in a weak ground ball.

played enough years to draw a pension. You know I had some good years in the minor leagues and I always had confidence that I could make the Yankees. I was small but I could throw hard. Every year I'd be playing with some minor league team and there'd be some big stud pitchers, and yet I knew that I was better than they were and that if given a chance I could pitch up there. I think I would have had a nice career if I had been with some other organization.

What happened to your career after '61?

Well, in the spring of '62 with the Angels I had worked my way up to the fourth starting pitcher. I never really told anybody, but I was pitching batting practice in the off-season just to some cronies. I threw too long and my elbow started hurting. In spring I was pitching a game against the old Houston Colt .45s over in Apache Junction [Arizona]. I threw a curveball and you could hear my elbow pop all over the ballpark, they tell me. That was kind of the end of it—I never did get well. They gave me cortisone shots but it never did get well enough to pitch right.

I always tell people I was really fortunate that when I got out of baseball when I retired, I had gotten it all out of my system. Over the years, and up until very recently, I'd hear from guys I played minor league ball with who never got above B ball or C ball. They tell me that they knew they could have made it, but they couldn't have. I had my shot and I wasn't good enough and off I went. I had a really good life after baseball.

A couple of years ago I went on the computer and got a list of every player that had ever played or pitched for the New York Yankees. At the time I think the number was 1,276— it was the early '90s. Roughly 485 of them were pitchers, so I was one of 500 guys that pitched for the Yankees up until that point. I was really lucky to have done that.

Have you ever been back to Yankee Stadium?

No, I haven't. I had a birthday a couple of weeks ago and as a birthday present my son wanted to take me back to the stadium to see a couple of games, since it was the last year of the stadium. I like the outdoors and I like to fish—my son and I fly-fish. So I thought about it for a day and said to him, "Why don't we take a fly-fishing trip up to Colorado? We'll hire a guide and have him float us down the Gunnison River." And that's what we're going to do.

I don't mean to demean the stadium and all that history—my God, it's a fabulous place— but baseball was 50 years ago and I've gotten it out of my system. I don't have an affinity for it anymore. We have the D-Backs here in Phoenix, and if there's nothing else on TV I'll watch the Diamondbacks. But the game has changed so much in a lot of little ways—like if the pitcher throws the ball in the dirt it's immediately thrown out of the game. Well hell, if a ball's been thrown in the dirt three or four times it becomes a good ball to pitch with. Batting gloves and armor and all sorts of things that I don't like about the game anymore. I think the ballplayers of today are much better athletes than we ever were. Someone like me, 5' 10" and 145 pounds out of high school— I wouldn't even get a look from a scout.

TOPPS

JAMES, JOHN PHILLIP
Born: July 23, 1933 Bonners Ferry, Indiana
Bats: Left Throws: Right
Height: 5' 10" Weight: 160 lbs.

Year	Team	G	W-L	SV	GS	CG	IP	SO	W	ERA
1958	YANKEES	1	0-0	0	0	0	3.0	1	4	0.00
1960	YANKEES	28	5-1	2	0	0	43.3	29	26	4.36
1961	YANKEES	1	0-0	0	0	0	1.3	2	0	0.00
1961	Angels	36	0-2	0	3	0	71.3	41	53	5.30
	Total 3 Years	66	5-3	2	3	0	119.0	73	84	4.76

1960s

National Baseball Hall of Fame

JACK REED
1961–63

You were born in Silver City, Mississippi, and still reside there. I guess you were not a Yankee fan growing up?

[Laughs] Nope, I was a Cardinals fan. We would get the Cardinals games at night on KMOX out of St. Louis.

That's right. I believe they just stopped broadcasting the Cardinals games recently.[42]

Yes, they sure did.

Did you play a lot of baseball growing up in Silver City?

Oh yes, I sure did. We used to have a good semipro league here in the summertime. We had a lot of college boys, and of course local boys. I had a good high school coach named Mr. McClanahan. He was one of the best fundamental coaches I've ever been associated with, and that includes any of them I ran into in the pros. That was right here at Silver City High School. We're a small town but we were a consolidated school in a district. I played shortstop in high school but I wasn't an infielder really—the outfield was my place.

After high school you moved on to the University of Mississippi. You had a very good college baseball career and led the S.E.C. [Southeastern Conference] in hitting.

Yeah, I did. I played football and baseball at Old Miss and ran track.

You're still just one of four men to have played in a World Series and a major college bowl game [Sugar Bowl, 1953].

Well yes. I guess I was at the right place at the right time.

Was there any interest in you from the NFL or AFL when you graduated college?

Well NFL, yes. I don't know if you remember Jimmy Patton, who played with the Giants as a defensive back. He made All-Pro about six years in a row. He went to Old Miss, and he played one corner and I played the other. I don't know if they were interested in signing me or not, but I talked to Jim Lee Howell, who was the Giants' coach at the time, and he asked me if I was interested in playing football. I told him no, that baseball was my game. I enjoyed playing football, but baseball was what I loved.

---

42. Cardinals games could be heard over KMOX in most of the continental United States for 52 years, ending in 2005.

You were scouted by the Yankees while at Old Miss, but were you aware of any other teams that may have been looking at you?

Oh yes. I went to St. Louis for a week and worked out with the Cardinals. I also went to Detroit and worked out with the Tigers for a week. I guess the Yankees had a better offer. Looking at the Yankees, they were winners and that's what I liked. The guy that scouted me was an old Yankee pitcher named Atley Donald.

You signed with the Yankees as a 20-year-old and went to the minors right away, but had your career interrupted by a two-year stint as a lieutenant in the army in Korea.

I went through the ROTC program at Old Miss. I was in the infantry—bad. [Laughs] When I signed in August of '53 I actually went to Kansas City [AAA] for a month right at the end of the season. Then the next year I played at Winston-Salem [B], North Carolina. I then played at Binghamton [high A], New York, the next year before going into active duty. I had a bit of a delay going into the army. I don't know why I got that deferment, but I did. Jim Coats, John Blanchard, Zach Monroe, and Fritz Brickell—we all played together at Binghamton. I hit .308 or .309 and I tied Bobby Richardson with the lead in base hits.

Did you have any contact with the Yankees while you were on active duty?

None whatsoever. The only time that I had any contact with them was when I got out. I got out of the service in September of '57 and I went to Panama—they sent me to winter ball. After that I went to play at New Orleans in the old Southern League [AA], and I had a good year there, too.

During your time progressing through the Yankee minor league system did you ever get discouraged with the apparent lack of opportunity for an outfielder with the big club? They had Mantle, Maris, Bauer, Enos Slaughter, Norm Siebern, Elston Howard, Bob Cerv, Hector Lopez, and even Yogi, who had moved out to left field.

[Laughs] Well, I guess I didn't get discouraged—or didn't have sense enough too. Of course I knew back then that the only way you could make the Yankees was if you were a hot-prospect pitcher or if somebody retired. The whole time I was in the organization I don't think they had a retirement in the outfield. I guess Bauer, but I can't remember exactly when he retired.

When you played in the club's minor league system, some baseball people say that the Yankees AAA teams were actually better than some major league teams. How do you feel about that?

Like I said, when I signed it was August and I went up to Kansas City. I would say that team they had at that time could have played in the big leagues. They had Moose Skowron at first base, Alex Grammas was the shortstop, Rudy Smith was the third baseman, Elston Howard was the left fielder, Bob Cerv was the center fielder. They had a pretty good ball club. I was just taking up room, really. [Laughs] They just sent me up there because they needed a body.

Did you make the big club out of spring training in 1961?

Yes I did, but the biggest thing was that Ralph Houk took over the ball club from Stengel. What he said was that I was going to be a backup to Mantle,—a late-inning replacement— and that's what I did, really. I actually took Yogi's place more than I did Mantle, when he started playing left field.

What was it like that first time you put on a Yankee uniform and walked out onto the field at Yankee Stadium?

The best feeling I've had in a long time. I can remember the first game I played in. I took Yogi's place in left field. I don't know if you remember or not, but Yankee Stadium used to slope off behind shortstop before they renovated it. I don't know how they used to play football there myself—they had to be running uphill sometimes. Anyway, when they put me in I said to myself, I hope they don't hit a ball to me—I'd hate to make a screwup the first time I get on the field. Luckily a guy hit it right to me.

The only time I had been to New York City previously was when I was with Binghamton. I'd been there once. Listen, I live in a town that has about 250 people. Silver City is a farming area. They've got a lot of bright lights [in New York City].

Where did you stay during your three years on the team?

Well, when my wife wasn't up there I stayed at the old Manhattan Hotel. It's right behind Times Square, right behind the Waldorf Astoria. When she was up there I lived over in Ridgewood, New Jersey.

At 28 you were an old rookie on arguably the best team in baseball history. How did your teammates treat you?

Oh, just fine. Johnny Blanchard and I kind of grew up in the Yankee organization together ,and he's probably one of the best friends I've got. Clete Boyer is kind of like I was. He came from a small town in Missouri and he was a country boy like I was. Everybody got along fine.

Is it true that you were called "Mickey's Legs"?

Yes. [Laughs] That's what Ralph Houk told me I was going to do and I think that probably some sports writers picked that up.

You were known for your speed. In fact you had more runs scored [39] than hits [30] in your career. You weren't disappointed when you finally made it to the big leagues that you got cast into this bench role?

No, not really. Like you said, I was 28 years old, and back then when you hit that 30 mark you felt like it was going downhill. I was just glad to be there.

Was Mickey Mantle the greatest hitter that you ever saw?

He was the best *player* I ever saw! He was the best talent I ever saw in a uniform. There wasn't anything this guy couldn't do. You know, he used to wrap his legs—the one that he had osteomyelitis in his knee; he used to wrap that. He never complained though, he really didn't.

Some fans today forget what a great player Roger Maris was. His career sometimes gets overshadowed by the 61 home runs. He won two MVP awards and was one of the best outfielders in the game.

Yes, he was. Roger was a complete player. I played against him in the minors when I was at Binghamton. He was at Reading. You could tell the guy was a good ballplayer. He was an excellent outfielder and excellent base runner, and he had one of the most accurate arms I ever saw.

You were there on October 1, 1961, when Roger Maris hit his 61st home run. After touching home plate he just wanted to go back into the dugout, and you and your teammates had to push him back out onto the field to take a bow.

Yes, I played in that game. Roger really didn't want all that hoopla, you know. Roger was kind of an introvert type of guy. A nice guy—I don't mean that in a derogatory way—he was a nice guy to me, but he just didn't want all that hoopla about the whole thing.

You have been asked this question a thousand times, but I have to ask it again. On June 24, 1962, the Yankees were in Detroit on a Sunday afternoon and jumped out to a 6–0 lead in the top of the first inning. At that point nobody would have guessed that there were still 21 innings of baseball left to play. At the end of nine innings the score stood at 7–7. Houk sent

you in to right field to replace Pepitone [219 career home runs], who had earlier replaced Mantle [536 career home runs]. Were you tired by the 22nd inning?

Not really. Bobby Richardson said I was the only one still in the lineup that wasn't tired.

With one out Maris walked and you came to the plate to face All-Star pitcher Phil Regan. Do you remember the next events?

Oh yes. Hey listen, you're talking about my only claim to fame here. [Laughs] I played against Phil Regan in the minors. He pitched for Birmingham when I played at New Orleans. I didn't remember that much about him. I was really supposed to bunt on the first pitch and move Maris over to second base. I thought the ball was outside but it was called a strike. Crosetti, the third base coach, took the bunt off and he threw me a pitch right down the middle. I didn't watch it, but it went to left center field and I really didn't think it was a home run. Yeah, I hit it good but I thought it would be a double. When I hit second base the umpire was waving me around and that's when I knew it was a home run.

Your teammates must have been pretty thankful that you ended it?

[Laughs] I think so. I know Yogi was. He caught all 22 innings!

Did you get the ball?

No, I didn't. I didn't think about it at the time, really.

Did Ralph Houk say anything to you after the game?

He was just congratulating me and glad to have it over with.

In 1963, your third year with the team, Mickey Mantle broke his ankle and you played in 106 games. Did you think that you would be back in '64?

Well, when they made Yogi the manager I knew I wouldn't be back. Yogi liked pitching and he carried an extra pitcher instead of an extra outfielder. I guess I was expendable, since my job was just picking up Mantle or whoever in the late innings. I went down to Richmond in 1964 and I was a coach. I played some but then I started managing. I managed minor league ball for three years, from '65 to '67, in their system. I never played for anybody else or worked for anybody else except the Yankees. After my father died I went home to take care of the family farm.

What type of farm?

We raised cotton, soybeans, and I raised catfish. Have you ever had any catfish?

No, I never have.

You need to eat some. It's good! [Laughs]

Did the team give you a World Series ring for either 1961 or '62?

Yes sir, I have both of them.

Have you gotten back to the Bronx since you retired?

I've been to eight or nine Old-Timers' Days. I've also been up to card shows and things like that. I was in New York last June [2008]. I took my grandson to see Yankee Stadium. He likes baseball.

Did you contact anybody from the organization?

No, I didn't. We flew in and went to a ball game that night and again the next afternoon, then flew home the next morning. I'll tell you one thing, though: the guy who's their trainer now, [Gene] Monahan, he was my trainer when I managed Binghamton, New York, in 1967. He was just a young kid then.

Are you going to come back to see the new Yankee Stadium?

I don't know. I might. I'm getting to the point where I don't want to travel anymore. My son lives in Holland and my wife and I just flew over there last year. The nine and a half hours on an airplane was a little much for me. I'd like to see it though. Are they going to tear down the old stadium and make it into a parking lot?

I think they're still discussing what they're going to do with that space.

You know what I can't understand? If it's going to be a parking lot, what's the purpose? If there hasn't been a parking space up there in 50 years, why now? About the only way you can get there is if you come on the bus, or catch a cab, or subway.

BRACE Photo

REED, JOHN BURWELL
Born: February 2, 1933 Silver City, Mississippi
Bats: Right Throws: Right
Height: 6' 0" Weight: 185

Year	Team	G	AB	H	2B	3B	HR	AVG	RBI	R
1961	YANKEES	28	13	2	0	0	0	.154	1	4
1962	YANKEES	88	43	13	2	1	1	.302	4	17
1963	YANKEES	106	73	15	3	1	0	.205	1	18
	Total 3 Years	222	129	30	5	2	1	.233	6	39

Narional Baseballl Hall of Fame

JAKE GIBBS
1962–71

You were born in Grenada, Mississippi. Is that where you grew up?

That's correct. Believe it or not, as a boy, of course I followed baseball since I was big enough to walk, but somehow or other I got to listen to the Game of the Week and I became a Detroit Tiger fan. It seemed like the Yankees were always playing Detroit [on TV] and I somehow or other got involved with Detroit. It was Virgil Trucks, Dizzy Trout, Art Houtteman, Johnny Lipon, and Vic Wertz. I'm looking at back when I was about eight to ten years old and it was about 1951 when Detroit and the Yankees went down to the last game of the year and the Yankees won it. That's when I really started to listen to baseball games. I followed baseball ever since that time. I grew up outside of Grenada and we had our own little team back then. We had enough guys to make up a ball team and we just played all the time.

Mississippi is a place where you can probably play all the time, so you must have played a lot growing up.

Well, you can't play all year round because we do have some wintertime weather in December and January and February. But you can probably play eight months out of the year.

After sandlot you moved on to your high school team at John Rundle High.

I did. As a matter of fact I made my high school team while I was still in the seventh grade. I played six years of high school baseball in Granada.

Were you scouted in high school?

Oh yeah, sure. There was a guy who pitched for the Yankees named Atley Donald. He saw me play about as much as anybody. He's the one who followed me through my high school and college days, and eventually I signed with him to be a Yankee.

Originally you were not a catcher but an infielder, I believe.

I've always been an infielder. I never was a catcher until I had played two years in AAA. In '61 when I signed with the Yankees I went straight to AAA and played third base and some second base that year. Then in 1962 I played just about the whole year at shortstop. I was made into a catcher in the spring of '63. I think the decision was made before spring training took place.

After high school you went on to play for Ole Miss, the University of Mississippi. Were you their third baseman?

I was a third baseman and I was a shortstop one year. You see, at that time freshmen couldn't play on varsity so I only played three years of varsity. So one year at shortstop and two years at third base. I signed as a third baseman.

Despite your being a baseball All-American, the most notable thing about your college sports career was being an All-American quarterback and coming in third in the Heisman Trophy voting in 1960.

That's correct. Deep down I loved baseball, though. College football was the exciting sport on campus. We had outstanding college football teams and I loved playing college football. I also loved playing baseball, and I thought that I could have a longer career in baseball.

At the end of your Ole Miss career both the Houston Oilers and the Cleveland Browns offered you contracts. Instead you signed with the Yankees as a bonus baby for $105,000. Was that a lot of pressure for a 22-year-old joining an organization that had just won 19 pennants and 15 World Championships in the last 26 years?

Well, the way I looked at it was, I had an opportunity to sign with the Milwaukee Braves and the San Francisco Giants, and those teams were offering me almost the same money that the Yankees were. What influenced me about signing with the Yankees was, I had followed them and knew their players, from Lou Gehrig, Babe Ruth, Mickey Mantle, and Whitey Ford and all those guys. I just felt like we were winners at Ole Miss—we won the SEC [Southeastern Conference] baseball two years when I was there, and if I was a good enough athlete then I wanted to sign with the best. I wanted to play with the best.

You broke into professional baseball with a five-hit day. That's not too bad of a start.

Yeah, it was a doubleheader against Toronto. In fact I don't think I hit a ball hard the whole night, I just got lucky.

You wouldn't have to wait long to be a Yankee. Just a little over a year after signing you were called up to New York on September 11, 1962. Were you surprised at being called up so quickly?

What happened was, we finished the season at AAA in Toronto. When that season was over I got recalled by the Yankees and flew from Toronto to Detroit. It was Pedro Gonzalez and me. I played in my first game at Tiger Stadium when I pinch-ran in the eighth inning, I believe. I wound up scoring on a fly ball to right field, where Al Kaline was playing. My run tied the game 1–1, but we got beat the next inning. That was my first game as a big-leaguer.

I noticed that you went into the army in 1962 also. Were you drafted during the season?

I enlisted in the army! I was at Richmond in '61 and the Yankees sent down word for me and a pitcher named George Haney to go and enlist because they were going to close the six-month tour of duty.[43] George and I went and enlisted in St. Petersburg, Virginia, at Fort Lee in July or August, and when the baseball season was over I came home and joined the Mississippi National Guard.

In '62 when I get home from playing baseball, that's when I went to Fort Jackson for my basic training. I went there for three months, and then I went to Fort Gordon in Augusta, Georgia, for my advanced training. I got out of Fort Gordon sometime around the first of February. My wife was over there with my baby, who was about eight months old. We went to Grenada and changed clothes, repacked, and went to Ft. Lauderdale [for the Yankees spring training]! That was in '63, when I walked into Ralph Houk's office. He called me in, and he said that they were thinking about making me a catcher.

When I was at Fort Gordon we were setting up a military auditorium theater and this army captain comes up to me and says, "Are you the Gibbs who plays with the Yankees?" I said, "Well, it could be." He saw my name on my fatigue shirt and he said to me, "You're gonna be a catcher when you go to spring training." That was the first time I ever heard anything like that and I looked at him and I said, "I don't think so, Captain, I'm an infielder." It struck me that an army captain would say something like that. He told me that he knew the general manager at Augusta and that the rumor was that they were going to make me a catcher when I went to spring training! I said, "Well, that's just talk. I don't think I'm going to catch." When I was in Ralph Houk's office and he told me that they were going to make me a catcher my mind went back to Fort Gordon to that army captain. He knew what he was talking about.

Before you were called up with the Yankees had you ever been to New York City before?

Yeah, when I made All-American in football. I went on the Ed Sullivan football awards show. There were about 11 guys up there for that.

What was it like that first time you got to Yankee Stadium and put on that uniform and walked out onto the field?

I remember it because when I signed with the Yankees it was the 25th of May and I flew up the next day on the 26th. Roy Hamey, who was the general manager of the Yankees, and Jack White, who was his assistant, were with me. Jack White was very familiar with Ole Miss because of his

---

43. The tour of duty was expanded to one year during the Vietnam War.

football background. Anyway, we flew into New York and had a nice conversation on the plane. I didn't get nervous until we kind of got close. We flew where you could see Yankee Stadium and I thought, God, in maybe an hour I'm going to be in the locker room and meeting and shaking hands with people that I've been following through the papers and TV. I got excited and got nervous too.

When I walked in locker room I met Mickey, I met Houk, I met Whitey. Moose Skowron came over and he said, "Hey, whatever these guys say they're just glad you're here, and welcome." Yogi came over and gave me a handshake and said, "It's about time you got here." So they made me feel real at ease when I got there. Putting on that uniform and running out on that field—it was exciting times.

When you made the switch to catcher there were plenty of experienced guys there to guide you, between Houk, Berra, and Howard. Did any of them more than the others help you?

Well, I'll tell you, there were two guys. Jim Hegan was our catching coach. I only had about three weeks or maybe a month in spring training to learn how to be a catcher. Then they sent me to Richmond [AAA] and they brought up a guy named Lamar North. Lamar North was a catcher in the Yankees organization and had been down in AA. He was a well-known defensive catcher. They brought him up to Richmond, I guess as a player-coach, and he worked with me the whole year in '63. I have to give him a lot of credit because he was with the team and with me every day. He taught me the good, basic fundamentals of catching. So I learned quite a lot from him. Of course I learned a lot from Ellie Howard just by going to spring training with him and watching him catch and how he does things. We also would talk a lot about different things. Yogi at that time wasn't catching that much; he was in the outfield. But between them and Jim Hegan every year—the whole time that I was with the Yankees Jim Hegan was my catching coach. He was great teacher and a great man. I respect him very much.

Did the Yankees put you on any of their postseason rosters in either '62, '63, or '64?

I don't think so, because I started all of those years in AAA. The only World Series that I was going to be in was in 1964, when the Yankees played the Cardinals. I had gotten called up from Richmond to the Yankees and about a week before the season was over Tony Kubek hurt his throwing hand and was kind of unable to grip a bat or throw. They had to make a decision and they dropped Tony from the World Series list and put me on it. We won the pennant on the next-to-last day of the season. Then on the last day of the season, it was a Sunday against Cleveland. The game is in the 13th inning and it's tied 1–1. I'm catching and I get a foul tip off my throwing hand. It broke a bone in my index finger and chipped a bone in my middle finger. Then they took me off the World Series list and put Mike Hegan on it. That was my only chance to have ever gone to a World Series.

During your time with the team you caught some fine pitchers, including Ford, Stottlemyre, Fritz Peterson, Al Downing, Stan Bahnsen, and Ralph Terry, among others. Did any of them stand out in your mind as the best?

Well, I'd say Whitey was the best pitcher I ever caught because he had great command of all of his pitches. Mel Stottlemyre was another great pitcher that I caught. I caught him two years in AAA. I wound up catching him for nine years and I knew him like a book. They would have to be two of my favorites. Al Downing was fun to catch, and so was Fritz Peterson.

Obviously you got to know Mickey Mantle during your time with the Yankees. Was he the most talented hitter that you ever saw?

Well I would say so. I saw him more than anybody else. He was an inspiration to all the players. He was such a leader in the clubhouse and on the field. He led by example. As a player you'd watch him wrap his own legs and get in the whirlpool, and you knew that when he played his legs were probably in a good bit of pain. He would play through that and he played every game, you know. He was that kind of guy who was great in the clubhouse, and we looked up to him and followed him.

Roger Maris was another teammate who was very talented, but who similarly struggled with injuries.

Roger had a beautiful swing and was a very good outfielder who could run and had an accurate arm in right field. He had that perfect swing for Yankee Stadium.

After the 1964 season the Yankees' fortunes turned quickly. After coming in first in all but two seasons since 1948, the team plummeted to sixth place in '65, followed by a tenth-place finish in '66 and ninth place in '67. What would you say could be the reasons for this?

I don't know. It's kind of hard to put your finger on it because in '65 we still had Bobby Richardson, we had Clete Boyer back, we had Mickey back, we had Roger Maris back, Elston Howard back, we had Whitey Ford back, Stottlemyre back, Downing back, we had Hector Lopez back. Tom Tresh was there. We had Horace Clarke, who came up with me. I think Kubek retired after '64. You know, I don't know what it was in '65.

After '64 they let Yogi go and brought in the guy from St. Louis—Johnny Keane. That was the year we wound up in sixth place. We didn't play in '65 like we did in '64, but I don't know what the reason was.

Were you surprised when Johnny Keane got fired 20 games into his second season [1966]?

Gosh, you never know about those things. We weren't doing good. We got off to a bad start in '66. We went out to a West Coast road trip. Ralph Houk was on the plane with us and I think we were something like 3–12 or 4–12—it wasn't good. Of course it's hard to read into anything and I don't think anybody was expecting it to happen, but it did happen out in L.A. They fired him when we were out on a road trip playing the Angels.

In August of 1969 the team promoted Thurman Munson to New York. Did you have an early impression of him that made you think that he was going to be something special?

Yeah, the fist time I saw Thurman was in batting practice and he could swing the bat. You could tell that he was going to be a good ballplayer. He came up in '70 and I backed him up. You could see that he was going to be a good ballplayer because he had a lot of leadership ability, he could swing the bat, and he had a quick throw to second base. You know, he just had to learn the pitching staff, and once you learn the pitching staff you're ready to be a catcher.

That's one thing about being a Yankee—everybody would work with you. We ended up being good friends. We talked together about different pitchers and blocking balls in the dirt—you know, just trying to be helpful whenever we could. We got along real good those two years.

You fell into the role of Thurman Munson's backup catcher for 1970 and '71. That seemed to be a good role for you and the team as a veteran catcher behind a young player. The Yankees never released you at the end of your career. Did you just decide to retire after the '71 season?

That was my own decision. What happened was, the University of Mississippi offered me the opportunity to come home and be their baseball coach and football recruiter. That's what we did, we left the New York Yankees and came back to the University of Mississippi and I worked until 1992, when I retired.

When you told the Yankees that you were retiring did they try to convince you to stay?

Well, Ralph Houk was my manager and he kind of knew my feelings toward Ole Miss. Back in '65 I started working with the quarterbacks at Ole Miss. When I would get through playing with the Yankees I would come and work with the quarterbacks here. I did that for five years. Ralph knew my association with Ole Miss, so I don't think that decision surprised him when it came about. I know that they didn't want to lose me because when I told him in Kansas City that I was retiring at the end of the year, he told me in his office that Ted Williams, the Washington manager, tried to get me to be their number one catcher in the spring of '71 and the Yankees turned it down. About a week before the June trade deadline in '71, the Senators called the Yankees and made the same offer again, and the Yanks still said no. So the Yankees turned down the trade for me twice.

The final game in which you were a Yankee was a very strange affair that occurred on September 30, 1971. The Yankees were in Washington for the final game of the season, which also happened to be the last Senators game in history. It is still the only forfeit the Yankees have been involved in during the past 80 years. Do you remember that game?[44]

I left that morning! Ralph wanted me to catch the night before. I caught Mel Stottlemyre and we won the ball game. When the game was over I went to Ralph Houk and I said, "I know you're not going to catch me tomorrow. Can I just leave a day early?" and he said, "Just take off and go." I was on my way back to Mississippi when the Yankees played that night and all the people ran out onto the field and wouldn't get off. The Yankees won 9–0,[45] but I wasn't there—I was back in Mississippi.

As you said earlier, you became the baseball coach for the University of Mississippi Rebels and became their winningest coach, finishing with a 485–389–9 record.

It was good to get back home and raise our family—we have three boys. You get to cut out all those road trips and travel, too. I loved playing baseball, but being a college baseball coach was exciting. Getting to work with young kids was good. Even when I was in high school I thought I might be a coach one day.

Ole Miss has produced 28 major league ballplayers.

Yeah, there've been a few and we've had a good program down here. It's been fun; it's been a great run.

After retiring from Ole Miss you made it back to the Yankees!

---

44. The Yankees were losing 7–5 in the ninth inning and down to their last out when Washington fans, angry that their team was moving to Texas, stormed the field and tore it up.
45. In a forfeited game the team that is awarded the win is automatically credited with a 9–0 victory regardless of the actual score.

Yeah, I was the catching coach in New York in 1993. I worked with Matt Nokes, Mike Stanley, and Jim Leyritz. Those were the three catchers I was responsible for. In '94 I became the manager of the Tampa Yankees and I managed there for two years. In 1995 when the season was over my wife and I said, "Let's go home," and that's what we did.

Did you manage to get back to New York this year [2008] for the Yankee Stadium finale?

No, I did not. As a matter of fact I haven't been to New York since '05.

Are you going to come up and see the new stadium?

Well I hope so, one of these days. I'd like to see it.

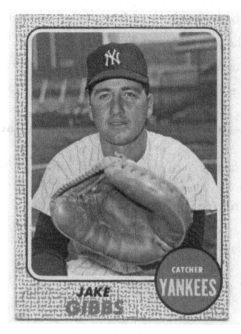

TOPPS

GIBBS, JERRY DEAN
Born: November 7, 1938 Grenada, Mississippi
Bats: Left Throws: Right
Height: 6' 0" Weight: 185

Year	Team	G	AB	H	2B	3B	HR	AVG	RBI	R
1962	YANKEES	2	0	0	0	0	0	.---	0	2
1963	YANKEES	4	8	2	0	0	0	.250	0	1
1964	YANKEES	3	6	1	0	0	0	.167	0	1
1965	YANKEES	37	68	15	1	0	2	.221	7	6
1966	YANKEES	62	182	47	6	0	3	.258	20	19
1967	YANKEES	116	374	87	7	1	4	.233	25	33
1968	YANKEES	124	423	90	12	3	3	.213	29	31
1969	YANKEES	71	219	49	9	2	0	.224	18	18
1970	YANKEES	49	153	46	9	2	8	.301	26	23
1971	YANKEES	70	206	45	9	0	5	.218	21	23
	Total 10 Years	538	1639	382	53	8	25	.233	146	157

Photofest

THAD TILLOTSON
1967–68

You were born and still live in Merced, California. Were you a San Francisco Giants fan growing up or an A's fan later on?

Yes, that's correct—well, I now live in Winton, California, just a few miles away. [Laughs] I wasn't a fan of either the Giants or the A's. I wasn't a fan of any of the local teams. I was a Dodger fan and a Yankee fan. As a kid you always remember the big names—they're the ones that are publicized the most, you know. Of course Mantle and Berra and all the ones who were name players at that time.

It's interesting that you were a Dodger and Yankee fan. You played for the Yankees but the Dodgers signed you as an amateur free agent at 19 years old.

I pitched on the Merced varsity High School team from when I was a freshman through my senior year, so I had four years on the varsity team. Normally they don't have freshmen on that team. Usually the freshmen had to work their way up through the freshman and sophomore teams. I was scouted by Red Adams. He came and talked to me and my parents about signing a contract with the Dodgers. Yeah, it was special.

You spent seven years in the Dodgers' minor league system. During that time they had great teams at the major league level—they went to the World Series several times. Do you feel that your advancement to the majors was blocked by their quality pitching staff?

Most definitely. I've always said that I probably could have pitched five years earlier in the big leagues if I had been with another organization, one that wasn't so deep in pitching. You just couldn't break that pitching staff at that time. I went to the AAA division and that's where I stayed at. I pitched for the Spokane Indians Pacific League team for years.

On September 10, 1966, you were traded from the Dodger organization to the Yankees for a 20-year major leaguer, Dick Schofield. By that time some of the aura of the Yankees was wearing off and they certainly weren't as good as the Dodgers. Did you view the trade as a chance to finally get to the majors?

Yeah, I really did. It gave me a chance to get away from trying to break into that Dodgers staff. That was an impossibility unless you were a superphenom.

In 1967 did the Yankees invite you to the major league camp?

Yes, I went directly to the major league camp. I had a good spring training with them—I had 13 innings of scoreless ball. When it came time to break camp Ralph Houk called me into his office and told me, "Tilly, I got no choice—I've got to take you with me because if I don't, the media will just eat me up, because you had such a good spring training." So that's how that came about. I wasn't in his plans to be on the Yankee staff—Stan Bahnsan was supposed to take the pitching spot that was there. Their plans had already been made to take Stan, but because of my spring they sent him back to AAA and kept me on the major league team.

In 1967 they kept you on the Yankees the entire season and you were actually used quite a bit.

Yes, in 1967 I was with them the entire season and I pitched in about 43 ball games.

You pitched one inning on April 14 against Boston at home for your first major league game. You stuck with it for a number of years before getting to the big leagues. What was that like, to finally put on a New York Yankee uniform and walk out onto the field at Yankee Stadium for the first time?

I don't think there are any words that could describe that. I mean it's just a dream come true, wearing the Yankee pinstripes. The walk from the bullpen to the mound was just something I'll never forget, because Elston Howard was waiting on the mound to give me the ball and Ralph Houk was there, you know, and it was neat! [Laughs]

Had you ever been to New York City before?

Never did. I had no idea what New York City was like. The city just blew me away because I never knew anything like that existed—except you read about it in books and things, the Big Apple.

You did pretty good for a while on the Yankees.

Yeah, the first year I thought I did quite well. My win-loss percentage wasn't really good—I think I was 3–9. But it didn't really show the effectiveness of my pitching. You see, I was a long reliever so I'd come in from the third inning to the sixth or seventh inning, anywhere in that line. I would pitch one or two or three innings to get us down to the short relief, and then Dooley Womack would always come in as the closer. He really got all of the recognition for being the top reliever. But of all the games I pitched, I really did well but I never got the recognition of being the relief pitcher that I thought I was.

Do you think there was any reason why you had the nine losses in a row, or was it just a coincidence?

Some of it was just unfortunate situations, and others were times when there were errors and stuff made. You know how that goes—there's always somebody making an error when you really need them not to. [Laughs]

Whitey Ford's final game for the Yankees came on May 21. You weren't on the team a long time with him, but was he helpful to the younger guys. Could you approach him?

Oh yeah, if you had some question that you wanted to ask he would take the time and explain things and tell you what you wanted to know. I never sat in the bullpen with Whitey Ford because he was starting all the time. He would sit on the dugout bench when he wasn't starting—usually the pitcher who was starting the next day would sit on the bench and chart the game. I still got some of my old pitching charts here at home. But just being in the same locker room with him was pretty neat.

Whitey finished '67 with a 2–5 record but had an ERA of 1.64. Did he just have enough, or was there some other reason he decided to leave?

Well, he was injured. He went on the injury list—he had to have been out a good five to six weeks. You know, the Yankees do things right, though. They had a special night for him when he retired out around home plate, just like they did for Mantle and all their other superstars that retire.

In '67, despite going 72–90, the Yankees actually had a pretty good starting staff even without Ford. Stottlemyre was one of the starters, along with Fritz Peterson, Al Downing, and Steve Barber, who was somewhat injured but a former 20-game winner.

They had Fred Talbot, who they fit into the rotation a lot of the time—I don't know if you remember Fred. And we did pick up Bill Monbouquette. He pitched with us that year. I forget who they picked him up from, but he fit in there, too.

How was Mickey Mantle to you, or did he not get involved with the rookies?

Oh no, you know, he was really wonderful to me. He took me under his wing when I first went up there for some reason. Maybe he thought I was a country boy or something, with him having that country-boy background. I needed a place to stay and he told me, "I'll get you a room at the St. Moritz right next to mine," so he did! I got an adjoining room to his room. There were times when he told me that if I wanted to go into his room and listen to his music and stuff like that, that I could go in there. We played a lot of golf together whenever we would go out—he and I and Phil Rizzuto. That was exciting. He was very good to me.

How was your pitching coach on the Yankees at that time?

Jim Turner. He was helpful. Jim just did the normal things that a pitching coach would do—he'd come down and work with you. Most pitching coaches would tell you that you had to keep the ball down and you have to follow through. But he was up in years pretty good and he couldn't demonstrate, you know what I mean, like a young pitching coach could. He could just tell you with the knowledge that he had as far as pitching goes. He would always run the pitchers in the outfield before the game.

After the 1967 season what did you think your chances were of returning to the Yankees the following season?

Oh, I thought they were good, because I had a good enough season where I thought Ralph Houk would like to have me back. I think I did a better than average job in relief and my arm was strong. He used me as a starter a few times when Whitey Ford went on the disabled list. He threw me into the rotation and I started five games until Whitey came back on the active list.

In fact you had one complete game [June 5].

Oh yeah, it was against Washington, if I'm not mistaken. It was my first win as a starter. One of my other games was a 3–0 shutout—I kept the baseball.

In 1968 on June 29 you picked up a win. That must have been a pretty good feeling, to break that streak.

Oh yeah, when you get a losing streak going it's always a good feeling to win one.

After seven games the Yankees sent you out.

Yes, the Yankees sent me back down to Syracuse, where I finished out the year. I came back and played one more year at Syracuse, but that was my last year because I got an opportunity to go over to Japan and play there, so I went. I played with the Nankai Hawks for one year in 1970. It was tough because they play a totally different brand of baseball than the United States. If their pitchers come close to a batter they'll bow like they're saying, "Excuse me." I was a typical American pitcher. If I brush you back I brush you back—I'm not going to bow and tell you I'm sorry. So I was kind of one of the bad guys—I didn't show remorse to them when I knocked them down.

It was a real experience; I enjoyed it. I learned another aspect of the game. They're hard workers, the Japanese people. They do a lot of exercising and stretching and all that—they're very physically fit.

After the '70 season I figured that if nobody wanted me over here and I had to go over there to play, well then, I figured I'd just go ahead and retire. I was fortunate enough to be able to pick up a job locally with a spaghetti sauce company, Ragu, and I worked with them for about 30 years and retired in '99.

Even though you had a relatively brief tenure with the team, you're a part of Yankee-Red Sox lore.

Yeah. [Laughs] We had that big brawl there at Yankee Stadium that one time.[46]

You hit third baseman Joe Foy in the helmet.

Yes. I hit him in the helmet. It wasn't intentional or anything. I wasn't trying to brush him back; I was just trying to cut lose with a good fastball and it happened to get up. Every batter has a blind spot when they're at bat and have their head turned looking at the pitcher. It got up in his blind spot and he didn't see it. He didn't see it coming and it nailed him. They thought I did it on purpose because the night before he hit a home run to beat us. They thought I did that in retaliation but that had nothing to do with it.

So in the bottom half of the inning Red Sox pitcher Jim Lonborg hit you.

Yeah, I knew he was going to do it. I told him after he hit me, "That's OK Jim, you've got to come up to bat and you'll get yours too." Ralph Houk knew me well enough to know that I would. That was part of my Dodger training—they were always that way. When I was in the Pacific Coast League I used to lead the league in hit batsmen every year. I had a good friend of mine, Earl Averill, who used to play for Seattle [PCL]. He had a tendency to stand up close to the plate and I told him, "Earl, don't crowd the plate on me 'cause I'm gonna have to push you back." Well, what did he do? He crowded the plate on me and I threw him inside and he got hit! [Laughs] On his way down to first I said to him, "I told you, Earl."

---

46. June 21, 1967.

So when Lonborg hit me I started walking out to the mound. Foy came in from third base, the first baseman came in, and both teams came out and gathered in the center of the field on the pitching mound. The thing that really made me mad was that Lonborg didn't even stay out there—he ran in the dugout. He wasn't going to be around when the scuffle was taking place. He stayed in the dugout while all the fighting was going on.

Any final Yankee memories?

One game that I remember pitching in was when Mickey got his 500th home run. And then I kept some headlines when my name was in the headline with Mickey's, "Mantle and Tillotson," etc. You start to think about things. I remember back in spring training when I was with the Dodgers and Stan Musial was still playing and we had a game against the Cardinals. I had the opportunity to pitch to Stan Musial and was fortunate to get him to ground out. So that's something that's stuck in my mind all these years—that I pitched to Stan Musial and got him out.

Have you stayed in touch with the Yankee organization?

No, I get a Christmas card and a newsletter every couple of months, but I never did stay in contact with anybody.

Have you been back to New York since your playing days?

No, I sure haven't. That was my first and last time in New York. I sure hate to see them get rid of the old stadium, but I guess you have to keep up with the times. I never got over to Shea either.

TOPPS

TILLOTSON, THADDEUS ASA
Born: December 20, 1940 Merced, California
Bats: Right Throws: Right
Height: 6' 2" Weight: 195

Year	Team	G	W-L	SV	GS	CG	IP	SO	W	ERA
1967	YANKEES	43	3-9	2	5	1	98.3	62	39	4.03
1968	YANKEES	7	1-0	1	0	0	10.3	1	7	4.35
	Total 2 Years	50	4-9	2	5	1	108.7	63	46	4.06

BRACE Photo

FRANK TEPEDINO
1967, 1969–72

You were born and raised in Brooklyn. The Dodgers moved away when you were ten. I suppose you were a Dodger fan?

A lot of the family was Dodger fans and Yankee fans. I'd been to Ebbetts Field quite a few times growing up. I just loved baseball. I was a Boston fan, Yankee fan, Cincinnati too—I liked Frank Robinson.

Were you a star Little Leaguer or American Legion player?

My father wouldn't let me play Little League when I was growing up. I didn't start playing organized ball until I was about 14. Growing up in Brooklyn we played stickball, softball, baseball. My father felt that all Little League was going to do was burn me out and nobody was going to teach me anything better than he could. My uncles had played professionally too—my uncle Johnny and my uncle Frankie, who was a player-manager in the Southern League in the '50s.

You were drafted in 1965 by the Orioles at 18. You must have been scouted in high school.

Seventeen.

Wow, even younger.

Usually what is done is, the scouting is done a lot during the summertime. In the summertime you play more baseball and you play against better baseball. I played for the Cadets and we were "unlimited"—guys who played in college would come home for the summer and play with us. That's where your good brand of baseball is. High school ball is tough because you have a limited schedule and every school has a team, so it's not necessarily the best players in Brooklyn or Queens or wherever. The scouts would go to the Parade Grounds or Marine Park or other places like that.

How did it feel to be drafted by a major league ball club?

Well, they were looking at me in '63 and '64. They can't talk to you personally, so they would talk to my father. So I knew that I had the ability to play baseball. I knew I could hit but it was the other parts of the game—I could run and throw. . . . I was an adequate fielder. But when the time comes and you have big-league scouts talking about you signing a professional contract, it's big. Especially since that's been your dream since you've been five years old.

After playing in the minors briefly the Yankees acquired you in 1967. How did that come about?

What had happened was I was in the Marine Corps down in Camp Lejeune in North Carolina and the Orioles put me on their AAA roster along with Charlie Sands. I was just 18 at the time and was a third-round draft choice. They had just signed Terry Crowley in 1966, and I think gave him quite a bit of money. So it was either protect me or Terry Crowley, and they went with Crowley. Lee MacPhail and Harry Craft were with the Orioles—MacPhail the GM and Craft their top scout. When they made the change and came over to New York, I think that was a big part of it—they took two of the Orioles top players, in their opinion, at a young age with them. That's why we had to spend most of 1967 in the major leagues.

Could the Yankees have possibly lost you?

Well, what it is, no money ever changes hands. After [the Yankees] had us they had to offer us back to the Orioles at half the price. That's the way things go; that was the tough times for the Yankees, in 1967. They needed pitching and they worked out a deal with the Orioles to get Steve Barber. They picked up his salary and told the Orioles, "You don't claim Tepedino." That's how that worked.

How did you feel when you learned that you were a Yankee?

I was happy, being from Brooklyn and rooting for the Yankees. I was glad I had a chance to move. I had been in Rookie League and A ball. I'm not realizing that I'm going to be in the majors. That's too young, with only two years' experience. I was never groomed for anything that quick; it was just like an instant shock. Then I realize, "Oh my God, I'm going to be playing in Yankee Stadium." But I wasn't playing in Yankee Stadium—I was *sitting* in Yankee Stadium. [Laughs] The team left me and Charlie [Sands] in extended spring training to play with the minor leagues. I had just gotten out of the Marine Corps and a few weeks into the '67 season they brought us up.

In 1967 you were the fourth youngest player in the majors at 19.

Yeah.

You felt that was too young?

Definitely too young. Looking back at my age now, it was unbelievable at the time, but it was probably one of the worst things that could have happened. Eventually it did work out, not with the Yankees but to play in the big leagues for [eight years].

That must have been overwhelming, to be 19 and on the same team as Mantle, Ford, Howard, Stottlemyre . . .

Tresh, Houk. Yeah, it was like a kid in a candy store. You don't know which way to turn; every way you turn there are idols sitting next to you getting dressed in the clubhouse, going on the field, warming up in the bullpen, or going up to bat. Also, playing with the Yankees at 19 years old, what everybody seems to forget is that you're in the major leagues. I'm getting a chance to see Carl Yaztremski, Harmon Killebrew, Rod Carew, Al Kaline—all the players that you see on TV—and here I am watching them play. Like I always said, I had the best seat in the house.

Did Mickey Mantle say anything to you when you got called up?

Well, with the older guys it's always like, "How ya doin', rook?" and things like that. They all take you under their wing. They know I'm 19 and have only played at A ball, and this is just a situation where the Yankees have to carry me. I roomed with Charlie Sands. We were two 19-year-olds traveling together. The traveling secretary was outstanding and Houk was good. Those were the '60s—helping players was not on everyone's mind, players' or coaches'. Don't forget, hitting coach—really nonexistent. Fielding coach—nonexistent. Frankie Crosetti would hit you a few ground balls, but that's it. At that particular time those guys cared about *their* job. The game has changed so much, even in minor league teams. They all have a manager, pitching coach, bullpen coach, hitting coach. When we played, the manager was your hitting coach and he coached third base. One of the pitchers usually coached first base. Baseball now has gotten in such specifics that you have a person that takes care of every aspect of the game. With the Yankees we had Jim Hegan, who was the bullpen catcher and took care of the bullpen, but then we had Jim Turner as the pitching coach, who was there for 40 years. What was he going to transfer to players of the late '60s, as far as the game has changed from the '30s, the '40s, and '50s? It's things like that that I look back on and I say, "My God, I'm playing in the major leagues at 19 and I'm not getting any help at furthering [my skills] or getting better." When there was extra batting practice *I* went out and threw to Tresh, Bill Robinson, and the players. They would ask me, they wouldn't ask the coaches to come out early because the coaches were elderly. You know, really, they couldn't go out there and throw for an hour. We took it upon ourselves to go out there.

Whitey Ford only pitched in seven games in 1967 before retiring. Did you get to meet him?

Yeah. Whitey Ford, as a matter of fact, is the person I got my first at bat for; I pinch-hit for him. To this day every time I see Whitey we laugh about that season and me pinch- hitting for him. I didn't get a base hit and when I got back to the bench Whitey said, "I could've done that."

Being a Brooklyn guy, did you already know Joe Pepitone, who was still with the Yankees in '67?

I had played ball against his brother Billy. I knew Billy Pepitone growing up when we played with the Cadets. I never met Joe but eventually in 1967 we were on the same team.

In 1967 after the Fourth of July you got sent down to Greensboro in the Carolina League and hit .222. After a couple of very good seasons in the minors, why did your average drop?

What it was, after April, May, June—three months of just throwing batting practice and getting five at bats, you can't go into a game situation facing live pitching. This is why we have spring training for four or five weeks, to get you ready for the season. My time in Greensboro was my spring training. I didn't even realize that I hit that high; I needed to go to a place to get back into shape and play. What they should have done was sent me down to the minors to play and then to winter ball and that would have been my season. So now when it comes down to going to spring training in '68 I'm trying to catch up from missing all of 1967.

After hitting .300 in the International League in 1969 the Yankees called you back up. Did you think that it was for good now and that you would have a career in pinstripes?

What I thought was that I'd have a chance to play and I think I had about 35 at bats.[47] I didn't get called up until the end of the year because at Syracuse we went to the Little World Series and that extended our minor league season for a couple of weeks, so that cut back on me a little bit. So now I get to play again in the major leagues and that was fantastic; I get to feel a little bit more comfortable. But now I was playing right field. In AAA I was playing DH and a little first base and a little bit of right field. So in 1969 I finished the season playing right field and then they send me to winter ball. Ralph Houk tells me, "You're my right fielder." I'm at winter ball playing right field and the Yankees make a deal for Curt Blefary! So now here I am, you sent me down to play right and I was going to platoon with Billy Robinson—he was going to play against left-handers and I was going to play against right-handers. I don't have a problem with that—I know my position on the team. Now I go to spring training in 1970 and I'm playing first base. I had a good spring, but then I start the season and I'm not playing.

After 39 at bats in '69 and 19 at bats in '70, you started the 1971 season with the Yankees but after just 6 at bats you were traded to the Brewers on June 7. Was this expected, or were you taken by surprise?

---

47. Actually 39.

That was probably the biggest surprise of my career. I started the season with the Yankees and then they send me down to AAA. I think I was hitting .190 and the manager, Frank Verdi, calls me into his office and tells me they're calling me back up. Never in a million years did I know that the reason I was being called back up was they had the deal with the Brewers—myself for Danny Walton. So now it doesn't look good on paper, trading a AAA player for someone as popular as Walton was in Milwaukee, so they called me back up and made the deal. Ironically, in 1972 me and Danny wind up rooming together in AAA [with the Syracuse Yankees].

After playing the rest of the 1971 season with the Brewers, they traded you back to the Yankees at the end of spring training in 1972 and you're back in New York for at least part of the '72 season. Why did the Yankees do that after basically not playing you for four years?

What that comes down to is filling spots in their minor league system. I was a popular player at Syracuse. I had good years there and my manager, Frank Verdi, liked me. So what it comes down to is, they had a spot and I'm either going to play in Evansville in the Brewers system or another organization's AAA team. I had no effect on the majors so what it is is a minor league ballplayer moving around.

Did that disappoint you, going back there?

No, I wanted to go back there. If I was going to play in the minor leagues that's where I wanted to go, I wanted to play in Syracuse. When you play in a place for a few years you become comfortable in the surroundings—the people, the ballpark, the area—especially if you have a couple of good years.

You spent the year in Syracuse and at some point the Yankees briefly called you up.

They called me up at the end of the year. They bought my contract and brought me back to the major leagues. But then again, it comes down to coming up for the last month of the year to get eight at bats. Getting eight pinch-hit at bats is tough.

In 1973 you were back in AAA for the Yankees and they traded you to the Atlanta Braves on June 7. Was that a relief for you? Did you view this as an opportunity to play more at the major league level?

That was a relief, that particular trade was. My manager at Syracuse was Bobby Cox. They wouldn't let me play the night before. He says, "I can't play you." I said, "What do you mean, you can't play me?" He said, "I can't take the chance on you getting hurt. Come to my room at three in the morning." [Laughs] So I said, "What?!" He continued, "Come to my room at three in the morning and I'll give you a little more information." I told him to just tell me where am I going. He said, "I can't tell you. There are a couple of things in the works, but I'll tell you that tomorrow morning you won't be here." So I went to the room at three in the morning and he told me that the Yankees and Atlanta had made a deal. The first thing out of my mouth was, "Don't tell me I'm going to Richmond," because Richmond was great for right-hand hitters, not for left-hand hitters. I think it was 360 down the right-field line and 420 into the alley. But he said no, that the Atlanta Braves were calling me up right away.

You said that you didn't understand why you never really got a shot with the Yankees when you had a career average of .270 and they said you couldn't hit. Did someone in the organization really say that?

Yeah. I think they got that messed up because I wasn't as good of a fielder as a hitter. Hitting comes down a lot to you have to play to hit. Batting practice is batting practice. There's nothing like game situations, which is very hard for someone not associated with baseball at that level to understand. They think that when you take batting practice and fielding practice you're ready to go out and play. It's completely different when you play the game—it gets quicker. Everything about practice is just to stay in shape for the game.

You had two good seasons for the Braves and played in about half of their games. Did they use you as a defensive replacement, or in a platoon with Davey Johnson or Mike Lum?

I was used more or less for Hank Aaron. If you look at the 1973 Braves roster, we all had good years—it was a good hitting team. We just ran into the Cincinnati Reds that year. If Aaron didn't play and it was a right-hander pitching, then Lum moved to the outfield and I would play first base. I was also pinch-hitting. Our manager was Eddie Mathews. He told me shortly into the season, "From now on I'll only use you to either tie or win the game against a right-handed pitcher." So I knew my position on the team. So I had a good year and if you look, I had a real good year in '74 up until the All-Star break, when they fired Mathews and Clyde King took over. I think the second half of '74 I got only 30–40 at bats. Once again it comes down to not playing, which is hard.

Being his understudy, how was Hank Aaron to you?

Excellent. He let me know when he was playing and when he wasn't. We had a little thing worked out where Hank would give me a thumbs-up or thumbs-down. He told me, "It's not fair—you never know when you're going to get into a game or not. Everything hinges on me and I'll try and let you know when I come into the clubhouse," and he did.

You said that one of the biggest thrills for you during your career was being on the bench for both Mantle's 500th home run and Aaron's 715th home run.

Yeah, there are only two people that were there to see those, myself and Al Downing. We were both on the Yankees and Downing gave up Aaron's 715th.

You're in the picture of Aaron at home plate.

Yeah. [Laughs] And the funny thing was that the person who was the calmest with all this going on was Aaron himself. He had said, "I'm going to hit the home run but I just don't know when, so as far as pressure, there's no pressure on me." When they asked him how it felt to be chasing Babe Ruth, I'll never forget what he said: "I should be chasing Willie Mays, because if the Giants had never moved out of the Polo Grounds I'd be chasing him."[48] This is somebody who is an instant Hall of Famer giving that respect to another ballplayer.

You got rid of the sideburns.

From the picture, yeah. [Laughs]

Pepitone was also a member of the 1973 Braves with you.

Pepitone was there early in the season, but just for about a month. They worked some sort of deal out so he could go to Japan. That's when they needed another left-handed first baseman or outfielder, or just another Italian kid from Brooklyn, I don't know. They made the deal for me after he left.

You started the '75 season with Atlanta but were gone fairly early in the season. What happened?

They sent me down to Richmond. I was [in Atlanta] for about two months but didn't get any playing time. I think I pinch-hit about seven times, that's it. I didn't play, I never got into a game, was never used at first base. I hit about .280 at Richmond and naturally I was disgruntled when I went down. I didn't have a good attitude.

Was that your final year as a player?

In 1976 I was still there and they wanted to cut [my salary]. Not that I was making a lot, but they wanted to cut me from $23,000 to $12,000 and I said, "Just release me." So I just didn't report. I didn't go to spring training and I started working at a sporting goods store—for more money! I talked to Jack McKeon, who was the manager of Richmond at that time, and told him

---

48. The Giants used the Polo Grounds in Upper Manhattan from 1883 to 1957, until they moved to San Francisco. The Polo Grounds had a very unusual "bathtub" shape. The distance to the left and right field walls was very short, making it easy to hit a home run over those walls. But center field was unusually deep—possibly 480 feet (the exact distance is unknown)— and no home run was ever hit out of center field. Candlestick Park in San Francisco had average dimensions. Willie Mays hit 660 career home runs, to Aaron's 755 and Ruth's 714.

to just release me. They wouldn't do it. I thought I had forced their hand but they put me on the restricted list.

I was going crazy working in the store so I called Atlanta and told them that I was ready to report and that I was still working out and would report in shape and ready to play. They said OK and to go join the team in Pawtucket. Once I got there the manager watched me work out and said, "You really are ready to play." So he called Atlanta and they said to wait until the team got back to Richmond, which was the following day. After we got there he told me Atlanta said to wait a couple of days. I said to him, "With pay?" And he said yes, so I did. A week goes by and nothing happens. Atlanta didn't know what to do with me so I just went home.

So I didn't play in 1976 or '77. I wound up talking to a lawyer and asked him what I could do about this.[49] He said, "What we have to do is send a letter to every major league ball club offering your services, and naturally they will all say no." This was February of '78. Don't you know that two clubs called me and accepted. The first one was the Pirates. The GM called me and said, "We would like to invite you to spring training." I said, "You're kidding." He said, "No." Pittsburgh had no left-handed-hitting first baseman. They wanted to use me as a pinch-hitter and to spell Willie Stargel. About three hours later the St. Louis Cardinals called me, Bing Devine. He said he wanted to invite me to spring training, but I told him that I had just committed to the Pirates. So I go to spring training. Chuck Tanner is the manager, and for the first couple of weeks there was no problem. Tanner even said to me, "You haven't skipped a beat for a guy who's been out for two years." But then Pittsburgh was making a week-long trip during spring training to Miami to play, and Puerto Rico, and I wasn't on the trip. What they were going to do was release me and then resign me to go play in Portland and I said, "That's it." It wasn't so much going to AAA, but not getting the opportunity to stay. From the time I committed to them until I got to spring training, they had signed John Milner and Mike Easler. I thought that I had a great shot, but it's business—they were just protecting themselves.

After that I didn't do anything for baseball until Rusty Torres and Tom Sabellico got in touch with me about Winning Beyond Winning. This is an organization that has former major leaguers go out and talk to kids about drugs and alcohol, anywhere from five years old and up. We've been around now ten or eleven years.

You worked in the fire service in New York City, actually in downtown Manhattan, for about 25 years after you retired as a player. On 9/11 you were off duty but responded from your home to the scene.

---

49. About Atlanta still controlling Tepedino's status.

Yes. My one son had just gotten off at 8:00 a.m. that morning and my other son just happened to already be on medical leave.[50] My brother also still was working in Fire Patrol Company 3 but was also on vacation. I was home watching on TV and thought, bad weather or maybe the pilot had a heart attack. I went back to my firehouse, got my gear like everybody else, and tried to get down to the site.

Were you ever in contact with the New York Yankees after you stopped playing?

No. The only time they ever got in touch with me was right after 9/11. We lost one member of my firehouse, Keith Roma, who was a big Yankee fan. We found his Yankee hat on the rig and his family wanted something from the Yankees if possible, maybe to have his hat signed by Joe Torre. I said, "I don't know, this is a tough one." I had called my former roommate Bobby Murcer, whose brother was a fireman in Oklahoma, God bless Bobby. Bobby got the ball rolling and then the team got in touch with the family and me. They had me throw out the first pitch against Oakland in the playoffs [2001] and they had Keith's family there, so it was great for them.

Anything else about the Yankees that you remember?

That first time going from the clubhouse down the runway into the dugout and getting your first look from that spot is priceless—that's when you hear the word "priceless." You will never, ever duplicate that experience again. You'll get that feeling every time you go there—it's one of the few ballparks that does it to you, but never like the first time. I liked Fenway a lot, Wrigley too. Playing at Chavez Ravine in Los Angeles is special. But there's nothing like Yankee Stadium. And as far as the new ballpark, it's progress. We live in a different age—we live corporate, and baseball is corporate. Baseball is cable TV and it's corporate. The only thing that I had said was that when they open up the new ballpark, every living Yankee should be there. Let Steinbrenner cut the ribbon and have every player with a hat and his jersey and a handful of dirt from the old stadium and throw it on the field. We transfer the hallowed ground from the old ballpark to the new one. They could then auction off the shirts and hats to charity.[51]

---

50. Both sons are New York City firefighters.
51. The first game at the new stadium in the Bronx was on April 16, 2009, against the Cleveland Indians. Yogi Berra, then 83, threw out the first pitch. Forty Yankee alumni were in attendance and honored on the field.

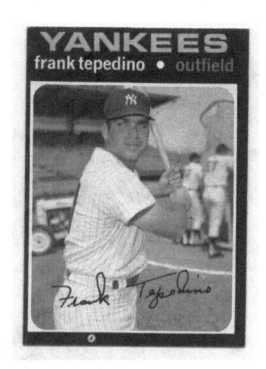

TOPPS

TEPEDINO, FRANK RONALD
Born: November 23, 1947 Brooklyn, New York
Bats: Left Throws: Left
Height: 5' 11" Weight: 192

Year	Team	G	AB	H	2B	3B	HR	AVG	RBI	R
1967	YANKEES	9	5	2	0	0	0	.400	0	0
1969	YANKEES	13	39	9	0	0	0	.231	4	6
1970	YANKEES	16	19	6	2	0	0	.316	2	2
1971	YANKEES	6	6	0	0	0	0	.000	0	0
1971	Brewers	53	106	21	1	0	2	.198	7	11
1972	YANKEES	8	8	0	0	0	0	.000	0	0
1973	Braves	74	148	45	5	0	4	.304	29	20
1974	Braves	78	169	39	5	1	0	.231	16	11
1975	Braves	8	7	0	0	0	0	.000	0	0
	Total 8 Years	265	507	122	13	1	6	.241	58	50

National Baseball Hall of Fame

BILL BURBACH
1969–71

You were born in Dickeyville, Wisconsin, so I guess you were not a Yankees fan growing up.

[Laughs] No, I was a Braves fan. They were in Milwaukee then and were the closest team to us.

The Yankees drafted you as their number one choice (19th overall) in the 1965 free- agent draft, which was the first year of the draft. So you're actually the answer to a Yankee trivia question.

[Laughs] That's correct.

They must have seen something special in you at 18. Were you a standout high school player?

Yeah. I went to high school in Iowa. We didn't have a high school here and we lived on the border, so I went about fifteen miles to school. Dickeyville then was probably about 600 people. Where I went to high school was about 40,000. I guess I had a pretty impressive record.

Were you always a pitcher?

I did a little bit of both. I played some infield and I pitched.

When you went to Johnson City of the Appalachia League in '65 did you think you had any chance of making it to the major league Yankees, who had just won 15 pennants in the previous 18 years?

Well, when I was drafted I was really surprised. I hadn't really talked to them. I had talked to other teams, or they had talked to me. So when I was drafted I was kind of half in shock. They scouted me. I had known the scout was there but I had never talked to him.

That first year you finished with a 6.16 ERA but the following season (1966) at Greensboro you lowered it to 2.19. That's some drop—how do you account for that?

Well the first year I had some control problems. I don't know if I was awestruck or what. Plus we didn't have a very good team.

The next two seasons were pretty good for you, including a no-hitter in '67. When you went to spring training in 1969 did you think you could stick with the big club?

Well, I thought I had a shot. I knew the people that were there and I was fairly confident in my ability. They really didn't have that many young pitchers. Stottlemyre and Peterson were starters,

119

and they had some older guys like Lindy McDaniel, Jack Aker, and Steve Hamilton. Bahnsen was there and he was young, but they really had an older staff. I had a pretty good spring training. I think I was voted co-rookie of the spring. I pitched pretty well. My record and ERA was good and I pitched quite a few innings.

The Yanks' pitching coach was Jim Turner, who had been in the game since the early 1920s. Did he help you in any way?

Hmm, not really. [Laughs] No, I don't know what it was, if he didn't care to work with me, or what it was. He just didn't seem to help me that much.

Do you think the pitching coaches years ago just didn't get involved like they do today?

I don't believe they did, no. I don't know what they were but the whole game is different now from what it was then.

When the Yankees opened their season in '69, was that the first time that you had ever been to New York or Yankee Stadium?

Yes. I enjoyed New York and had a great time there. I enjoyed the people—they were as critical back then as they are today, I'm sure. [Laughs] I think we were about .500 in '69.

In 1969 the Yankees actually had three catchers. Jake Gibbs was the senior member of the team. Did you throw to him the most, or Munson or Frank Fernandez?

Well, I threw mainly to Jake but Fernandez caught some. I don't know if Munson was there that full year or not. I don't believe he was. John Ellis was there. He was the third catcher and played some first base too. I threw to Munson the next year a little bit and I played winter ball with him, but it didn't matter who I threw to.

Your first major league game was a start at Tiger Stadium on Friday, April 11. If you were nervous it didn't show. You pitched six innings, giving up just one earned run in a game that was eventually won by the Yanks and Lindy McDaniel 9–4.

I had good vibes about it. I pitched against them two or three times in the spring and I did really well against them, believe it or not. They had a strong team.

Sure, defending World Champions.

Right. Kaline, Freehan, and Cash—they had quite a few big names in there, but I pitched pretty well against them.

Your second game in the majors was also against the Tigers, but at Yankee Stadium now and on a Sunday in front of 35,000 fans. What was it like walking out to that mound at Yankee Stadium wearing pinstripes?

It was exciting. You're nervous before you start, but once the game starts you're not that nervous. The most nervous I was, was the day before the season opened and we played an exhibition game against the Giants and I pitched. The first hitter was Willie Mays and what did I do? I hit him! I almost got booed out of New York. I got out of the inning and [Mays] came by me and said, "Relax kid, relax."

Back to your second game. You were facing Denny McLain, who had won 31 games in '68 and was probably the best pitcher of the late '60s, and all you did was outpitch him. You threw a complete game shutout, striking out seven, and for good measure hit a single and scored twice.

It was a relief to get the first win out of the way, and it was just exciting. And you think you're on your way.

On Sunday, May 18, you were pitching another shutout against the Angels but had to be relieved in the seventh by Steve Hamilton, who got the win when the Yankees won 1–0 on a ninth-inning home run by Joe Pepitone. You lost a different game 2–1 a few days later. Did you ever feel that you were a victim of low run support?

Well, I was kind of used to it. In the minor leagues it was that way. When I was in A ball in Greensboro I either led the league in ERA or was close to it, and I was 3–14. I was getting beat 2–1 or 1–0 every game. I was used to that lack of run support.

Sunday, June 8, was Mickey Mantle Day at Yankee Stadium. Mantle had retired a few months earlier at spring training. The first game of the doubleheader was won by the Yanks 3–1 behind a brilliant complete game thrown by Mel Stottlemyre. The ball was handed to you for game 2. With over 60,000 people in attendance, you made it a perfect day in New York by throwing another complete game win, besting the White Sox 11–2. You doubled and scored twice, too.

I remember that day well. I remember it so well because they retired Mantle's number, but also being in the clubhouse before game 1 with Mantle, Ford, and a lot of the old-timers and hearing their stories and taking part in the celebration. And then to go out and do that it was the capper of the day, really. Mantle was probably as nervous with his number being retired as I was getting ready to pitch. But that was a fun day and it was probably the highlight of my career, to tell you the truth.

You pitched two innings of shutout relief on September 25 to finish with a 3.65 ERA. How did you feel about your season?

I was halfway satisfied. I got taken out of the rotation at the end of June or July, and I was surprised at that, but I ran into some control problems.

Did the Yankees tell you anything about their plans for you in 1970?

Well, no, but I had a good spring training again and made the ball club. I made about two or three starts, but I had a little bit of sickness in the spring and it took me a while to get my strength back. I had a touch of mononucleosis and it affected my stamina. I was just getting it back when they sent me down to AAA, Syracuse.

In 1971 you appeared in just two games for the Yankees and were traded to the Orioles on May 28. How did you feel about the trade?

I made the club again in '71. I didn't pitch but I was traded to Baltimore the year they had four 20-game winners, so that didn't excite me too much. I joined the big club in Baltimore and was never on the roster. Part of the reason was they thought I was injured. They had just signed Dave Boswell. I was there a week and they sent me down to Rochester. They told me to win a few games and said, "We'll call you back up." So I went down and I was 7–0—and I haven't heard anything yet. [Laughs]

The Orioles traded you to the Tigers after that.

Yes, they told me that I'd go to AAA and I probably wouldn't pitch much to start with, so I told them to release me. So I finally got my release and later that year found myself with Minnesota in their AAA club. I did pretty well [there]—I pitched a lot in relief. The following year I went to spring training with the Twins, but there again it was a numbers thing and I wasn't going to pitch much and I quit—which I thought I never should have done; I probably should have bit the bullet.

Mel Stottlemyre won 20 games in 1969, making him the best pitcher on the team. Could you see anything in him back then that would have led you to believe he'd become a great pitching coach?

Well, yeah, he was very intelligent. He was a student of the game. I think back then he relied more on control and setting up hitters instead of throwing hard—which he did too; he threw fairly hard. I think that those things are very valuable for a pitching coach.

Who was your roommate in '69?

John Ellis. We lived in New Jersey—a lot of the players did. I lived in Paramus, and then I lived in a little bit in Fort Lee.

Did you ever get over to Shea Stadium?

Yes I did. We played an exhibition game there in '69.

Do you ever get back to Yankee Stadium?

I went back to the World Series once. My nephew was going to college down here in western Kentucky and he had always been a Yankee fan. I just called him out of the blue one day and I said, "Let's go to the World Series." So we went up to the World Series. That was in the '80s, but that's the only time I've been back.

Are you going to make it back this year [2008]?

Well, I don't know. I thought they would invite a lot of the players back being it's the final year of the stadium, but maybe not. [Laughs] I thought all along that they would do something, but I don't know how many players that would involve.

TOPPS

BURBACH, WILLIAM DAVID
Born: August 22, 1947 Dickeyville, Wisconsin
Bats: Right Throws: Right
Height: 6' 4" Weight: 215

Year	Team	G	W-L	SV	GS	CG	IP	SO	W	ERA
1969	YANKEES	31	6-8	0	24	2	140.7	82	102	3.65
1970	YANKEES	4	0-2	0	4	0	16.7	10	9	10.26
1971	YANKEES	2	0-1	0	0	0	3.3	3	5	10.80
	Total 3 Years	37	6-11	0	28	2	160.7	95	116	4.48

National Baseball Hall of Fame

JIM LYTTLE
1969–71

You were from Ohio. Were you a Reds fan growing up?

I was born in Ohio and grew up in Indiana, but Cincinnati was only 20 miles away, so yes, I was a Reds fan.

Were you a standout player in high school?

Well, yeah, but we only played a ten-game schedule. It was very small—we only had 350 in the school. I was even hurt my senior year and didn't play.

You wound up playing baseball at Florida State University, though.

A Cincinnati scout had seen me play and he wanted me to go to FSU. Also, there was a basketball coach down in Indiana that I played against my whole career. [He] went to FSU and played basketball there, and I wound up getting a basketball scholarship to FSU to play baseball also. I didn't play the outfield until I got to college. I pitched and played shortstop in high school.

You were a big guy for a shortstop—six feet, 185 pounds.

[Laughs] Not now.

When the Yankees drafted you in the first round in 1966 did that surprise you?

Yes, it did. I was All-American that year at FSU. I was only a sophomore. Every team had spoken to me *except* the Yankees. We were ranked number two in the country so we had 20–30 scouts in the stands every night. There were no rules back then and the big question was, "Will you sign if we draft you?" My answer was, "I don't know." [Laughs] I did sign.

By 1969 you hit .313 at AAA Syracuse and the Yankees called you up for 28 games. Your first game was on Saturday, May 17, at Yankee Stadium against the Angels. How did you feel walking out onto that field wearing pinstripes?

Well, for a small-town Indiana boy it was overwhelming. [Laughs] When I signed, being the first draft choice that year, they brought me to Yankee Stadium and I worked out with the team for a week. Then they sent me down to Ft. Lauderdale. When I walked into the clubhouse, [clubhouse manager] big Pete Sheehy met me at the door and said, "I have someone for you to meet." He took me right to Mantle's locker to meet him, where Mickey was sitting getting dressed. He stood up, and I was taller than Mickey! I had always thought that Mickey must be about 6' 8" and 250 pounds—that was just the image I had of him. Mickey started talking to me and I don't remember a word he said. The only thing I can remember is thinking, I'm bigger than Mickey

Mantle, you gotta be kidding me. I actually met Bouton and he tried to get me to Fleer bubble gum.[52] I got to speak to most everybody.

After growing up in a small town, [New York City] was a little overwhelming. The mile after mile of buildings was not what I was used to, but I got used to it.

In your first big-league game you got your first hit out of the way going 1 for 4 and singling off of longtime major leaguer and All-Star, Eddie Fisher. That must have felt good.

He was throwing the knuckleball at the time and as I recall, I hit a line drive back off of his glove for an infield single. There were guys on first and second.

The Yankees played you a lot in May and June before sending you back to Syracuse. Was someone hurt?

[Laughs] Me, the way I hit! No, when we left spring training they had said, "We're going to be calling someone up pretty soon, and whoever is doing the best is going to get the call." At the time me and Tommy Shopey and Frank Tepedino were the three left-hand-hitting outfielders. Well, we were all hitting about .340 at Syracuse! It seems to me they told us all, "If you do well we're going to call you up," so it was a tough decision for them to make.

After the '69 season did the Yankees tell you anything about their plans for you in 1970?

No, they never told you anything back then. You go back home and wait and see if they sent you a contract, or cut your salary, or gave you a raise. There was really no communication between the front office and management and the players.

I had a decent spring in '70 and actually made the starting lineup. The Yankees at that time played spring training in Ft. Lauderdale. I was married and we lived in an apartment. I liked the area so much we bought a home down here so I could be home during spring training, and the day we moved in they traded me! But we started the [1970] season, I think, in Boston and then went to D.C. and I had an appendectomy. When I had that they called Bloomberg up.

So that knocked you out for a little while?

Well, yeah, and then when Bloomberg got there that really knocked me out! I kind of caddied for Cater in right field and pinch-hit quite a bit.

---

52. Fleer Corporation, founded in 1885, was the first manufacturer of bubble gum in the U.S. It began producing baseball cards in 1959, signing Ted Williams to a contract to feature his career on a series of cards.

After playing for the White Sox and Expos you finished up your major league career in '76 with the Dodgers. Being that there was expansion coming in 1977, did you try to extend your major league career thinking that there would be more job openings?

No, the Dodgers wanted to send me and Leron Lee to Albuquerque because they had all those young kids there and they had great years. They wanted to protect them, so they had to take them to the big leagues for a little while. So they told us, "After the first month of the season we'll call you guys back up." I had three kids and was 30 years old and had moved around enough. They had signed me as a free agent and told me, "If you don't want to go down there we'll release you and you can go wherever you want." I took the release and then I got a call from a friend of mine who was playing over in Japan asking me to go over there. So that's how I wound up in Japan.

I played for Hiroshima and played in their World Series. I hit three home runs, drove in 11, and was 11 for 24 and scored 14 or 15 runs. My first year was 1977 and I won the MVP in '81. I already had a three-year contract at that time. After the '82 season they released me and traded away all the guys from the [Japanese World] Series. All the guys were like 36 years old and they just got rid of all of us. Our first baseman went to the other league and won the batting title. The relief pitcher went over too and won MVP of the league, and I went and played in the other league also for the Osaka Nanki Hawks. [Laughs] But '83 was my last season over there.

During your time in New York, how was Ralph Houk as the Yankee manager?

My impression was that Ralph never liked me a whole lot. He liked guys like John Ellis who were tough and boisterous, and I was always quiet and went about my business and played the game hard. Ralph liked guys who produced and I didn't produce that well. As a manager I liked the way he managed, but he seemed to have favorites and it was obvious. We didn't really have a hitting coach at that time. Ellie Howard was there, Dick Howser was there, so it was by committee.

Who was your roommate on the Yanks?

Basically the whole team. [Laughs] I roomed with Lindy McDaniel the most time.

During your time with the club, Roy White and Bobby Murcer were the All-Stars in the outfield, along with Thurman Munson catching. Did White or Murcer help you in any way as an outfielder?

Well, I was a better outfielder than both of them, so I would say no. [Laughs] Bobby was a nice guy. Roy was a nice guy too; he and I got along really well. He came over to Japan and played with me. He was with the Tokyo Giants.

Was the outfield at Yankee Stadium the biggest one you ever covered?

Yeah, I played center field there a few times. There were some balls hit in left center field that you used to just run as hard as you can for as long as you can. One day when I was playing right field Murcer went through the monuments[53] and picked the ball up, then came out and threw the ball in.

Have you ever been back to Yankee Stadium?

The last time was '93. I went back to Old-Timers' Day.

---

53. At the time referred to (pre-1976), three monuments stood in center field to honor manager Miller Huggins, Lou Gehrig, and Babe Ruth. Later plaques were placed on the outfield wall. Although more than 450 feet from home plate, the monuments were nonetheless in the field of play. They were finally moved off the field when the stadium was renovated in the 1970s, to an area known as Monument Park.

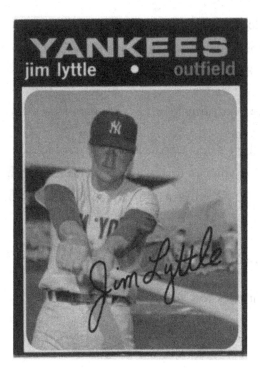

TOPPS

LYTTLE, JAMES LAWRENCE JR.
Born: May 20, 1946 Hamilton, Ohio
Bats: Left Throws: Right
Height: 6' 0" Weight: 186 lbs.

Year	Team	G	AB	H	2B	3B	HR	AVG	RBI	R
1969	YANKEES	28	83	15	4	0	0	.181	4	7
1970	YANKEES	87	126	39	7	1	3	.310	14	20
1971	YANKEES	49	86	17	5	0	1	.198	7	7
1972	White Sox	44	82	19	5	2	0	.232	5	8
1973	Expos	49	116	30	5	1	4	.259	19	12
1974	Expos	25	9	3	0	0	0	.333	2	1
1975	Expos	44	55	15	4	0	0	.273	6	7
1976	Expos	42	85	23	4	1	1	.271	8	6
1976	Dodgers	23	68	15	3	0	0	.221	5	3
	Total 8 Years	391	710	176	37	5	9	.248	70	71

1970s

Photofest

RON KLIMKOWSKI
1969–70, 1972

You were born in Jersey City, New Jersey. Is that where you grew up?

No, I actually grew up in Jamaica, Queens. I went to parochial school on Sutphin Boulevard, St. Joseph's. We had no gym whatsoever, just cement. And I was an altar boy, believe it or not. So I really didn't play any organized sports or had gym until we moved out to Westbury [Long Island] when I was 12. But I was a Yankee fan from Queens. Always a Yankee fan, a Knick fan, and a Ranger fan.

I read a story about you getting a Yankee uniform from someone as a kid, maybe a friend's mom?

No, actually my mother had a relative who had a dress shop in Ohio and she made me a whole outfit with my favorite, number 5, Joe DiMaggio, on it and I used to wear that.

You attended W. Tresper Clarke High School in Westbury and received 10 varsity letters in baseball, football, and basketball. Was there any interest in you from the NFL, NBA, or colleges looking for football and basketball players?

No. This was the first time I had gym and I was All-County football, basketball, and baseball. For some reason just baseball, but I was a first baseman then and was a good hitter and pitched every so often.

You were signed as an amateur free agent by the Red Sox in 1964.

Well, I went to school first. I attended Morehead State College in Kentucky, where Steve Hamilton and Phil Simms went. I had a baseball scholarship there and then I signed in my second year with the Red Sox. The scout who signed me was [Frank] "Bots" Nekola, who was Boston's top scout. He signed Yaztremski, Petrocelli, and Frank Malzone. By this time I had switched to pitching along with being a first baseman, but when he saw me he saw something and wanted me as a pitcher.

When you went to the minors with the Red Sox did they use you as a reliever or a starter?

In the minors I was a starter; all the time I started. I pitched 200-plus innings one of my first years and was something like 12–14 and completed 20 games. They sent me a raise at the end of the year of $50 a month! [Laughs] I was really mad and I sent a letter to the farm director, Neil Mahoney. I remember it like it was yesterday. I explained in the letter what I did during the season and I asked for a four- or five-hundred-dollar raise. He wrote back, believe it or not. He said, "You're right," and they gave it to me!

133

Wow! That's not what I was expecting you to say, baseball being what it was back then.

No, I know, I know. But they did give me the raise.

So you were a New York kid and a Yankee fan playing for the Boston Red Sox in their system. On August 8, 1967—

Yeah, I cried. [Laughs]

Boston trades you to the Yankees for Elston Howard, of all people.

I was in Pittsfield, Massachusetts, AA ball when I went over in the deal.

How did that feel, being traded for a Yankee MVP?

Ah, you know, I was just happy because I was a Yankee fan and grew up a Yankee fan and it was home.

Did you feel that being traded for a Yankee icon put any extra pressure on you to perform?

No, at the time I really didn't think about it that much.

By 1968 the Yankees, who had been a great team for 50 years, had fallen on some hard times. Did you view the trade as an opportunity to make the majors due to the pitching staff not being as talented as it had been in years past?

When I got traded the Yankees never actually used me as a starter that much. They tried me at all different things. In 1968 I had a terrible season and they sent me down to AA. In 1969 I was 0–3 as a starter at first. Then I won ten games in a row and that's when the Yankees brought me up, in September.

In 1969 you led the International League [AAA] with a 15–7 record and a 2.18 ERA. Then the Yanks recall you in September.

Right, I was an All-Star in the IL and I think I even hit a home run. When the Yanks called me up the first batter I faced was Al Kaline when I came in in relief in a 2–0 game. I pitched three innings in relief and gave up one hit to Bill Freehan. It was a Texas League single.

How did it feel, being from New York and a Yankee fan, to walk out on to that mound at Yankee Stadium for your first major league game wearing pinstripes?

I was so nervous I couldn't even get my warm-up jacket off when I got to the mound—you know how the car used to bring you in. I couldn't even get the zipper down to get that jacket off. But it felt fantastic. I'd love to get a tape of that game, but you know, there wasn't that much coverage back then, not like today.

When you pitched that first game you were facing Denny McLain. Then in your second major league game you relieved Kekich against the Orioles, and now you're pitching opposite Jim Palmer. That's some way to start your major league career.

Not only that, but then about four days after that they gave me a start up in Boston at Fenway against the Red Sox. But when I came in against Baltimore and pitched a couple innings of relief, that's when they had their real good team with Brooks Robinson and Frank Robinson—they had everybody. In two innings of relief I gave up one run when somebody—a right-hander, I don't remember who—inside-outted me and got it down the first baseline, got a base hit off me, and scored a run.

That start against the Red Sox was your third major league game [and final game of the 1969 season]. You faced Ken Brett, who was pitching his seventh major league game. It turned out to be a classic pitching duel.

Yeah, I went nine innings and gave up three hits and left a 0–0 ballgame. The first batter that I faced was Mike Andrews. He hit a double off the Green Monster, but that was about it. I got the start because I thought they were testing me out—they had just brought me up from the minors and Houk wanted to see how good I was. I always figured that I'd be a starter because I was a starter all through the minors. But to make the big leagues you don't argue too much.

The Yankees lost 1–0 in the 14th inning. Brett similarly went nine innings without giving up a run.

In 1970 I didn't give up a run the whole spring training. I missed the rookie of spring training award when they gave it to John Ellis. But they never used to give it to pitchers. My first exhibition game I went five innings, which was a lot for early spring training, against the Washington Senators in Pompano Beach. I was a sinker-ball pitcher so I didn't throw a lot of pitches. They used me a lot that spring training.

We went on from there in the 1970 season, and as a matter of fact they started me one game last minute in Detroit. I don't remember who I was facing, but the Tigers had all those stars. I had a no-hitter for five innings until I think Dalton Jones got a base hit off me. I went nine innings for a complete game and got my first major league hit. I won 5–0 on a three-hitter.

1970 was a fine season for you. You appeared in 45 games [3 starts] and you wound up with a 2.65 ERA. At the conclusion of spring training in 1971 the Yankees traded you to the A's for Felipe Alou. Why did they trade you?

I don't know. It was on Good Friday, too. As a matter of fact my father and I cried because, again, I left New York, where I had always wanted to be, and they traded me to Oakland, 3,000 miles away. I guess they needed a right-handed batter for Yankee Stadium. I was disappointed. Finley called me up and wanted me to report to Oakland.

I was actually with the Yankees at LaGuardia Airport where we were leaving to go play a weekend series. Ralph Houk and Lee MacPhail came walking over to me and told me. They had to take all my gear off the plane. I said good-bye to my teammates and now I'm walking through the airport with all my baseball stuff. As it turned out the earliest I could get out to California was Saturday night. [The A's] were leaving Monday for Minnesota. I told [Finley] that I would meet him there and went home for the weekend. I wound up having a very good series [in Minnesota], striking out Harmon Killebrew three or four times in a row. They made me a long reliever and I pitched good.

That road trip was where they took Rollie Fingers out of the rotation and made him a reliever for good. We also had Vide Blue, Catfish Hunter—we had a hell of a team. We won everything until we got to Baltimore and lost three straight to the Orioles [in the AL Championship Series]. I think I was going to start the third game, but they decided to start Diego Segui, [who] wound up getting knocked out. So I never go a chance to appear in the playoffs. Yeah, we lost three in a row.

Was Dick Williams as good as everyone says?

Good coach, he was a good manager, but Ralph Houk was a good manager too. You know, things were different back then, though. If you started and didn't go eight or nine innings you were terrible. There was no such thing as 100 pitches. You can see it on my baseball cards. I think I pitched about 900 innings in the minor leagues.

In 1972 you were in spring training with the A's and you got injured.

Yes, what happened was, it was outfield practice and they had the pitchers as guinea pigs run the bases as base runners. They would hit to the outfielders and then they would hit to the cutoff man. It was early in the morning and the grass and dirt were still damp, and while running I hurt my right knee. I still had a great spring training, but every time I pitched I had to have my knee drained. My knee was drained about 60 times that year. It would blow up after I would pitch—it was the medial cartilage. After the season I finally had it operated on. Back then they cut you; there was no arthroscopic. It was a tough recovery situation.

On May 22, 1972, the A's released you, but on that same day the Yankees picked you up again. They must have thought you still had something left.

Yes, I went back to Syracuse [AAA] and from there they brought me back up.

You appeared in 16 games for the Yanks in 1972 and that concluded your major league career. What happened after that? Was the knee too bad?

Well, that was when they operated on me after the season, and the recovery in 1973 was horrible. I had tears in my eyes trying to break the adhesions. There was no physical therapy back then; they didn't send you for anything like that. It was a different era—I made $12 a day in meal money. [Laughs] If I'm not mistaken, now they get more than $200. In the minors I got $3 a day.

I went back and played some amateur ball but that was it.

You played with two men who would become the most prominent pitching coaches in baseball. Could you tell that Mel Stottlemyre or Dave Duncan were headed in that direction, or had that in them?

Well, Duncan was a catcher and a teammate, but the person I really liked and was on the same wavelength with was Thurman Munson. I had my best games with him.

Jake Gibbs was the senior member of the Yankees at this time. Did you throw to him much?

Oh yeah, but for some reason we just didn't gel that well with the thinking and what to throw the hitter. It should always be up to the pitcher what to throw anyway. You have to think for yourself out there.

Do you ever get back to the stadium?

I used to but I haven't done so lately. I used to play in the Old-Timers' Game going back about 12 years ago. I'd like to get back this year [2008] before they move out.

You are involved with the QuesTec pitching system as sports advisor and marketing director.

Right, we developed that for monitoring the umpires.

When most fans hear "QuesTec" they immediately associate it with the strike zone in major league baseball, and maybe they can picture Curt Schilling attacking a device with a bat.

[Laughs] Right, but I think it's a good product. First of all, it should be in every ballpark. It's a good tool that can be used by the teams for training purposes, especially if a pitcher has had Tommy John surgery or something similar, you have a record if his curveball breaks the same amount of inches and such. The problem with umpires is that they each had their own individual strike zone—they still do. So now it's just monitored by Major League Baseball, and ESPN has copied it.

My advice was to go into things like virtual lines on TV, say like in football for first-down lines. That should have been developed by the company, interactive content. But their main product is the QuesTec pitching monitoring system.

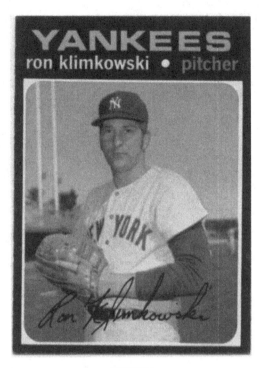

TOPPS

KLIMKOWSKI, RONALD BERNARD
Born: March 1, 1944 Jersey City, New Jersey
Bats: Right Throws: Right
Height: 6' 2" Weight: 190

Year	Team	G	W-L	SV	GS	CG	IP	SO	W	ERA
1969	YANKEES	3	0-0	0	1	0	14.0	3	5	0.64
1970	YANKEES	45	6-7	1	3	1	98.3	40	33	2.65
1971	A's	26	2-2	2	0	0	45.3	25	23	3.38
1972	YANKEES	16	0-3	1	2	0	31.3	11	15	4.02
	Total 4 Years	90	8-12	4	6	1	189.0	79	76	2.90

BRACE Photo

ROGER HAMBRIGHT
1971

You were born in Sunnyside, Washington. Is that where you grew up?

That's where I was born, but we moved to Vancouver when I was six years old.

Were you a PCL fan back then?

We went to the old Portland Beavers games. They were associated with the Indians back then. Tiant and Sam McDowell and some of the other guys came through there. I wasn't a Yankee fan but my dad and my brother were. My mom and I always liked the old Milwaukee Braves.

Were you involved in organized baseball prior to high school?

I played Little League, Babe Ruth, and American Legion. I started playing when I was about nine years old.

You played for Columbia River High School, where you had a very nice baseball career.

Yeah, the Columbia River Chieftains, I did. When I was a sophomore I was on the varsity team and when I didn't pitch I was playing third base.

In 1967 the Yankees drafted you in the 67th round of the amateur entry draft [954th overall]. Were there any other teams watching you?

It's kind of a strange thing, because the scouts were talking to my mom and dad and I was told that I was going to be drafted by the Pittsburgh Pirates. When you go to these All-Star games, high school and American Legion, there's quite a few scouts around. I didn't know who they were at the time. Carl Taylor is the one who signed me. He was the Yankees scout in the Pacific Northwest. He's the one who signed Steve Kline and Mel Stottlemyre.

I didn't sign in '67; I signed in '68. I wasn't going to sign—I was going to go ahead and go to college. After talking to my mom and dad and everybody, because I was drafted so low they said I may never get another chance, so I finally went ahead and signed. I went to Johnson City, Tennessee, in '68. It was just a rookie league that played for three months. It's an orientation league basically. I was 5–0. [Laughs] The next year I went to spring training and started out in the Florida State League.

Did you think that you had any shot at making the major leagues?

I think everybody thinks down deep in their heart that they can make it. I always thought that I could. It's really strange when you get into professional baseball, because a lot of the guys that had great ability, like number one draft choices, a lot of them just didn't have the determination or desire. They liked to screw around too much. The guys that had to work for what they got were a lot more dedicated and determined, and they seemed to actually do better than the higher draft choices. That's what I saw.

At some point the organization switched you to a reliever.

That actually happened in Johnson City. What happened was, when I got down there I hurt my back. At these instructional leagues you don't go to a spring training; they have their own four- or five-week "spring training." During that preseason I threw out some vertebras in my back and I wasn't able to start, so they just put me in the bullpen. Once I went into the bullpen I never got out of there, and that started me out to be a short reliever.

You preferred starting, though.

Well, that's all I'd ever done. In high school the guys who threw the ball were all starters. We didn't have a reliever. If a starter was having a bad game they'd bring in another starter as a reliever. Everybody prefers to start. I had the ability of getting up and warming up pretty fast, so ideally I was suited for being a short reliever.

You moved up the system pretty quickly before getting called up to the majors. Were you in Syracuse [AAA] in 1971 prior to getting the call?

No. I was in West Haven, Connecticut, AA. I played the rookie year in Johnson City. Then I played in Fort Lauderdale, and then the next year I played in Kinston, North Carolina, before going to West Haven in '71. Yeah, I jumped AAA.

In July of 1971 the Yankees called you up after you posted a 2.08 ERA in AA. How did you find out that you were being recalled?

My manager called me into his office and told me that I was going up. It was a shock to me. You hope that call is going to come one of these days, but when it happens it really shocks you because you have no idea. They didn't say anything to me before that, but I had had two good years prior to that and at West Haven I was having a good year.

By that point you had posted a 2.79 ERA in four seasons in the Yankee system. Did you think that you would have an opportunity to stay with the big club after that?

You know, I don't know how aware you are about baseball politics. There's a lot of politics in baseball. There's a lot of things that have to happen. I was almost positive that I was going to stay the next year, but they had a guy, Wayne Granger, who was on his way out, basically, and they had no way of getting rid of him. He was making a lot of money. So they wound up keeping him instead. Whitey Ford called me in and said, "We shouldn't be sending you down, but we have to because we want to keep you busy. As soon as we can get a trade or do something with Wayne Granger, we're going to call you back up." That never happened. When I got sent down to AAA Frank Verdi was the manager. He had won the Little World Series the year before. He had his players coming back from the year before that had won the championship. He was like anybody else, looking to get a big-league job. So they didn't use me. I hadn't been part of the team the year before because I came up from AA. Basically they didn't use me at all. I was the type of pitcher that I had to be used three or four times a week in order to stay sharp. You get too strong if you don't pitch—your arm gets too strong and you overthrow the ball. Once you haven't been used in five or six days and then they send you in, you're not real sharp. You don't put the ball where you want it and wind up walking a few guys. I ended up not having a real good year there [in 1972].

Had you ever been to New York City before being called up?

No, I'd never been there. [Laughs] Vancouver had about 30,000 people.

Did you meet the team on the road or at home?

I joined the team at Yankee Stadium. They were home playing either the White Sox or Minnesota, I can't remember.

What was it like putting on that pinstripe uniform and walking out onto the field at Yankee Stadium that first time?

That was an awesome feeling. Well, the Yankees are the greatest team of all time. You've seen it and heard about it, but it still doesn't prepare you for when you walk into it. That was the old Yankee Stadium that I played in, not the remodeled one. It was quite a place.

Did Ralph Houk or Jim Turner say anything to you when you got there?

They introduced themselves to me and told me that I would be pitching in short relief. Ralph Houk was a good manager, he was a good guy. So was Jim Turner, but he was really up in age at that time.

Your first game went pretty well. You replaced Alan Closter to start the ninth inning at the stadium in a losing game (3–1) against the White Sox. In a sign of the times for the team, barely 10,000 fans were in attendance for the Monday night game. You gave up a single to Rich Morales but otherwise recorded three quick outs. Were you nervous?

I think we wound up in fourth place that year. The Yankees at that time were by no means a dynasty and we were playing another team that wasn't that great. That had a lot to do with [the low attendance].

You're always nervous the first time that you get called in, especially at Yankee Stadium. I was nervous a little bit. Not like a lot of the others that I saw come up after me. A friend of mine named Terry Ley got called up right at the tail end of the season. The first time he went out there he couldn't even throw the ball! He was just dumbstruck and was just standing there. Of course everybody on the team was just laughing at him. He was so awestruck he couldn't even pitch and everybody had to go out to him and calm him down. Munson had to go out and shake him and say, "Hey, you gotta throw the ball."

By the end of the 1971 campaign you were 3–1 with two saves. That seems to have been a pretty good job for your first taste of major league baseball. Did you think that you would be back for the 1972 season?

I did a pretty good job even though they used me sparingly. They had Jack Aker and Lindy McDaniel, but they were getting up there in age and they didn't have great years. There were a lot of situations where I wish they had brought me in, where I thought I could help.

The year that I left was the year George Steinbrenner bought the team. After the season [1974] they called me and wanted to cut my contract and I said no. To be honest I was in Syracuse and didn't have that good of a year playing for Bobby Cox. I didn't want to take a cut, and it's not that easy living out of a suitcase every six months either. I had a family and had to make a livable wage to continue to play there, but they wouldn't negotiate. I semiretired and told them to either trade me or release me or sell my contract. Then I get a call from Mexico [Laughs] and they told me they bought my contract. I said, "Oh you did, did you?" They came up and paid me more than the Yankees were paying me!

The team I was playing for, Juarez [Indians], didn't have a very good team. The first year I went down there I threw a no-hitter against Tampico [Lightermen], who were the Mexican League champions. The reason I went down there was I was hoping somebody from the States would pick me back up, but I never heard from anybody. I was in a situation where I didn't have to live in Mexico. I lived in El Paso, which is a border town right across from Juarez. I lived in the States every night unless we were on a road trip. I didn't ride their buses either—I was the only one on the whole team that flew. I told them to fly me or I was going home. I wasn't riding in those stinkin' buses for 16 hours and then getting out and be expected to play, I don't think so. The conditions down there aren't real good. Mike Kekich was down there, George Brunet was down there, Jim Ray Hart was down there. There were a lot of big-leaguers who went down there.

Did the major leagues have scouts down in Mexico?

Oh yeah, all the time. Down there I was a starter and thought someone would pick me up.

After you went back to being a starter in Mexico you became a workhorse. In 1976 you were 17–11 in 250 innings pitched, and in 1977 you were 21–12 in 263 innings pitched. It is estimated that you threw over 4,000 pitches each season.

Yeah, that's a lot of pitches, isn't it? Down in Mexico we didn't have a reliever either, so I was usually out there for the duration. Very rarely did I get taken out of a game, and you threw about 140 pitches a game. I was there for three seasons—1975, '76, and '77— all for the Juarez Indios. I left after the '77 season when I was 28 years old. I figured that if nobody picked me up after winning 21 games, what were the chances of going back down there and somebody wanting to pick me up next year? I just hung 'em up.

You had mentioned the game earlier that happened on May 20, 1975, just after you arrived in the Mexican League.

It was at Tampico and I threw a no-hitter against them. It actually should have been a perfect game, but I walked one hitter in the second inning and then the batter behind him hit into a double play. He was the only guy to reach base the whole game.

Oddly enough, both of those teams, Juarez and Tampico, are defunct.

Oh really? I didn't know that. I haven't followed them. I know Juarez won the Mexican League Championship about three years after I left.

Thurman Munson was only a couple of years older than you but was already an All-Star and Rookie of the Year by the time you joined the Yankees. How was he to work with as a rookie pitcher?

Thurman was a good friend of mine. In spring training we lived in the same complex together and our kids played together and all that stuff. Thurman was a good guy and I really liked him a lot. He was a good catcher and had been in the big leagues a couple of years by the time I got up there and knew all the hitters. When you're a rookie and don't know all the hitters you have to relay on the catcher. He called all the pitches. I didn't always agree with him—he would get that number one stuck. If he didn't know you he would want you to throw a lot of fastballs. I

145

had a good fastball but I also had a real good slider. I liked to throw the slider a lot more than he wanted me to, but I let him call the game. [Laughs]

You played with Gene Michael also. Does it surprise you that he's still with the Yankees 38 years later?

He was the shortstop then and I got to know him even though he wasn't someone I ran around with. For being a ballplayer at that time he was fairly old, but he loved baseball. It's like they say, it gets in your blood. You miss it when you leave.

The Yankees had some good starting pitching in '71 with Stottlemyre, Fritz Peterson, Stan Bahnsen, and Steve Kline. Those four pitched a total of 64 complete games and 15 shutouts for a team that came in fourth. It was a different era for pitchers then.

Yeah, it was. It was actually just the beginning of pitching becoming specialized with middle relievers and short relievers. Right after that Sparky Lyle was purchased by the Yankees for short relief. I'm sure if you looked at Baltimore with Palmer, McNally, and Dobson and those guys, they had a lot of complete games too. That was the era that starting pitchers pitched. If you had the lead and hadn't thrown that many pitches you stayed in.

We had a good staff. They taught me how to throw a changeup, a palmball. That was something that I really didn't do in the minors. They did teach me how to change speeds.

You also finished with a .500 batting average in the majors.[54]

[Laughs] Well, you know, you go up there and they think that pitchers can't hit. They didn't know that I didn't sign as a pitcher—I signed as a third baseman and I could always hit. That kind of surprised them. That pitcher threw the ball right in there and I hit a line drive right over the shortstop's head. They all looked and said, "What the hell?" [Laughs]

Have you been back to New York since you retired?

No, I haven't. I really didn't get to do too much sightseeing while I was there and I wish that I had. When we were home we were always playing. My daughter went to Yankee Stadium and she told them who she was and they let her in. It was closed at the time but they opened it and she took a tour.

Are you coming out to see the new Yankee Stadium?

---

54. 1 for 2 with 1 RBI.

I would like to but it's a long way out there. It's a bit of a journey. I still get all kinds of mail from the Yankees. I get a newsletter and every year. You get a Christmas card and Christmas ornament, and I get paraphernalia to sign.

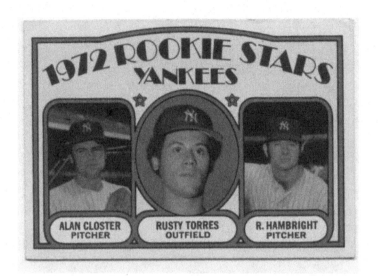

TOPPS

HAMBRIGHT, ROGER DEE
Born: March 26, 1949 Sunnyside, Washington
Bats: Right Throws: Right
Height: 5' 10" Weight: 180 lbs

Year	Team	G	W-L	SV	GS	CG	IP	SO	W	ERA
1971	YANKEES	18	3-1	2	0	0	26.7	14	10	4.39
	Total 1 year	18	3-1	2	0	0	26.7	14	10	4.39

BRACE Photo

Dave Pagan
1973–76

You were born in Nipawin, Saskatchewan, in Canada. Do you still live there?

I lived in a smaller area outside of Nipawin—there were just 100 people there, smaller than a village. It's about 30 miles from Nipawin. I was just now out in my garage getting some bats for a guy.

Nipawin isn't even close to the U.S. border. How did you start playing baseball as a child?

[Laughs] The same way as everyone else, I guess. We organized our own baseball. What happened was a friend of mine and I had a raffle to buy equipment when we were 12—of course it's illegal, but years ago it didn't matter. We made enough to buy catcher's gear and two bats. Then we had to find a coach, who was more of a babysitter than a coach. We went to little tournaments around. There was no league. All the little towns had kids play, no uniforms or anything, you know. Then we got leagues the next year and I started playing senior ball the next year. When I was 14 I started playing senior ball, which is like your semipro only not as good.

Was there a baseball team at your high school?

There was the first year I was there and that was it. They disbanded it—there wasn't enough interest.

A few NHL players came from Nipawin, but you seem like the only baseball player.

Yeah—well I'm the only one I know of. [Laughs] There's not too many that even come from Saskatchewan. A few but not a lot. Reggie Cleveland came from Saskatchewan but I think he was raised in California mostly. Harmon Killebrew and Maury Wills had that World Baseball [Classic tournament] for kids a few years ago down in Regina. They asked me to come down and I talked to Reggie Cleveland for quite a while. The closest major league team to Nipawin was the Twins, but I wasn't interested in them.

The Yankees signed you as an undrafted free agent in 1970. How did that come about? How did they become aware of you?

A guy that I played senior ball against in Prince Albert, which is a little bigger than where I came from—they had about 11,000 people—he played ball in college and the coach from Belleview asked him if there was anybody up there who could play baseball and he mentioned my name. So I went to a baseball school in Oliver, British Columbia, and he met me there. They put up a game against the Vancouver Mounties, which was a junior team at that time. I pitched against them for six innings and never gave up any runs or anything, so he gave me a scholarship there to Belleview Junior College. Other colleges were after me after this—I could have gone to a four-year college in California, but not after I gave my word to [Belleview's baseball coach].

Is Belleview Junior College where the Yankees scouted you?

Oh yeah, Eddie Taylor did.

Did you think that you had any chance of making it to the majors when the Yankees signed you?

Yeah, yeah. There was no doubt. [Laughs] When I signed with the Yankees the Expos wanted me, and so did the Pirates.

You played 13 games in the low minors in 1970 before moving on to Ft. Lauderdale in '71. Did playing in that heat bother you?

Nope, it didn't bother me. Well, it was hot—it was hot for everybody. You mean because I'm from Northern Saskatchewan? [Laughs] No, it didn't. You get climatized.

After a decent year you were moved up to Kingston in '72 and responded with a 14–9 record. You led the Carolina League with a 2.53 ERA and 192 strikeouts.

It was a good year. See, when I was with Ft. Lauderdale I was with Bobby Cox and he was my coach. I went home during that year because my wife was having my second baby and I thought, "Are they going to leave me at home?" because I was having a poor year—my win-loss record was not good. I talked to him later when he was coaching in Venezuela when I went down to winter ball, and he said that there was not even a thought of getting released or anything, "Because you were right in the games and it wasn't your fault most of the times when we lost." He said I pitched well but I didn't have a good record—I think it was 9–14—and you start thinking about that.

In 1973 you were in AA at West Haven, where you started out great, going 6–2 with a 1.86 ERA.

I went there for two months and I was doing fine. I think I lost all my games by 1–0—we never scored any runs.

Do you remember finding out that you were being promoted to the major leagues?

[Manager Doc Edwards] called me into his room—because we were on the road; in fact I believe we were in Quebec City—and I was supposed to pitch the next game. He said, "Dave, I've got good news for you. You're going up and your flight is leaving tomorrow at seven o'clock." . . . Never slept all night that night. I flew into Cleveland and met them in Cleveland.

When I got there I remember that they played a trick on me, Bobby Murcer did. He said, "There's a press conference for you." I was already dressed and I said, "Now?" I didn't know there was no press conference—there could have been, you know. I said that I would change back into my civvies and he said, "Oh no, you don't have to do that." So I went walking down there to the restaurant in the Cleveland stadium in my uniform and my shower shoes. I got there and I said [to the staff], "Is there anyone else here?" They said no and I walked back. As soon as I walked back through the door of the clubhouse they all started laughing. As soon as I saw there was nobody else in the restaurant I said to myself, "OK, they got me."

When you got back to New York what was it like walking out onto the field at Yankee Stadium wearing a Yankees uniform?

It was something, and this was old Yankee Stadium. This was the one that really meant something. What I meant was, compared to the new one, when we came back to it wasn't the same. It wasn't the feeling where center field has got the monuments and things like that. I was surprised at the drainage though. When I sat in the dugout I couldn't see the left fielder. But it was really something seeing the façade and all that stuff that I knew was there, but I never thought I'd get a chance to see it.

You were a starter in the minors and you started your first major league game on Sunday, July 1, 1973, at Yankee Stadium against the Indians in the second game of a doubleheader.

Right, Canada Day.

Really?

Oh yeah. Like you have July 4th, we have July 1st.

It probably didn't go as well as you would have liked it to.

No!

You got through one inning giving up six hits with two earned runs and walking a batter while striking out none.

I think Ralph, if he'd have pitched me one inning on the road just to get the nerves out of my system—I'm not using this as an excuse, but it might have been better. After Cleveland we went somewhere else, and if he'd have pitched me just one inning I would have been good. I would have gotten the butterflies out of my system there instead of at Yankee Stadium during the second game of a doubleheader on a Sunday in July.

I warmed up in the bullpen and I was loose before I even started the game, you might say. There were 55,000 people there. Sam McDowell pitched the first game, and I moved that day! What a stupid thing to do. I moved my wife and kids into New Jersey, mostly clothing and stuff, because I was still living in West Haven and I would go back there at night. We got back and I got to the stadium about halfway through the first game and never had much chance to realize what was going on. I remember warming up in the bullpen and not feeling anything, and then going out to throw my warm-up pitches. The first pitch bounced in front of the plate; I threw it about 56 feet. My first out was Buddy Bell, who hit a groundball to me.

Munson was your catcher. Did he come out to calm you down?

I can't remember. I was so up for it I can't remember much of anything. It was the biggest crowd I ever pitched in front of. We were a decent team and Cleveland was decent, but they weren't a great draw. It may have been a promotion game too, where they give away something.

After that first game your ERA stood at 18.00. You would pitch 12 more innings for the team that year, striking out 9 while not allowing a walk and allowing just 2 runs. You got your ERA down to 2.84. Were you satisfied with the way your first season went?

I think that's what it was, getting familiar with things. I was a little disappointed the next year when they sent me down to the minors. I thought I would stay up. I was in the major league camp and they sent me to AAA.

You were on the team for the final game at old Yankee Stadium on September 30, 1973. There was such a big celebration and send-off this year [2008] with the renovated Yankee Stadium, but that seems not to have been the case in '73. Obviously the players were aware of the stadium's closing, but was there any sentiment about it?

I don't think it was a big deal, because we were coming back there. I can't remember it being anything, but I think that also we knew that we were going to be back in two years, whereas now they're not going to be back there.

You did great at AAA in 1974, posting a 1.29 ERA before going back to New York, where you pitched in 16 games. Did you get hurt that year?

It was the year I tore my rotator cuff. The first game I pitched for them was against Kansas City and I tore my rotator cuff. I felt it in about the sixth inning. I wondered, "What the hell?" but I finished up the game because it was my first start and first complete game. They didn't put me on the disabled list because I had options, so they just sent me down. That's why I traveled up and down so much, because I'd go down and pitch a little in AAA in '74 and '75, and then I'd come back up and I'd sit, and then all of a sudden pitch and it would hurt again. It would help to pitch a little but when I would get back up to the major leagues I never pitched much. Then surgery wasn't a big thing for rotator cuff. You just had had it, I guess. That's about the way it was.

How was Thurman Munson to throw to for a young pitcher?

I liked Thurman as a person but Rick Dempsey would catch me more than Thurman. I played with him in the minors and we came up at the end of '73 together. I threw to him quite a bit in Baltimore when we got traded over to Baltimore in '76.

You seemed to prefer starting.

Yeah, I did. The bullpen wasn't bad, but other than a fastball I never had a pitch that could do anything, so starting was best for me.

How did you find Bill Virdon as a manager?

He was different. The guys, from what I saw, didn't care for him; they didn't respect him.

Were you surprised when he was replaced by Billy Martin?

No. We used to have meetings and stuff, just the baseball players without Billy Virdon, and we used to talk about him. It was not a good scenario; he didn't seem to get along with the guys that well.

That surprises me, because he was a quieter guy, whereas Billy Martin was explosive.

Yeah, he was, I know, but Billy stuck up for you on the field. He stuck up for you and he was more vocal on the field. I don't know if you remember this, when he took that home run away from Money off me? We were playing in Milwaukee and I came in in relief in the bottom of the ninth He hit a home run but the umpire at first base called time because Billy [wanted to talk the me]—he wanted me to go into the windup instead of from the set. The umpire put his arms up just as I was delivering the ball. Billy came flying out of the dugout after Money was circling the bases and I didn't know if he was coming after me or what he was doing. [Laughs] He went running right by me to go over to the first base umpire. That umpire said, "Yes, I called time before the pitch was made." It won us the game instead of losing it. I got the next two guys out and we won the game. [The Brewers] were already leaving the dugout going into the dressing room. That's how he stuck up for the players very much on the field.

Roy White was the senior member of the team by this point.

Oh yeah, I still remember him. I got to know him quit well. He was very quiet but I liked him.

In 1976 you started the year with the Yankees when they went back into the renovated Yankee Stadium. You have an interesting perspective for someone who was only on the team for four years: you played in three different home ballparks.

I thought [the new stadium] was good. By that time I kind of forgot what the old one was like, but then you see some of the things that were still there and it brings it back. The clubhouse was much better. In the old one there wasn't much room. This one had a lounge or a games room, you might say, and things like that. It was much better.

Were you surprised when New York traded you to Baltimore on June 15, 1976?

I was, yeah. Rick Dempsey was my roommate at the time and he came home and asked me if I'd heard that we got traded and I said, "What?!" He said, "Yeah, we're going to Baltimore." Really, the coach never did tell us, or the manager Billy Martin. We never heard [from a Yankee official)] that we got traded.

That wound up going down as one of the worst trades in Yankee history. They gave up Tippy Martinez, Rudy May (who the Yanks would bring back four years later), Rick Dempsey (who caught until 1992), and a minor leaguer named Scott McGregor (20-game winner and All-Star). In return they got a washed-up Ken Holtzman and Ellie Hendricks, who was clearly finished, along with Doyle Alexander and Grant Jackson, both of whom the Yankees let go after the season.

Tippy and Rick Dempsey would have a big part in winning the World Series that one year [1983]. What happened was, the Yankees were going for it that year and they got rid of a lot of their young players. Just to make up for that year, because they wanted to win it, they gave up a lot of young players.

After you played a lot for the Orioles in '76 the fledgling Mariners took you in the expansion draft for the 1977 season. Did you view this as an opportunity to stick in the majors?

Yeah, a little bit, or stick longer. In fact Baltimore called me in at the end of the year and was going to renew my contract. I told them that I didn't see me in any of their plans, so I said that if they wouldn't mind, I'd like to go in the expansion draft. I thought I would go to Toronto, you know, because of being a Canadian and they were looking for Canadian players. But no, Seattle got me.

You'll always be an original Seattle Mariner.

I guess so. [Laughs]

Do you ever get any fan mail in regards to being an original Mariner?

No, no. Other than getting Topps bubble gum cards to sign your John Hancock on, no.

During the 1977 season the Pirates GM inquired about you for their pennant drive. The Mariners traded you to Pittsburg on July 27 for Rick Honeycutt, but you only appeared in one game for the Pirates. What happened?

I don't know. They only called me up at the end of the year. They sent me to Columbus, Ohio [AAA]. Then in 1978 I went back to Columbus and the following year I went to Portland with the Pirates for AAA again, and that's where I got released. I went down to Mexico and played one month down there with the Mexico City Reds and didn't like it too much. [Laughs]. I asked to go home! [Most people] stayed in and around where the tourists were, but I used to walk all around. I just didn't like the travel and everything else—it was second rate. I came home and played ball locally in a senior league, and then I played with a semipro team here and that was about it. Canada has an Olympic team but I never got involved in that because I had a family to feed and I never made a lot of money playing ball.

Looking back, are there any other Yankee memories?

I remember getting fan mail. You would come to your locker and you see it sitting there from fans that wanted autographs. That I remember; it was like the second day I was there. When we came back from that first road trip and I was up for about a week, there were about six letters there already! A couple days later there was more. I remember guys like Bobby Murcer and Sparky Lyle. [Laughs] Mine was just a drop in the ocean compared to theirs.

I think this is true too: Sparky Lyle and I are the only pitchers that went back to Yankee Stadium, from the old Yankee Stadium to the new Yankee Stadium, the one that's now going to get demolished.

Your Yankee baseball card looks better than your Mariners one, where it looks like they painted a hat on you.

[Laughs] That's right. You know, I never chew. I don't know what I was thinking, but in the Mariners one I've got tobacco in my mouth. I think I did put it in and never did think anything of it until they took the picture.

Did any one particular hitter give you a hard time?

Yes, Freddie Patek of the Kansas City Royals.

Freddie Patek!

You know why? Because I was a fastball pitcher and he liked the fastball and he was a poke hitter. The home-run hitters I never had any trouble with. If you look at my stats, I never gave up many home runs for the amount of innings pitched. They never bothered me. It was the little Punch-and-Judy type of hitter.

In fact, when I was in Seattle I came on in relief and I remember there were two outs with a runner on second. Freddie Patek was who I had to face. People started getting up and going home and this put a negative thing in my mind. I was thinking, "You people are going home? Don't go home, it's not over yet." I put it in my mind that way and I shouldn't have. Anyway, he got a hit and drove in the tying run. Then the next batter hit an ordinary ball through the infield and Patek scored from first.

He also went 3 for 4 in my first win in the majors when I was with the Yankees. I won but he still got three hits.

Did you ever get to meet George Steinbrenner?

Oh yeah, lots. In fact he came up to me after I hurt my shoulder and said to me, "How's your shoulder?" I told him, "Not too good." He replied, "Well, if it's not good we'll send you down." It was the way he said it that turned me off, he was being . . . a boss. And the next day I was sent down. He sent paintings to my house for Christmas. He was good when I was playing, but it was just the way he said it that I didn't like.

He sent paintings to your house?

Yeah, I think he sent them to all the players. He sent the team picture that was about 18" X 24" with a frame. It's still hanging up in my living room.

Have you ever been back to Yankee Stadium since you retired?

No. I was back in New Jersey a couple of years ago doing an autograph show but that was it, I've never been back in New York. [Laughs] Excuse me, but the lifestyle we've got here is a lot different and I wouldn't want to change it. I never went downtown much. I went downtown more as a Mariner and an Oriole because we lived down there in the hotels. I only went downtown once or twice (while a Yankee) and that was to go to the Empire State Building.

Are you going to make it to the new Yankee Stadium?

If I get there. [Laughs] Not a special trip, though. I'll see it on television.

TOPPS

PAGAN, DAVID PERCY
Born: September 15, 1949 Nipawin, Saskatchewan, Canada
Bats: Right Throws: Right
Height: 6' 2" Weight: 175

Year	Team	G	W-L	SV	GS	CG	IP	SO	W	ERA
1973	YANKEES	4	0-0	0	1	0	12.7	9	1	2.84
1974	YANKEES	16	1-3	0	6	1	49.3	39	28	5.11
1975	YANKEES	13	0-0	1	0	0	31.0	18	13	4.06
1976	YANKEES	7	1-1	0	2	1	23.7	13	4	2.28
1976	Orioles	20	1-4	1	5	0	46.7	34	23	5.98
1977	Mariners	24	1-1	2	4	1	66.0	30	26	6.14
1977	Pirates	1	0-0	0	0	0	3.0	4	0	0.00
	Total 5 Years	85	4-9	4	18	3	232.3	147	95	4.96

BRACE Photo

RICK BLADT
1975

You were signed by the Cubs in May of 1966 when you were 20 years old. Was that a tryout, or were you scouted?

I was scouted after my second year of college at Foothills Junior College.

Were you a standout in high school and college?

Well, in other people's estimations. I was never good enough in my own. We can be our own worst critics sometimes.

Were you always an outfielder growing up?

No, I was a shortstop and second baseman and pitcher. In my first year [in the minors] at Caldwell, Idaho, rookie league one of the kids in right field came up with tendonitis in his throwing wrist. George Freeze, the manager, asked if anybody could play the outfield and I said, "I don't see why not. I can catch a fly ball in the infield." And that started it. He told me to take right field tonight. A couple of my throws were over the third baseman and into the stands. That was in Ogden, Utah. That was because I had no clue how to throw that far, because at shortstop your longest throw is from behind the third baseman to the first baseman.

Did you have any favorite teams or players growing up in California?

The Giants, because they were so close, with Mays and McCovey and Cepeda and Marichal—they were fine athletes. I wasn't a Yankee fan but only [interested] because of Mantle and 61 in '61 and that sort of thing, and Whitey Ford and Yogi and Maris.

Once you were in the Cubs' minor league system you made it to the majors in just three years on June 15, 1969, when you got called up and put in as a pinch-runner against the Reds at Crosley Field. That must have been quite a thrill?

It was. My sister had just come up to visit me in the Bay area. She was a teenager and it was just a short few hours after she had arrived and I got her at the airport. I had to turn around and put her on a plane back home and then I got on a plane and went to Chicago.

Prior to the following season the Cubs traded you to the Yankees on January 6, 1970. Was that a surprise to you after making it to the big club so quickly?

Yes. I hoped they were considering me a prospect and I had just come off a .300 season in the Coast League. I was stunned and I didn't know what to think. I had no delusions of going directly to them and pushing somebody onto the bench or starting, or anything like that. I didn't go to the big-league camp my first year in 1970. I went to the AAA camp for Syracuse.

Had you ever been to New York City before, even as a Cub?

No. The Mets may have been in Wrigley during my time with the Cubs, but I would have remembered Shea.

After getting to the majors quickly you stayed in the Yankee minor league system for five years. What do you attribute that to?

Well, they didn't have all that great outfielders, but they had quality people. I think I was—and I hate to say it—an insurance policy, if you know what I mean. In case of one or two injuries I was next in line, but not good enough to be there, in their estimation. I was on the bench to pinch-run or whatever was needed.

I'd like to ask you what you thought of the revered Yankee Stadium, but your timing was off.

Right—I only drove by it; I never was in it.

Did you ever make it back to Yankee Stadium after your playing days?

No. I've never been there and I've never been invited to an Old-Timers' Game or anything. The only contact I have is a quarterly magazine from the old-timers' association.

Regardless of your never having played in Yankee Stadium, what did it feel like putting on a Yankee uniform and walking out on a major league field for the first time as a Yankee?

To be frank, I was scared shitless! [Laughs] I was also a 28-year-old rookie, which is an old rookie. I was about 20 with the Cubs and 28 with the Yankees. I got called up around the All-Star break [July 19]. I was treated very well. I palled around with Catfish and Thurman and Ed Brinkman. When Catfish's wife and kids had to go to South Carolina for school, Thurman, Ed Brinkman, and myself all moved into Catfish's house in New Jersey. I don't remember anything bad about any man on that team.

You were fast. Were you used as a defensive replacement in the outfield?

Yes, often, in center field. Shea Stadium had a big center field and I had Piniella on one side and Bobby Bonds on the other, Barry's dad. That's how I got into center, because Billy Martin exploded one day and asked if there was any S.O.B. on the bench who could play center field and

I stood up and said, "I've been doing it for nine years." He exploded after a few overthrows when Bobby was trying to show his arm off. He called me into his office after one game and told me, "From now until the end of the season you're starting in center field." Bobby moved to right field. That was some feeling. Here's a guy with 300 and something home runs, and I ended up with one! Bobby and I got along well, though. We used to sit together on the planes. We got along well—I don't have any clue why, but we did. He was physically a hell of a lot more imposing than me. Piniella didn't hit well until late in the year. I saw him again later when he was managing Seattle. I met him and Roy White and Yogi. My wife couldn't believe I was standing there talking to these guys like it was old-home week, but to me it was.

One day that stands out in Shea was when I stepped into that trench in center field right before the warning track and caught a line drive. I promptly dislocated something in my hip and back and had nerve pain for the next ten days clear down to my heel. [Yankee pitcher] Doc Medich and Monaghan, the trainer, worked on me—Medich was premed at that time. You didn't want to go on the disabled list, hell no. Nobody does. When that man says, "Play ball," you're in heaven.

Actually, when you were called up Bill Virdon was the manager.

That's right. Ten or twelve days later when we got back from Texas and Cleveland he got fired. When I got called up that's when Guidry and I left a hurricane in Virginia, where we were playing the Tidewater Mets. Everything was flooded and for seven or eight days we didn't do anything but stay in a hotel room. We joined the Yankees in Texas.

When the Yankees recalled you your first at bat was in Minnesota and you got hit by a pitch! Was there a story behind that?

Yep. Tom Johnson threw kind of a screwball/fastball. I think it just got away from him and when I reacted it was too late and it hit me in both forearms. It bounced off the left one and hit me in the other one. That hurts. [Laughs]

Well, you came around to score, so he shouldn't have hit you.

Yeah, then I singled off him later in what wound up being my first official at bat.

You hit your only major league home run on August 23 off the Angels' Andy Hassler, a pretty good pitcher.

Yes, he was. I was in Shea and I was running for a double because I didn't think it was high enough to get over the wall, so I was going for two. I knew I hit the blank out of it. I looked up at second and I saw Runge—I think he was the umpire—making the circle with his finger and I was amazed. I would hit 5–12 home runs a year in the minors, so essentially I was more of a doubles and triples hitter.

After the '75 season you spent the next year in the minors. Was that disappointing?

Yes, it was. I was a frozen player. I would have opted out, but they opted me to the minors so the only way to make it back to the majors was with anybody else. I had no option at all. There was no free agency, and it was even before Catfish had won his lawsuit against Finley.[55]

Did you view the trade to Baltimore in January of '77 as an opportunity to get back to the majors?

I thought so at the time, but then, I was also 29 and pushing 30 by then. So I spent '77 in the minors with the Orioles. The following spring I had a contract in my hand, but I had a decent job too back home and I thought, I'm so sick of being on the other side of the Mississippi; it isn't home. I'd have probably played another year if I'd gotten transferred to the Pacific Coast League, but that didn't happen. When I decided to leave I turned my back and left. I didn't talk about it very often to anyone other than immediate family.

Did you enjoy your time as a ballplayer?

Oh yes, immensely. I still miss it.

Well, I have your baseball card. There aren't too many people that can say they have one.

[Laughs] Well, don't be surprised if you have to pay someone to take it! I had an extended cup of coffee, as Rizzuto would say. Me and another kid in Ft. Lauderdale in spring training figured out that the odds would be 100,000 to 1 to put a minor league uniform on for one day as a male for the United States, Caribbean, and North and South America, and you had to add another two or three zeros to put on a major league uniform for one day. It's astronomically against you.

So, last chance, do you think you're finally going to get to Yankee Stadium in 2008?

No, I'm not. I'm just a working stiff and I'm not going to make it.

---

55. Charles Finley, owner of the Oakland Athletics, was known for his heavy-handed tactics and conflicts with the team. Jim "Catfish" Hunter sued Finley in 1974 over a contract dispute and declared himself a free agent. He won his court case and signed a million-dollar contract with the Yankees the following season, becoming the highest-paid player in baseball history.

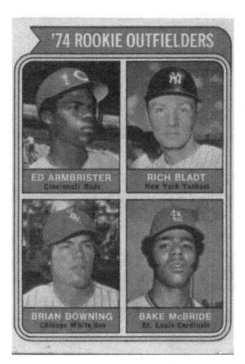

TOPPS

Bladt, Richard Alan
Born: December 9, 1946 Santa Cruz, California
Bats: Right Throws: Right
Height: 6' 1" Weight: 160

Year	Team	G	AB	H	2B	3B	HR	AVG	RBI	R
1969	Cubs	10	13	2	0	0	0	.154	1	1
1975	YANKEES	52	117	26	3	1	1	.222	11	13
	Total 2 Years	62	130	28	3	1	1	.215	12	14

DENNIS SHERRILL
1978, 1980

Growing up in Miami I suppose that you weren't a Yankee fan?

Actually the Orioles had their spring training here at that time, but the Yankees were in Ft. Lauderdale. To answer you question, probably no.

You must have played a lot of baseball growing up.

We had Little League and then we had a thing called Cory League down there, which was a little better than Little League because you could take leads and it was more like baseball. I played in both of them, and then after Little League, which went to about 12, I played American Legion when I was in ninth grade. I started and was better than most of the kids my own age—I had three older brothers so I learned to play at a higher level because of that. Also, being in Miami, where the weather is good all the time for baseball, I played a lot. Whatever sport was going on was what we played, but baseball was always the sport that I knew I could do the best in.

I'm the youngest but my [next] youngest brother played at [Florida State University] on a full scholarship. He got drafted twice but didn't sign either time, but played up in the Cape Cod League. My dad had a scrapbook. There was an article in it that the St. Louis Browns were going to sign him after the season. The war broke out and for whatever reason that never happened, but he was a pretty good ballplayer.

At South Miami High School you were a standout player. Were you always a shortstop?

Yeah, I was [a standout]. I pretty much was always a shortstop. I pitched in Little League and played shortstop. When I got into high school I didn't pitch anymore, which truthfully—I coach a high school team with my son now, and if I had a kid on our team right now that had an arm like I had back then, he would have pitched unless his parents told me that they didn't want him to pitch. My dad may have said that; I don't know.

My oldest brother played in this senior league. I don't know how old I was, maybe nine or ten, and I went to his game at night. Me and my buddy were throwing a ball around on the side. There was a Chicago White Sox scout there watching the game and he ended up paying me more attention more than the game. He told me, "You're going to make some money someday playing this game." When he was getting ready to leave he called me over and opened up his trunk and gave me a major league baseball. I thought that was just the coolest thing. I guess it was pretty evident at a young age that I could play, but then it's, "Is he going to get bigger, stronger, and continue to get better?" As a ninth grader I played in the American Legion. There were even some college guys playing there and I did real well. The scouts knew my brother and knew the family name, too.

On June 5, 1974, the Yankees drafted you with their first pick in the first round of the amateur draft, 12ᵗʰ overall pick. Were you surprised that you went so high?

You know, I was just a kid who wanted to play baseball and professional baseball. The scouts all talked to my dad. My dad hit it right on the head on draft day, because he was talking to all the other scouts and was getting info from the super scouts who were there because it was later in the season. They were telling him, "If he's available we're looking for a shortstop and we're going to get him." This team was looking for a pitcher but they didn't know if they were going to get that pick, and then they may opt for an infielder. So a week before the draft [my dad] said I was going to go to the Yankees. I don't know who the super scout for the Yankees was at that time, but he pretty much assured him that if I was there they were going to get me.

I was excited. I always got a lot of attention because I could play, but never at this level. Newspaper articles and the local news were coming over to my house to interview me, and there was a lot of that stuff going on.

The number 1 pick in that draft was Bill Almon. You were chosen in front of number 13, Gary Templeton, and a couple of fellow shortstops.

[Laughs] Yeah, the Yankees screwed up there.

Did the team hold a press conference with you when you signed?

You know what happened? A couple of days after I got drafted the Yankees flew me and my mom and my dad up to Shea Stadium, because [Yankee] stadium was being renovated at that time. They had a press conference and it was funny, because they took me aside before the conference and were kind of asking me, "The Yankees have always been a dream of yours to play for, right?" I said, "Well, not really. The Orioles were the team that I would go watch in spring training"— the Orioles were pretty good at that time. They go, "No, that's not the answer that we want." [Laughs] So they basically told me that this had been a lifelong dream of [mine]. Any big-league team would have been fine. There's so much history with the Yankees, everybody knew who the Yankees were, so you could say that it was. But they did have a press conference and they schooled me on what to say to a point.

You went to Ft. Lauderdale right away and joined the A ball team there where you hit .180 for the rest of 1974. Were you nervous or overwhelmed being a professional player at 18, and all the attention?

I use that a lot in dealing with younger players. I hit like .470 as a senior and then I went to the Florida State League, where you're playing against men and polished players, and yeah, I was overmatched. Offensively, at least—defensively I could play. Looking back on it, they pushed me quick because I could play defense. I had a real good arm and good hands, which is why they drafted me as high as they did. What it kind of does to a young player, you're used to being the best and you go to the Florida State League and not only are you not the best, but you're hitting a buck eighty, and a very weak buck eighty at that. Then they moved me up the next year to AA, where I got a little better, but it was a big adjustment—I had never been away from home before.

The Yankees kept promoting you every year. Do you feel they may have rushed you because you were a first-round pick?

Yeah, and I guess they were kind of in need of a shortstop at that time. I don't really know what their thinking was. Defensively I could play. I made a lot of errors but they didn't seem to be too concerned with that. You really don't know how to play when you leave high school. Actually, these things that I'm teaching these kids at this high school now, as far as their knowledge of the game, they're far more advanced than I was. Instead of making an easy play a tough play, you learn how to make an easy play an easy play.

In 1976 you played in just 42 games, and in only 7 in 1977. Were you injured?

Yes, I was injured. What happened there was, I wound up breaking my toe in spring training. You know what? The world came crashing down on me at that time. I went from A to West Haven [AA], to Syracuse [AAA], and in the spring of that year going into Syracuse I broke my big right toe and I couldn't throw. Every time I went to push off I couldn't get anything on the ball, and the ball was all over the place. They sent me down to A ball back at Ft. Lauderdale and I said, "You know what? I need some time away from this game," and sat out the rest of that year. At the end of that year they called me up and asked me if I wanted to play in the Instructional League over in Sarasota or Bradenton, and I did. I went to AA after that and had a pretty good year.

In 1978 you were back at West Haven AA and had a breakout year. You managed 142 hits with a .292 batting average, and a surprising 14 home runs. This earned you a promotion to the Yankees in September.

I needed to regroup from the injury and to get an idea of what I wanted to do in life. This is something that haunts a young player that didn't go to college: what am I going to do if I don't make it? The bonus money back then wasn't much—I signed for $55,000. Nowadays I don't know what a 12th overall pick is worth, but it's in the millions, I'm sure. There was no money to be made in the minor leagues, and I'm looking at my friends and they became firefighters or utility workers and are getting on with their lives. Everybody looks at you and says, "Wow, you're the baseball player," but you're only something if you make it to the big leagues and actually stay in the big leagues. Even then the money wasn't much back then—I think the minimum was $40,000. I have several friends who played five or six years in the big leagues back then, and there wasn't a whole lot of money.

Had you ever been to Yankee Stadium before this?

I went there one year prior to that when I separated my shoulder. I went to a doctor in New York and they had me go to the stadium as a minor league player. I forget why, but it was something to do with that injury.

Do you remember what it was like to walk into the Yankee clubhouse as a 22-year-old and suit up in a Yankee uniform?

You know, when you're a player it's just what you do. It's like, this is where I'm at in my career now. You're excited about going to the big leagues and you're awed at everything. I knew several players from the major league spring training, but not real personal.

Did your new manager, Bob Lemon, say anything to you when you got there?

You know, it's interesting, because people say, "Who was the manager?" The Yankees went through a lot of managers back then and I couldn't really remember who the manager was when I got called up, but you're saying it was Lemon.

When I got drafted they took me into the clubhouse and Bobby Murcer kind of took me under his wing and introduced me around. I just remember when I got drafted him talking to me a lot more [than the other players].

Backing up a little bit, I know that I had to sign a contract [when they brought me up]. They said, "Hey, you've got to go up and see Mr. Steinbrenner to sign your contract." I just said, "Oh, OK." So I went up and his secretary was there and I told her who I was and that I was there to sign a contract and she said to go on in. I go on in there and he's sitting at his desk and I introduced myself, "Mr. Steinbrenner, I'm Dennis Sherrill." He said, "I know who you are. What do you think, I just call you up and don't know who you are? Sit down." [Laughs] He just went on to tell me, "You're in the big leagues. This is a class organization and we want you to conduct yourself in a classy way. We give you good meal money and we want you to spend your meal money. I don't want you getting ham sandwiches and bringing them back to your room. You're a big-league player. I want you to act like a big-league player and tip like a big-league player. Play the role of a big- league player while you're up here."

What was it like walking out onto the field at Yankee Stadium wearing a Yankee uniform for the first time?

Well, that's pretty cool. I think I had only been to one big-league park and that was Fenway. That was when my brother was playing in the Cape Cod League and I went up there to stay with him for a week. That was the only time that I had been in a big-league park, and now I'm stepping into Yankee Stadium. Yeah, you're kind of awestruck. I was looking at it like, "Wow, what a cool park!" Then the thing that stuck out with me the most was when we started taking batting practice, and I guess it was about the time that we were taking infield practice, and they started playing *New York, New York* by Frank Sinatra out of the speakers. Then you're smelling the popcorn and the hot dogs, and you see the vendors and the people are piling in, and you hear *New York, New York* blaring and you're like, "Wow, man!" That was the moment that stood out more than anything. It was pretty cool.

Your first game was Monday, September 4. The Yankees were home playing Detroit and beat them 9–1 behind Ron Guidry, who won his 20th game, upping his record to 20–2. In the bottom of the eighth inning you pinch-ran for Jim Spencer and scored on a Thurman Munson single. That's a nice way to break into the majors.

I knew Guidry a little bit from playing in the minor leagues with him and that he was going good, but I didn't know that was his 20th win. I got to know Thurman a little bit. He was a really good guy. I remember from spring training—which is a little sad because it was the year he was killed[56]—we were in batting practice and I had taken my ground balls and had finished and went out to the outfield to shag fly balls. He was in the outfield shagging and he walked up and we were talking. I knew he had some shoulder problems so we were just chitchatting and I was saying, "How ya doing? How's your shoulder?" He was telling me that he wanted to play one more year—"I just want to play one more year so I can pay this jet off" that he bought.

He was a good guy. I remember being up at bat and what I thought was an outside pitch, I was called out strike three on it. I jawed at the umpire a bit and the umpire really got back in my face. Probably being a rookie it was like "Don't show me up," that kind of thing. When I came into

---

56. Catcher, team captain, MVP, and seven-time All-Star Thurman Munson played for the Yankees from 1969 to 1979. He died August 2, 1979, while taking flying lessons in his personal jet. The day after his death he received an eight-minute standing ovation from the fans at Yankee Stadium.

the dugout Munson was right there and he said, "What'd he say"? I told him, and as I'm running out there to shortstop I get out there and turn around and Munson is all in that umpire's face. I thought that was pretty cool, because he was a guy that stood up for his teammate there.

The only other game that you got into that year was on September 8 at Fenway Park. 1978 was some year to be a Yankee playing in Boston.

Yes, it was—that was the [Boston] Massacre. I knew we were down three or four games, and that they were big games.

The Yankees were in second place by four games at the start of the four-game series and came away tied with the Red Sox.

Yeah, that's what I thought it was—that's what I've been telling people, anyway. We went in there and just blew them away. I remember Tony Kubek was there [broadcasting] and I talked to him a little bit. I knew the magnitude of these games and I knew that the chances were good that I was not going to get into these games. When I did get in I remember we were up, so I went in and played the eighth and the ninth and didn't get to hit. Mike Heath was up and he hit into a double play, which kept me from hitting. The only thing that happened defensively was Carlton Fisk hit a ground ball to my left that I dove for. I was pumped and wanted to get that ball and make the play and show my stuff off. It was about six inches out of my reach. That was my highlight. [Laughs]

I remember the fans there hated the Yankees. [Laughs] This all being new to me, I remember them getting a chant going: "REG-GIE SUCKS, REG-GIE SUCKS!" I couldn't understand what they were saying and then one of the other players told me what they were saying. Then I see them walking around with their "YANKEES SUCK" T-shirts and was like, "Wow, I'm in a pretty hostile place here with this Yankee uniform."

Did you get to know Lou Piniella or Reggie Jackson at all during this pennant race?

Yeah, a little bit. I remember Reggie telling me during a game, which I'm pretty sure was at Yankee Stadium, "You know, you could play for a lot of teams, but this is not one of them right now." You know Reggie was pretty cocky—very cocky—but what he was saying was the truth and I took it as that. It was a bit of a compliment too. This was a World Championship team here, and you're coming in brand new to the big leagues, and this is just not a team that you're going to play for right now.

You know, it's interesting: when I was playing with the Yankees I didn't like the organization because they were always going and buying players and there were not a whole lot of guys coming up through the organization. I remember one year, I think in AAA, we won the International League by 20-something games. We just blew away the competition. I think Righetti was the only one that went up. We were that good. There was no doubt that we could have competed with half of the other major league teams, and yet no one went up. Willie Magee was in AA and the Yankees didn't protect him by putting him on the 40-man roster. The Cardinals picked him up—and look at Willie Magee. Back at that time the Cardinals had to give the Yankees $50,000, I believe, and bring him up to the next level, AAA. That was a guy that had that much ability and talent, and yet the Yankees were so loaded that he never saw AAA with the Yankees. He was in the big leagues in no time after that.

Were you on the Yankees for the 1978 play-off game in Boston?

No, and you know, I regret that. They knew I wasn't going to play much and they were looking at me as a utility infielder. They asked me to go to this instructional league where I could work on three positions. Whoever came up with that came to me and asked me to go, but Gene Michael was saying that he felt like this was a better experience for me, being in the big leagues. I just said, "Whatever you guys feel like is the best thing for me, I'll do." I wish I would have held my ground and said, "I'd like to stay here." So I did go and therefore wasn't part of that play-off game.

After the 1978 season did you think that you would be back in New York again?

No, I knew I was up there because they could expand the roster. The Yankees just won the World Series, so you're going into spring training knowing that this is the best team in the world right here, and the odds of me making this team are slim. Most every guy there, with the exception of maybe a couple of pitchers, felt the same way. You're not going to make the team in spring training. If that was the case I would have made the team because I always had real good spring trainings. I stayed with them until the last cut.

In '79 you went back to the minors and split the year between AA and AAA. Were you injured again?

I can't remember exactly that year. I know I separated my shoulder, broke my hand, got hit in the face with a pitch, and broke my nose. I had fingers broken several times. So yeah, probably.

You split the 1980 season between AAA and the Yankees, with your final major league game coming on June 28, 1980. Did you decide to retire after that season?

There again it came back down to in the back of my head, "What am I going to do?" I was starting to lose interest in the game, believe it or not. I didn't have the passion. My son was born in 1980 and I had bounced around so much, and I'm on the road half the time. Even when I'm home at Columbus you get called up to New York and sent back down. Then you've got spring training, then the instructional league. You're bouncing all over the place. I wasn't making enough money—that was the bottom line. They sent me my contract [for 1981] and it was for the same as the year before. I had sat down and figured out what kind of money I needed to sustain my family. You see, you get paid during the season and then come home and don't have a job. You try to get a job and they know that you're part-time, so it's hard to get one. Plus during that time you've got to stay in shape for the season coming up. I relied on my bonus money to get me through those times, but that started running out. It wasn't a whole lot of money that I signed for. What happened was, I had an opportunity to work full-time here in Florida.

It was great being called up to the big leagues and I was happy with that. All the excitement of that was not enough to keep me going. I wrote them a letter back and told them that I need X amount of dollars. It was well below the major league minimum and it was not outrageous by any means. They said, "Well, you didn't have a good enough year." They sent me my contract back with the same amount on it and I sent it back with the same letter. I said, "This is not a matter of me asking for something whether I deserve it or not. This is me telling you that I need this much money to survive." Also in that letter I told them that I either want to be traded, released, sold, or I've got to make this much money. I don't regret that move; I don't. They wrote me back saying, "You're too valuable to this organization. If an infielder got hurt then you're coming up." [Laughs] Well, so I'm of *some* value to you, so pay me a little so I don't have to spend all of my savings. They were pretty tight with the money so I decided, that's it. We went back and forth with the contract a couple of times and then I never got it back the last time. I didn't show up for spring training and I never heard from them.

When I got out of baseball I was pretty bitter at the Yankees. But time heals. I never talked to anybody about it and never told anybody that I had even played baseball. Occasionally it would come up. I'd be coaching my son's Little League and throwing the baseball around and somebody would ask me if I had ever played. I'd tell them where and they would say, "Wow!" There were some really good times in baseball, but there were some really depressing times, too— when you don't know where your life is going, or you don't know from one day to the next if you're going to get released. It gets kind of nerve-racking. And then I had a kid and had responsibilities. I thought, if this baseball doesn't work out, and right now it doesn't look like it's going to, what am I going to do?

As time went on I started feeling proud of my accomplishment in baseball even though I got only one major league hit. The idea that I played in the big leagues and with the New York Yankees was a dream for so many different people. You don't realize that at the time because that's just what you do. As you get talking to people and they say, "Wow, that must have been neat," you realize, yeah, it was,—but it's neater now, if you can understand that. Now I'm an alumni and get the Yankee newsletter and the Christmas cards and that stuff. In 2002 they invited me to the Old-Timers' Game and I took my son. That was really cool because my last year was '80 and he was born in '80. They wined and dined us and then I played in a little game before the Blue Jays game and then went up to the press box to watch the game. He just thought that was the greatest thing. We were out there taking batting practice and talking and I pop one into the bleachers in left field. He thought that was so cool. It was a really, really good time. He got to talk with Boggs. We were both taking grounders during batting practice, and then he sat next to him on the bus ride back to the hotel.

Even though you weren't on the big club for long, did Buckey Dent help you at all?

Buckey was actually from Miami and had played against my brother in college. You got to that level because you can play. There is really not much people can do for you with the exception of hitting. There is really not a whole lot of instruction going on. I remember, though, Buckey told me one thing, because my ball would tail a lot. He said that you're always better to throw right at the guy at first base or just miss to his left. That way if it's off a little bit he can come and make the tag. Maybe I was going to his right a little and he picked up on it. That's pretty much it, my whole time in professional baseball as far as defense.

Do you think that you'll get to the new Yankee Stadium?

I'm hoping that they're going to ask me up there for a big shebang with all the old players. Everybody that played in the old stadium, let's do a little deal in the new stadium. That would be real good.

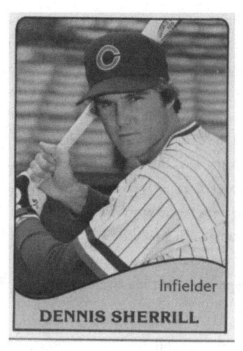

TCMA

SHERRILL, DENNIS LEE
Born: March 3, 1956 Miami, Florida
Bats: Right Throws: Right
Height: 6' 0" Weight: 165

Year	Team	G	AB	H	2B	3B	HR	AVG	RBI	R
1978	YANKEES	2	1	0	0	0	0	.000	0	1
1980	YANKEES	3	4	1	0	0	0	.250	0	0
	Total 2 Years	5	5	1	0	0	0	.200	0	1

National Baseball Hall of Fame

DARRYL JONES
1979

You grew up in Meadville, Pennsylvania, and still reside in the area. Meadville is about halfway between Pittsburgh and Cleveland, so I guess you weren't a Yankee fan?

Actually, I was a Chicago White Sox fan growing up. The reason was because I used to get WGR and transistor radios were a big thing. I remember keeping a transistor radio at night when I would go to bed underneath my pillow to listen to games. It was always the Chicago station that would come in very clear and always the Chicago White Sox. There was a guy named Smokey Burgess who was one of the great pinch-hitters in baseball and I can remember him playing. Al Smith, Louie Aparicio, all of those guys. So I was a Chicago White Sox fan growing up. Probably one of the players that I admired the most was Minnie Minoso. Do you remember that name?

Sure, the White Sox kept bringing him back to play in order to break age records.

Absolutely. He also played with the Indians. When I was a young kid and played Little League baseball, they used to have Little League Day in Cleveland. Cleveland is about an hour and a half from here. My father, who coached our Little League teams, would take all the Little Leaguers there. You would parade around the field and in front of the dugout. I would look in the dugout and I would see my hero, Minnie Minoso. That was at old Municipal Stadium.

You must have been to Forbes Field also?

Yes, I was. In fact I was at one of the last games at Forbes Field and saw Roberto Clemente play.

That area of Pennsylvania is not what you would call a warm-weather area. Did you play a lot of baseball as a kid?

I played on several teams and you're right, in the springtime we had many times when you would be playing a game and you'd have snow showers and it's cold and miserable weather. In the summertime I would play American Legion ball. We had a league called the Crawford County League, which was an older guys' league, and I played in that. One summer I played on three teams. I played on a traveling team about 40 miles from here and they picked me up. Yeah, I played a lot of baseball.

You attended Lineville High School along with your brother Lynn, who eventually played for the Tigers and Royals. Did you attract attention from a lot of baseball scouts during your high school career?

Actually scouts were not looking at me. I went to a very small school. My graduating class had about 65 kids in it. But there were no teams that could beat us. We lost three games in four years.

We had my brother and me, and another guy who played professionally for a year, and a bunch of other guys who could just flat out play. My mother always said that she thought I was going to be a pitcher because I was 19–0 as a pitcher and I threw hard. I probably ended up hitting about .580. I hold a lot of records there still. In my first year as a freshman I hit .600 and something. I could always hit. We had a few colleges nearby—Edinboro and Allegheny—and I wasn't even recruited to play at any of those, so I ended up going to a small school called Westminster College in Newcastle, Pennsylvania.

Fortunately for me my baseball coach had grown up with Chuck Tanner. You may remember a name, Doc Medich. At the time he was a pitcher at the University of Pittsburgh. During his senior year I was in my sophomore year and we played the University of Pittsburgh. Doc was pitching against us and I had two of our team's three hits. I had a double and a single and hit the ball real well off him. That's when scouts first started to notice me. The following year there were usually more scouts at our games than there were fans. That year I got drafted in the fifth round [110th overall, 1972 draft] by the Yankees. I actually thought I was going to be drafted by the Pirates. There was a guy named Harding Peterson who was the player personnel director for the Pirates. He brought Danny Murtaugh with him to my game at Westminster College and watched me play. Danny was an ex-manager who had a heart attack the year before, and so he was out of the managerial thing but he was going around scouting. I thought I was going to get drafted by Kansas City, too, because they had a guy there, and there were a few other teams, too. I had no idea the Yankees were going to draft me. I had no idea the Yankees even had a guy there to see me.

Where did the Yankees send you that first year?

Oneonta. I hit exactly .300. Then they sent me to Ft. Lauderdale the following year, where I hit .324 and then to West Haven, Connecticut [AA], where I was second or third in the league [in hitting].

By 1978 you were at Tacoma [AAA], where you hit .322 with 140 hits. Unfortunately, you were a victim of bad timing as the Yankees won their third straight pennant and second straight World Championship. Did it ever get frustrating being an outfielder in the Yankees system at that time and having to watch them bring in outfielders from different organizations, like Reggie Jackson, Mickey Rivers, Lou Piniella, Paul Blair, Jay Johnstone, Gary Thomasson, Juan Beniquez, and Oscar Gamble?

Well, I think you know what that answer is. [Laughs] The thing that was very upsetting was, even before the Tacoma year I played in the Eastern League [West Haven AA]. Hardly anybody ever hit .300 in the Eastern League because of the conditions—poor lighting and very tough to see. I hit .280–.290 one year, and then the lowest average I ever had was about .260-something. There were times when you looked at the Eastern League batting averages and nobody was hitting .300.

One night Joaquin Andujar was facing us and he threw a ball behind my head and I never saw it. That's how bad the lighting was. The catcher caught the ball right behind my ear and said, "Jonesie, what are doing?" I told him that I never saw it. That scared me because he could have killed me, because Andujar threw the heck out of the ball.

In 1977 I was at Syracuse and that was my fist year at AAA in the International League. I hit .330 and was on the International League All-Star team. Those two years that I put together at AAA (1977–78) were the two best years that I had.

We were only in Tacoma for one year before they moved us to Columbus. That was the only year the Yankees had a team in Tacoma,[57] but I'll tell you what—that was one of the neatest years I remember playing. I think that for proximity reasons they moved to Columbus, because you don't want to have a team all the way out in Tacoma, Washington. The following year [1979] I went to spring training and was sent back to AAA, and I wasn't even a starter at Columbus! Gene Michael was my manager. I was obviously very upset about this. He told me that he wasn't making the call, but there were a couple of phenoms that were coming up and he had to play them. I was not real happy about the fact that I just came off of my two best years and was not starting. I said, "Why don't you just trade me?" I know for a fact the Orioles inquired about me in a trade, but the Yankees wanted something obscene for me like a big-leaguer for a minor-leaguer, so Baltimore wasn't going to do that. Anyway, the guy that played in front of me, this phenom, was hitting about .120 and I got back in the lineup.

During that 1979 season at Columbus you finally got the call to go up to New York at 27. Do you remember finding out that you were being promoted to the big leagues?

Reggie had a calf pull and he went on the disabled list in June. My father was down watching me at Columbus. We were at home and George Sisler, the GM for the team, called me. He said, "Darryl, I want you to pack your stuff. You're going to New York tonight." I said, "OK. Who is this?" After seven and a half years in the minor leagues, who's going to figure that they were going to be calling me—especially since I hadn't been starting. I said to him, "This is Larry Murray [a Columbus teammate]. I know it's you, Larry. Quit messing around."

57. The Yankees AAA affiliate was located in Syracuse, New York, from 1967 to 1977 and in Columbus, Ohio, from 1979 to 2006.

Then he finally convinced me it *was* George Sisler. He told me that I had a flight that afternoon and that I would be in the lineup that night. I flew into LaGuardia and a car or limousine picked me up. I got to the ballpark, and there was my name in the locker. My locker was right next to Thurman Munson. Bob Lemon came in and he said that I would be in the lineup tonight.

What was it like as a 27-year-old, who by your own admission never thought you would get the call, putting on a New York Yankee uniform and walking out onto the field at Yankee Stadium?

Obviously it was exciting, but quite honestly, it was something that I felt that I deserved. I felt that I earned it and that I belonged there. When I looked at some of the players from other organizations that had been in the big leagues two or three years, I always felt that I belonged.

When Martin came back he was a big believer in veterans. I believe that many of those veterans I could outhit. One thing I could do was hit. My friend Eddie Ricks[58] told me that I used to just snatch the ball out of the catcher's mitt because I would just wait and wait. I didn't strike out much. I hit a lot of balls to right center field.

That night, June 6, was your first major league game. Against the Twins you went 1 for 3 with a double and scored a run off Jerry Koosman. In the bottom of the ninth, with the score tied 2–2, you sacrificed Nettles to third base with a bunt. He eventually came around to score the winning run. That's a pretty good way to break into the majors.

Standing at second base in the stadium and looking up at the scoreboard and seeing "DARRYL JONES' FIRST MAJOR LEAGUE HIT," I felt like all of those years were worth it. I would do it all over again to have that moment. I don't know how many people were at the game, maybe 20,000. People around here tell me, "Hey, the Yankees messed with you." Well you know what? That's life. I wasn't the only one that that ever happened to. Look at my buddy Eddie Ricks. He spends four or six weeks in the big leagues and they never even give him the ball. So I've never looked back at it like, "Oh, those damn Yankees." I always thought it was a privilege to play a game that was fun. I was earning a living, although it was a very meager living. The minimum pay was $20,000. When you broke in and you had guys like Chris Chambliss, Roy White, Willie Randolph, Thurman—class guys that welcomed young players when they came—it was incredible.

---

58. Former Yankee-system pitcher.

I remember talking to Thurman out on the West Coast during a road trip. I knew Thurman because we used the same bat in spring training—it was more of a thick-handled bat. It was the '78 major league spring training and I was being sent back to AAA after spring training. Thurman came up to me and said, "Jonesie, I don't have any more bats. Can you leave some of your bats with me?" So I left him some of those same model bats that I had. I have a bat that I'm looking at right now on my wall in a case and I have to turn it a certain way because it says, "To Darryl, Best F***ing Wishes. Thurman Munson." [Laughs] Anyway, we're riding on a bus together on the West Coast and Thurman says to me, "I know this is new to you and it's real exciting. I've won World Series and I've been on All-Star teams, and right now all I want to do is be with my family." That was the time when he was learning how to fly those planes. There was talk about him wanting to get traded to Cleveland because he lived in Canton, and he could fly back and forth. In a matter of a couple of weeks he was gone.

About ten days into your stay the Yankees replaced Bob Lemon with Billy Martin. Did that surprise you?

Lemon was a nice guy but he was not a . . . there wasn't a lot of enthusiasm. Billy did bring a spark—I think that was one of the things George liked about him. I can remember one time we were playing in Texas and it was late in the ball game and Lemon was at the end of the bench. Bucky Dent was coming up and Mickey Rivers had to holler down to the end of the bench, "Hey Bob, you got a pinch-hitter right here." We were in a situation where they could have used a pinch-hitter. He actually hollered it at him twice. [Laughs] I wasn't going to holler it at him—who am I? I'm just a rookie. Bob actually then called me down and I pinch-hit for Bucky Dent. That was pretty funny. My demise came when they hired Billy back, because Billy liked the veteran players.

A few weeks after your call-up you were doing very well when George Steinbrenner went back to his old strategy and traded to bring back outfielder and Yankee legend Bobby Murcer. That must have been disappointing to you.

I was wearing number 2 when I came up and Bobby asked me if he could get his old number back. I said yeah and went to number 27. No, it wasn't good news for me. It's like anything—the only way you get experience is to play. How do you get experience getting sent back to the minor leagues? I already had over 1,000 hits in the minor leagues. I'm probably one of the few people in the history of the game that had over 1,000 hits in the minor leagues.

The Yankees had a very senior outfield of former All-Stars with Piniella, Rivers, and Jackson. How were they to you when you finally made it to the major leagues? Did you get to know them?

Piniella, a fiery guy. He'd be the first one to flip a finger to someone up in the stands. The crowd could get on him and incite him. I'll tell you what—he'd give you the shirt off of his back. Great guy. Mickey Rivers was the most happy-go-lucky guy that you'd ever meet. He would have been happy driving a school bus. He was just one of those types of guys. Roy White was just a gentleman.

Reggie . . . I had hit a double against Cleveland to the part of Yankee Stadium that goes real deep, left center field. I hit it off of the wall there and I came in after the game and players were still congratulating me—"Way to hit the ball," or "Great game," or something like that. Reggie's comment was, "Well, you know, when I hit them they don't go against the fence." He was an arrogant son-of-a-gun, but as a player you respect the fact that he was a big-time player. You respect him for his abilities. I don't let too much bother me. I was just happy to be there.

Going to a team like that, the number of people that helped you was great. Catfish Hunter: Catfish was no different than I'm talking to you right now. They called him Catfish because he was just like my fishing partner.[59] A lot of time these athletes are put up on a pedestal, but they're no different than anybody else. I can see him chewing tobacco down on a farm somewhere with a fishing pole—that's just the way he was.

Do you think that you would have had a longer major league career if you had been with a different organization?

No doubt. I will say this, though: 30 years later my name is connected with the New York Yankees. I still get three or four mailings a week asking for an autograph or to sign a card. I don't know if that would have happened if I were a Cleveland Indian. There's that thing about being a New York Yankee and having played in Yankee Stadium. I'm one of the few and very proud of it.

Were you sent back down when Jackson came off the DL?

Actually there were two guys that came off the DL. Mike Torres, and Jackson was the other and obviously then there wasn't any room on the roster.

---

59. When Jim Hunter joined the Oakland Athletics owner Charles Finley thought he needed a nickname, so Finley invented a story about Hunter catching a catfish as a boy.

I was supposedly going to be called up again in September, and then I hurt my knee.

What happened to your career after the 1979 season?

That winter I was having problems with my knee and they wanted to do exploratory surgery to see what was going on. They wanted to scope it. I went to Lenox Hill Hospital over the Thanksgiving holiday. Whoever the doctor was that explored it found a bone erosion that's like a wear and tear. It was some injury that I'd had and was never going to get any better. They ended up doing some surgery.

Did you play anywhere in 1980?

No. I wasn't released until the '81 season. They had asked me if I was going to come back. I did a lot of rehabilitation and working out with the Nautilus [equipment], but it just never came back.

Have you been back to Yankee Stadium?

No, I haven't. My wife always says to me, "We've got to go back and spend a weekend there sometime."

Are you going to come back and see the New Yankee Stadium?

There's going to be a display there with all the former Yankee players. There's a guy in charge of that who sent a baseball to sign and send back so they could be on display. So yes, sometime in my lifetime I'm going to have to make a trip up there.

One of the neatest things that I did was just this past September. Cooper Stadium, which was the Yankees AAA stadium for years down in Columbus, closed. They held what was called the Final Weekend at the Coop. A lot of the players who played at Cooper Stadium came back, and I was representing the '79 team. We won the International League Championship that year.

TOPPS

Jones, Darryl Lee
Born: June 5, 1951 Meadville, Pennsylvania
Bats: Right Throws: Right
Height: 5' 10" Weight: 175 lbs.

Year	Team	G	AB	H	2B	3B	HR	AVG	RBI	R
1979	YANKEES	18	47	12	5	1	0	.255	6	6
	Total 1 Year	18	47	12	5	1	0	.255	6	6

1980s

BRUCE ROBINSON
1979–80

You were born in LaJolla, California, and grew up in southern California. I'd say you were not a Yankee fan.

I was from LaJolla, went to LaJolla Elementary and LaJolla High School, and I was not a Yankee fan. My dad detested the Yankees and the Dodgers—anything to do with L.A. So I grew up hating the Rams and the Dodgers.

Since your brother Dave played for the hometown Padres, were you a Padre fan?

You know, I was never really too much of a baseball fan. I liked Johnny Bench and the Cincinnati Reds. I was a fan of the Big Red Machine. I was never that much of a "fan" fan. I went to AAA Padres [Pacific Coast League] in Westgate Park before they became a major league team. That was my introduction to professional baseball. When the Angels became a major league team my dad took me up there a few times to see them play.

I actually saw my brother's first two games, and then they went on the road so I got to see him get a hit in his first at bat. I think he was 2 for 2 his first game. Gosh, he didn't play in that many games.

You must have played a lot of baseball growing up in that warm area of the country?

I did. Of course my brothers being eight and ten years older than me, I grew up around the game. My dad loved it. It's what I did—I was always around the ball field when they were in Little League and PONY League. I played all sports, including youth basketball and flag football.

You attended LaJolla High School, where you were a standout baseball player on the Vikings. Were you always a catcher?

I was. I was a pitcher and shortstop in Little League. As a 13-year-old in 1967 I decided to be a catcher because I thought it would be the fastest way to the big leagues. That's when I thought that I could do something with [baseball], that I could make it a reality. My brother was drafted in '68 by the Padres and I became a full-time catcher at about that time.

Did you attract any attention from major league scouts in high school?

Oh yeah. I don't know if you remember Terry Forrester? He was a big star in San Diego, a left-handed pitcher who made it to the big leagues when he was 19 years old with the Chicago White Sox, and went on to play for the Dodgers and a number of teams. He may have one of the highest batting averages for pitchers ever—the guy could mash. Anyway, he threw really, really hard. I got to play on the American Legion team the summer before my tenth year in high school, which was unheard of because it was only a three-year high school. I was a ninth grader playing with the varsity, and that summer we got to play against Terry Forrester, who was going to be a senior. They had a great team, and then that year we played them in our second game at home. There must have been 30 or 40 scouts there. I was a skinny 5' 11" kid. We did nothing off Forrester, but the first time I faced him I hit a line drive base hit to left center. The scouts were all trying to figure out, "Who's he? Oh, his brother plays for the Padres." So that's when I went on the radar. I was drafted in the fourth round by the White Sox but went to Stanford.

At Stanford University did you play anything else besides baseball?

I actually did. I played a little football in high school and then in 12th grade I quit in order to concentrate on baseball. But I could always kick. When I went to college I started messing around with soccer-style kicking, even though I'd never played soccer in my life. I could kick 55-yard field goals. At Stanford I went in and talked to Jack Christensen, the football coach, and he said he'd let me try out but couldn't let me play unless my baseball coach says it's OK. That was because I was on a full ride at Stanford for baseball as a scholarship athlete. The baseball coach said it was alright as long as I didn't play any other position. I never got to kick in a game because I was on JV, and the next year they recruited some hotshot kicker for JV. Then I decided that it was fun but I needed to concentrate on baseball.

During your college career you played on probably the most famous collegiate summer baseball team, the Alaska Goldpanners [1972–75]. How was that experience?

Yeah, I played with Winfield, Floyd Bannister, Steve Kemp. I played with some great ones. It was phenomenal. I love Alaska. I didn't play so much that first year because they had Steve Swisher, but the next year I was the starting catcher. I wasn't even considered a prospect in Stanford my first two years until I came back from Alaska for my junior year. I had hit one homerun my freshman and sophomore year combined and then I came back my junior year and hit 13.

The Oakland A's, who had just won three consecutive World Championships, drafted you in the first round [21st overall] of the 1975 draft. Were you expecting to go that high?

I was expecting to go somewhere in the later half of the first round, or maybe early in the second.

Was it intimidating to be picked by a team that had just won three straight World Series?

I thought it was great because it was just across the bay [from Stanford] and I had gone to World Series games with my dad when he'd come up with my brother. It was pretty exciting. They were a West Coast team and at the time they were a powerhouse.

I didn't sign right away because of Finley. Charlie Finley was known for his frugality and I don't think he signed his previous couple of first-round picks, because he didn't offer them enough money. He didn't have any money, basically, and he was known for being a cheapskate. At the time the 21st pick in the nation slot was worth about $75,000. Today it's about $1.4 million or $1.5 million. They offered me $10,000 and my last year of college. [Laughs] I got offered more by the White Sox in the fourth round my last year in high school. They came up to $20,000. So I didn't sign and I went back up to Alaska and wound up playing outfield because I didn't want to get hurt playing catcher. I thought I'd be up there and it would be a nice negotiating ploy, but [Finley] just let me sit unsigned. It got down to a point where my brother Dave told me, "The money you're going to make with the signing bonus is inconsequential if you're going to make it to the big leagues, which you think you are. . . .You need to get out there and start playing. You need to estimate whether you have an opportunity with this team to get to the big leagues quickly." I thought I did so I signed for $28,000.

The A's moved you up in their minor-league system pretty quickly and you wound up in Vancouver [AAA] in 1978, where you hit .299. The A's called you up to the major leagues in August. Were you surprised at how quickly you made it to Oakland?

Very quickly. I played three weeks in A ball for Rene Lachemann in Modesto in '75 and then they invited me to travel around with the big-league team the last month of the season. That was real fun. I wasn't on the roster, but just to get the experience. I was in uniform for batting practice and infield and I caught guys in the bullpen. It was cool because Reggie Jackson, Joe Rudi, Campaneris, Billy North—they were all there. I got the meal money and that was great. We won the division but lost in the play-offs so I got to go on the road trip for the play-off. It was good in that I got acclimated, and by the next spring training I wasn't intimidated being around those types of players.

I did make it to the majors very quickly—it was only about 300 games. Was I surprised? Not really, because I thought I could play up there. It was easier to hit at each level that I went higher, because I wear contacts and anytime there was a bad background or bad lights I was miserable offensively. With better conditions I did better.

Your first game in the majors came on August 19, 1978, for the A's in Oakland against Boston. You went 2 for 3 with an RBI against a former Goldpanner, Bill Lee. How did it feel to break into the big leagues that way?

[Laughs] The Spaceman! [Bill Lee] That was really exciting. I was really surprised that Jack McKeon put me into the lineup the first day because I had flown all day and was excited, and when I went into the dugout I look and I'm starting! I thought, cool! I didn't have a chance to get nervous, and in retrospect that's a great way to do it for a young player—just stick him in there.

You had 16 hits in your first 14 games.

I felt like OK, I'm on my way, I've arrived, but then sure enough it was just snatched from me! I did really well my first three weeks and I just tore it up. They were writing articles about me being the best young catcher they've seen in years, and some Dodger guy wrote I was the best young catcher in decades. I had been getting hits off Jim Palmer and had a streak going and went from hitting 8th to 7th, to 6th, 5th, and then finally McKeon put me in at cleanup. I always hated hitting cleanup. Even as a kid I hated hitting cleanup. Then I just put this pressure on myself and sure enough, I hit five line drives off Matlack, and somebody else in Texas and went 0 for 5 and went into a tailspin, and that was the end of my Cinderella story.

We were in New York when I was still hot and the first three nights we faced Catfish, and Figueroa, and I can't remember who else. Wayne Gross was my roommate. We get back to our room in the Sheraton downtown and he's looking at me lying on the bed and goes, "You know, it's not that easy!" I laughed and said that the ball was just looking really big to me right now. [Laughs]

How did you feel when the A's sold you to the Yankees for $400,000 on February 3, 1979, just before spring training?

It was probably the worst thing that could have happened to me, because if I had stayed with the A's I would have played. They had been dismantled in '76, '77, and '78. In '78 when I got called up we lost over 100 games and there was an opportunity for a young player to play. A lot of young players got up. With the Yankees, they were an established team and when I got over there they had Thurman. You kind of had to wait your turn and even if you were a big name and were good, there was a good chance that you weren't going to get to play because George would

Kenneth Hogan

trade for somebody. I did get my chance because all my cards were in place in '81, but the car accident with Righetti was the thing that did me in.[60]

Also, the A's actually sold me for $500,000. What happened was Bowie Kuhn voided that and set a limit of $400,000 on player sales. What the A's did then was throw in another player and called me $400,000 and him $100,000 and we were both sold.

Is that what is meant by the "Robinson Rule"?

Yeah, MLB put a limit on selling players because they didn't want the dismantling of teams like that.

Do you think the Yankees had you in mind as an eventual successor to Thurman Munson?

George had all these advisors and they wanted a left-handed-hitting catcher. The year they got me they also got Brad Gulden from the Dodgers. He was another top AAA catcher from the Pacific Coast League. So George got the two best left-handed-hitting catchers in AAA baseball, figuring that one of them will pan out. We both went to Columbus so we could play, and they let Jerry Narron be the backup. Typically I'm not a fast starter. I got off to a crappy start, and when the scouts came through early in the season I was hitting poorly and Brad was hitting well. When Thurman's plane went down I was hitting really well and Brad couldn't hit the ball out of the infield. Brad got called up and stayed the rest of the year.

In Columbus we won the [1979] championship, which is good and bad, because we had to play the Governors' Cup, so we had to go through two play-offs. We were missing out on big-league service time and meal money to play these stupid minor league play-offs. That was fine and we had a good bunch of guys, but by the time we got called up it was for only half a month—you might get an at bat and look like an idiot from not playing.

Your first game as a Yankee was on September 17 in Cleveland. You then flew with the team back to New York. What did you think about putting on a Yankee uniform and walking out onto the field at Yankee Stadium?

I think I felt it more the first time I went there as an Oakland A. It was just the whole novelty of being there. As a Yankee it was a little anticlimactic. I was a little miffed because I hadn't been called up earlier in the season, and then you get into so few games it's hard to get any continuity.

---

60. Robinson and Dave Righetti were rear-ended by a drunk driver. Robinson needed shoulder reconstruction surgery and never returned to the majors.

The Yanks were out of it and we had already won at Columbus, so you're ready just to leave.

The Yankees had you in the major league spring training in 1979. The catchers report early and work together. Did you get to know Thurman Munson that much?

Oh, I did. My locker was right next to Thurman's in Ft. Lauderdale. It's kind of funny. What they typically do is put guys that aren't going to make the team in between guys that are going to make the team. That was one of the games that Nick Priore and Pete Sheehy used to play, so when you would get sent down they would have more room! [Laughs]

When we were in Tampa playing a spring training game I was rooming with Chris Welsh, who was a left-handed pitcher from Florida. After a game we were staying at a hotel that George owned on the bay. We were on the balcony of our room and in the next room was Munson and Gossage. Of course they could get single rooms if they wanted, but they were buddies and they liked rooming together. They were sitting there munching on cheeseburgers and asked us if we'd like to come over and have some cheeseburgers and beer. We were like, are you kidding, go hang out with some veterans? So we hopped over and they ordered us a bunch of food. We were just sitting around and Thurman starts talking about this new plane he just bought, a Cessna Citation. I knew something about flying from my days in Alaska, because I actually learned to fly a little bit while I was there. He was interested and excited that I knew something about planes, and he starts telling me about this new plane. There was such demand for the Cessna Citation at the time that he could have sold that plane and made $700,000 by not even taking delivery on it! It had pinstripe seats and blue carpeting and the whole thing was really decked out. Of course two months later we're in Richmond, Virginia, and we hear that Thurman went down practicing takeoffs and landings in Canton, Ohio, where he commuted to where his home was with his wife and kids. I remember that one like I remember Kennedy being shot. We walked into this dingy old locker room in Richmond, Virginia, and we just got the news.

What happened to your season in 1980?

I thought in 1980 I'd have a chance, but they got Cerone and Johnny Oates to be the backup. Then they put me at AAA and Gulden at AA and Gulden was just livid! I played for Joe Altobelli and got in the accident in midseason. . . . Righetti was my roommate. He was 19 and I taught him how to write checks! He was good. I think the two most impressive pitchers that I ever caught were Floyd Bannister in Alaska and Dave Righetti.

Anyway, we were in a left-hand turn pocket after a game, turning into our apartment complex at a signal light intersection. I'm stopped at the light and all of a sudden, kaboom! The police estimated he was going between 45 and 55 miles an hour in an old beat-up sedan. He plowed into my new Chevy van from behind and my seat bent back about 30–45 degrees; Dave's didn't. The guy was on drugs and drunk. He was a derelict and went to jail. He was uninsured, too. We were wearing our seatbelts and didn't even go to the hospital. I got up the next morning and was sore, but we were OK. My shoulder, however, just kept getting worse. I got called up at the end of the season and my arm was just killing me. Altobelli had been my manager at AAA and he told me that it was my job next year and that they were going to platoon me with Cerone. They had gotten rid of Oates; they had gotten rid of Gulden and Narron to Seattle that off-season. It was just me and Cerone.

The Yankees were in the play-offs that year [1980] and they had enough catchers up there, so being that it was the end of the year I could just hide and not take infield. I was thinking that my arm was just sore and that it would get better over the winter and I'd be ready for spring training. Well, it never did. On my own I was going to doctors, and chiropractors, and reflexologists, and I did acupuncture. I went to every kind of doctor that I could think of and it wasn't getting better. I went to spring training with an arm that I couldn't even soap under it or push buttons on a radio, and I'm trying to go play baseball at the highest level. It was pretty frustrating because I had the job. After the first game I caught I did the hardest thing that I ever did and went and told them that my arm was hurting.

In 1981 you only played five games at Ft. Lauderdale [A+] in the Florida State League.

In '81 I was hurt; my arm was totally screwed up. One day we were playing the Dodgers up in Vero Beach and that's when I told them. Don Fehr, who was second in charge to Marvin Miller at the Players Association at that time, was there. He was sitting there at the railing and I told him that my arm was hurting. He said, "You've got to tell them. If they send you down you're done. If you stay up you stay on the disabled list at major league pay." I knew my arm was not going to get better without surgery. [The Yankees] kept trying to rehabilitate me and send me to physical therapy. They kept asking me if I was ready to go because as soon as I step out onto a field they can send me down, and I was not going to do that. It made no sense because they had more money than God. George was ticked at me because here I was hurt, and then Cerone gets hurt! Those five games that I played in Ft. Lauderdale I only agreed to if they sent me there on rehabilitation status. This way I was still disabled but just rehabilitating and getting major league pay. They were mad at me—they thought I was faking and they were trying to play games with me. So I DH like four games and then I caught one game. Oh my God, [Laughs] I tried to throw and it felt like my arm was falling off.

I told them that I wanted to go see a doctor of my choosing . . . and they told me that they weren't going to pay for it. They didn't have to because the rule was, if you wanted a second opinion the club only had to pay for it if it was in your region. I think that they didn't believe that I was hurt so I said, "Screw it, I'll pay for it." When I got to the appointment in Los Angeles there was a telegram there from Cedric Tallis, the Yankees GM, saying that I was authorized to have Dr. Curlin evaluate me, and "You're expected to be back in Ft. Lauderdale in 24 hours"! I looked at it and said, "Those jerks, they really don't think I'm hurt!" Curlin examined me and said, "There is definitely a question mark and we need to find out what's going on." He did an arthrogram that day and looked at it and said I needed surgery. When we told Tallis he told me that George wants me back there because I need to get ready to get back up to New York. I just laughed and said, "I'm hurt, Cedric. What part of that don't you understand?" So Jobe did the arthroscopic procedure in 48 hours. . . . After the surgery I got flowers and another telegram from Tallis saying, "We're glad you went to the West Coast to find out what was wrong and we are behind you 100% and pulling for a complete recovery"! [Laughs]

What happened was, I had a fracture in the shoulder capsule and they repaired that with a T staple in the rear of the shoulder. Then, because I played on it, I had damage to the labrum, which is the tissue inside the joint. So the fracture with the rough edges was just tearing apart the labrum. The surgery was called a "posterior reconstruction with staple."

In 1982 you went back to Columbus [AAA] but managed just 3 hits in 15 games. Did you think that now at 28 years old it may be over?

In '82 I go to spring training but I'm just not ready. I was out all of '82 and I showed up the last two weeks of the season. I just wanted to see where I was at. The manager, Joe Verdi, didn't even know I was coming, I just showed up in the locker room . . .. The Yankees knew I was coming but nobody bothered to tell him. He called up New York and they told him that I was supposed to play, so he put me in the lineup for a few games. The Yankees basically treated me like a leper at that point.

You wound up back in the A's organization after the Yankees released you and you finished your career as a player-coach at Tacoma [AAA]. Did you just decide to retire after that?

The A's at that time needed catching—all they had was Mike Heath. Mike Heath gets hurt every year. He's like crystal; he's going down. You can't have two catchers when you have Mike Heath; you need three catchers. My arm wasn't resilient now and I knew I couldn't be an everyday player. I wanted to be a platoon player or a backup catcher. I just wanted to get back to the big leagues. At the end of spring training I get sent down, but I know I'm coming back because

Heath is going to get hurt. About a month into the season they told me to be on alert because Heath got hurt. I'm thinking I'm headed back and Heath goes about four days not playing and they make it through with one catcher. I couldn't believe it—Heath went the rest of the season without getting hurt!

About halfway through the season they came to me and said, "We got a player down in Modesto [A] and we'd like you to work with him." He's a young player, he's 19 and his mom died. He's got some promise but it's just not clicking with the situation. I pack up and go down there and the player is José Canseco. Then shortly after that they told me they had another young player coming in from the Olympics, and that was Mark McGwire. So I wound up working with Canseco and McGwire, and I've got them up in my apartment each night with the tape and the video. I showed Canseco how totally screwed up his swing was, with his bat barrel pointed at the pitcher when his foot lands, and there's no way on God's green earth that his bare hands can catch up. He struggled— he was hitting .230 and I think he wound up hitting .260 or .270 on the season and he hit some home runs. He kept saying, "God, I'm so weak. I gotta get bigger, I gotta get stronger." He was 6' 3" and 190. Then McGwire got there and he was 6' 5" and 210. The following season I think they were both 250. They got really big; they lifted a lot of weights that off-season.[61] [Laughs]

During your time with the Yankees did you ever get to catch Ron Guidry?

I did. I actually got a hit off Ron Guidry as an A, too. He was 25–3 in '78 and I got a line drive single off him, and I almost hit one out off him. That's when Steinbrenner wanted me, because of the way I could hit left-handers.

He was a really quiet guy who never said a word, the way Willie Randolph never said a word. He was nice. He let me call the game.

Jim Kaat just retired last year as a Yankee announcer. In 1980 he already had over 20 years in the majors. Did you ever form a battery with him?

Great guy, yes. Jim Kaat loved to dance. [Laughs] In spring training you used to see him out in the discos. He loved to disco.

---

61. In 2005 José Canseco made allegations—in a *60 Minutes* interview and in his book, *Juiced: Wild Times, Rampant 'Roids, Smash Hits & How Baseball Got Big*—about widespread use of steroids among baseball players, including that he had personally injected Mark McGwire with steroids. His allegations led to a Congressional inquiry, and McGwire was called to testify before the House Government Reform Committee. At that time he refused to answer any questions about his steroid use. In 2010 he finally admitted publically that he had used performance-enhancing drugs throughout his career. However, he claimed that he took them for health reasons.

You have to remember this is 1979–80—he was there in '80. Really good guy. So was Gaylord Perry; he was really good to me.

Another guy was Reggie Jackson. I was with him on the A's and I remember he cried when he was traded to Baltimore. I was sitting with him in the stands at this minor league field where we were practicing, and he was in tears; I saw a different side of Reggie. He was an interesting guy. Obviously egotistical, but an incredibly talented, articulate, and bright guy who knew a lot about a lot of different subjects. If you were one-on-one with him he was a real nice guy.

Did you ever meet George Steinbrenner?

Oh sure, sure. He would hang out in the locker room. He desperately wanted to be one of the guys, so he would hang out and the guys would give him crap. It was a real dichotomy playing for Charlie Finley and George Steinbrenner. One had money and one didn't.

Did you stay in the game after 1984?

No, I didn't. As a catcher I had an aptitude for the game and the A's told me I could pick my job. I could manage at Modesto, or be a pitching coach, or hitting coach. My son was born in 1983. I was working at instructional ball that spring [1985] and I was in the locker room putting on my sanitary socks, and I just said to myself, you know, it's just not the same, it's time to go. I took my uniform off and went out and told Karl Kuehl.

[My son] Scott wound up playing for the Alaska Goldpanners 30 years after I did and led the team and league in hitting and led them to a national championship. He was MVP of the team. He signed with Houston and he played Rookie ball and A ball. He dove for a ball and tore a ligament in his wrist that needed surgery, and he got released. He wound up needing Tommy John surgery and [his surgeon] also removed a giant bone fragment from his arm.

Could you explain the Robby Pad?

It was invented in 1980 when I was in Columbus, when I was playing with the Clippers. The traditional chest protector always covered your left shoulder, leaving the point of your right shoulder—the point exposed to foul tips when you lean forward—uncovered. It never happened to me, but I'd seen guys go down for weeks when you get hit like that. I cut up a chest protector and made a little hinged flap that I attached with shoe laces. That was the very first one. I tried to have it patented but it wasn't patentable because of something in 1898, some hinged thing that wasn't for baseball applications but for something else. Wilson wanted to work with me on it. They took pictures of it in spring training in '81 and then they stopped contacting me. They stole it! [Laughs] There was nothing I could do because I didn't have a patent.

I forgot all about it and then one year I drove up to the Hall of Fame for the day. I met this guy, Greg Harris, who was working on audio and video displays at the Hall. He took me down into the bowls of the Hall of Fame and showed me all sorts of stuff that's not on display, which is like three times the amount of stuff that is on display because they rotate all the exhibits. He had me send him files and clippings of the Robby Pad and he has the pad I made and wore. It rotates on display. So I finally made it to the Hall of Fame.[62]

---

62. The Robby Pad is now in widespread use.

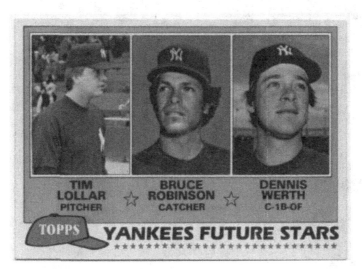

TOPPS

ROBINSON, BRUCE PHILLIP
Born: April 16, 1954 LaJolla, California
Bats: Left Throws: Right
Height: 6' 1" Weight: 185

Year	Team	G	AB	H	2B	3B	HR	AVG	RBI	R
1978	A's	28	84	21	3	1	0	.250	8	5
1979	YANKEES	6	12	2	0	0	0	.167	2	0
1980	YANKEES	4	5	0	0	0	0	.000	0	0
	Total 3 Years	38	101	23	3	1	0	228	10	5

Natioanl Baseball Hall of Fame

CURT KAUFMAN
1982–83

You grew up in the small farming town of Harlan, Iowa. You were probably not a Yankee fan.

You know, actually I think I was. I think most kids, when you grow up you're somewhat of a front-runner. For me it was the Cardinals in '67 and '68, and then the Miracle Mets in '69, then the Orioles of the early '70s and the Oakland A's, and then finally it was the Big Red Machine of the middle '70s. In 1976 they swept the Yankees and I don't know why, but I felt kind of sorry for the Yankees and I started following them and I've been a fan ever since.

You're not a Royals fan?[63]

I like them but I don't agree with everything ownership does. I wish Brett would get a little bit more involved.[64] The luxury tax is just not working out for the reasons it was designed for. Kansas City could put a much better product on the field, but they choose to pocket some of the money.

At Harlan High School you set a record for strikeouts. Was that for a season or your high school career?

Both. Nowadays you just don't see a lot of kids that have live arms like they did 30 years ago. I was one of probably a dozen around this area who had great arms. You just don't see it as much as you used to. Kids have other things to do now. They're not out playing games every day. They're sitting in front of the TV playing video games, and some of them choose to work for a little extra spending money. You just don't see the time spent on a baseball field playing baseball like you used to.

Were you scouted in high school?

I was, but not much came out of it. I was 6' 2" and probably 145 pounds. Bill Clark was a scout for the Cincinnati Reds and he said to me that the best thing would be for me to go to college and put on about 40 pounds. He was probably right.

You went on to Iowa State University on an athletic scholarship for baseball. Were you always a pitcher?

I was always a pitcher, but I played other positions all the time, too. When I was recruited at Iowa State I was recruited as a shortstop, too, but I never got that opportunity and it kind of soured

---

63. The closest major league city to Harlan.
64. Kansas City Royals star hitter (3,154 career hits, 300 home runs) and third baseman George Brett retired in 1993. He later became a Royals vice president and part-time coach. In 2008 he was considered a possible candidate to become the team's coach, but that didn't transpire.

me a little bit there. I felt like I was lied to. That's not what they said initially, otherwise I'd have chosen a different school. My college career was very unspectacular. I had a pretty decent freshman year and threw in more meaningful games than [later]. The second year we lost a lot of our pitching. I was our number one starter, so I always had to start against the other team's ace, so it was difficult. I was a .500 pitcher.

After three years at ISU the Yankees signed you as an amateur free agent in 1979.

The assistant baseball coach at Iowa State was a guy by the name of Gerry McNertney.[65] He's a fabulous human being. He actually was a minor league coach for the Yankees, too—a lot of people don't know that. Most of his years were spent in AAA in Columbus. He started going down to major league spring training in the early '80s full-time, so he couldn't help at Iowa State anymore at that point. He always liked the way I threw at college. He called me up that winter in January of '79 and wanted me to try out. Being here in the frozen tundra, it's kind of hard to get in shape on short notice, so we waited and I called him again in June. I played in an amateur league and the Yankees flew a scout out to see me play. Then they flew me out to Columbus where—what was the pitching coach's name?—Stan Williams, Big Stan, had me throw for him. He liked the way I threw and they flew me up to Oneonta the next day and I signed! Kind of a different route.

Your first year in the Yankee system was 1979 at Oneonta, low A. You went 4–1 with a 0.90 ERA and had 9 saves. You also had 50 strikeouts in 30 innings. You must have been pretty happy with the results of your first year.

What I took out of that first year was that I was 21 years old and a lot of the kids were 18, 19, and a lot younger than I was. I was already developed by the time I went and played there, and I already had 100 innings pitched. I was what you might say in midseason form and it showed.

Did the organization consider you a big prospect?

You know, I really don't know. They put me on the 40-man roster early. I was kind of caught between relieving and starting. If you look at the relief pitching who was ahead of me at that point, Ron Davis was still there as the setup man, and obviously Gossage was there, so it was kind of a dead end for me. I was the type who wanted to do what was the best for the team. I functioned well in the short relief role and they wanted me to do that. There's something about rocking out there in the ninth inning with the pressure on—you feed off that and I enjoyed that.

---

65. Nine-year major league catcher, 1964–73.

At Oneonta one of your teammates was an 18-year-old, Don Mattingly.

See, I showed up a little bit late after the season had already started in about mid-June or somewhere around there, and I didn't get there until probably around July 10.

The first thing I remember about Don was, the first day I show up and don't know anybody and I'm watching this guy take groundballs at third base. He's throwing across and he's right-handed. The next day he's out in left field and he's throwing in left-handed. I looked at somebody and said, "Isn't that the same guy who was taking ground balls the day before at third base?" They all laughed, because he's ambidextrous. He's the first person I've ever seen at that level to do that.

In 1980 the Yankees brought you up to high A at Ft. Lauderdale, where you were still too good. You went 5–1 with 8 saves and an ERA of 0.97. They promoted you to Nashville, AA, and you responded by going 6–2 in 11 games. Did you think the competition wasn't good enough for you at these levels?

In 1980 in spring training they gave me every opportunity to stick in AA, but honestly, I didn't have a very good spring training. I don't know why or what—I just did not have very good stuff and I couldn't explain it. So I worked it out in A ball and they moved me up to AA, where I became a starter. I liked it—it's a lot easier to be a starter versus a reliever, in the manner that it helps you to stay in shape. You pitch every fifth day and go through a routine the day after. You stretch out and run and there's so much more opportunity to lift and stay strong. I enjoyed that part. I was a fastball-slider pitcher and when I started I threw a changeup also.

In 1981 you had another great year at Nashville, while the big leagues are on strike for part of the season, 9–5 with 12 saves. One of your teammates in the bullpen was lefty Mike Morgan, who went on to a colorful 22-year major league career.

At the time I couldn't have told you that he would have that career, but in retrospect I understand how he did that. What I mean is he was a physical specimen—he was in great shape always. For longevity obviously that's very important, but his personality and how he approached everything was so important—he just never let things get to him. He was very matter-of-fact if he had a bad game. It wasn't like he didn't care, but he would just brush it off and move on. At the level he played at all those years you have to be able to do that; you learn that as you go. Great guy. He had good stuff obviously, or he would have never stayed there for so long, but his personality and his work ethic was why he was there so long.

In 1982 you're having a great year at Columbus [6–3, 10 saves] when the Yankees call you up in September. Do you remember being told that you were going to the big leagues?

It was rumored that I might get that September call-up along with some other people. There's always rumors among the team and with people you know on other teams. I don't think we found out until the [AAA] season was over. I remember we made the Yankees mad a little bit because we drove out there and they wanted us to fly up there. When they call you up they want you there that night. I drove up there with Mattingly from Columbus. I didn't think that it was that big of a deal because I had never done it. When we get there they said, "You guys actually drove here?" [Laughs] The traffic wasn't great but we got there.

Had you ever been to New York before?

No. We got to drive right to Yankee Stadium. We drove across the George Washington Bridge and down the Deegan Expressway the first time. It was an eye-opening experience. I got lost one time; well actually I didn't get lost but just missed my exit. When you leave Yankee Stadium you go north and have to get way left in order to get onto the George Washington Bridge. Well, there was a lot of traffic and they weren't letting me over and being a polite little midwesterner I didn't just force my car in like you need to do. I missed my turn and got off the next exit and doubled back down to Yankee Stadium and started over. The scout who had come out and scouted me was with me and he was scared to death. I don't know what's just north there, 20–30 blocks north of Yankee Stadium, but it wasn't too good and we were driving down those streets at one o'clock in the morning!

What was it like to put on a Yankee uniform and walk out onto the field at Yankee Stadium for the first time?

Having been a Yankee fan since '76, and even more than that, I was very much a baseball fan, I was aware of the history of the stadium and all that. The number one thing that I thought of first was the tradition and the history and who all played there. I think it actually winds up putting a little more pressure on you in a sense of the fear of failure in front of the baseball Gods, if you know what I mean.

The first game I got in Ron Guidry was pitching. The bullpen phone rings and, "Kaufman, you're up." I'm like, "What the heck am I going to throw that Guidry doesn't already have?" There's a difference between being nervous and being scared. Nervous you can get your adrenaline moving for you; scared you go the other way, and I was scared. Guidry got out of the inning, so I got a chance to sit down and kind of regroup and then I was fine.

That first game was against the Brewers at Yankee Stadium on September 10, 1982. You pitched 1⅓ innings, retiring all five batters that you faced: Ned Yost, Robin Yount, Paul Molitor, Cecil Cooper, and Gorman Thomas. Four All-Stars, two of them Hall of Famers.

[Laughs] That's a pretty good row right there.

Did it go through your mind when you were out there that you weren't getting a break here?

It did. That's why they called them Harvey's Wallbangers. I remember my first strikeout—it was Robin Yount. They were a notorious group of hitters, but most of them were free swingers and as a pitcher you like free swingers. If you make a mistake they'll let you know, but they're easier to pitch to also. Sometimes you like the challenge. I did well against them there, but I think they got me later in Milwaukee, where I threw two nights in a row. I didn't have a good fastball and Gorman Thomas and Molitor went back-to-back on me [with home runs].

You pitched six games in your first ten days in the majors and went 1–0. Did you think that you would be back the next year?

You've got to remember who was there. Ron Davis had been traded by then, but Gossage was still there. I went into spring training hoping that I would get a shot. Back then you didn't have as many roles in the bullpen, and not as clearly defined. Also, you have to look at who was the manager back then: Billy Martin. He didn't care for the young player that much. You really had to stand out to get used more by him, where you could win a position. Billy liked the veteran player. I guess deep down most managers do.

The 1982 Yankees are a case study in how not to run a ball club. They had three managers, four hitting coaches, and five pitching coaches. Who was your manager and pitching coach when you got called up?

The manager was Clyde King. Pitching coach . . . you know there was so many different ones there. I don't believe Dobson was there anymore, but Sammy Ellis was. Stan Williams was still around. I'm not actually sure who filled that position then.

King talked to us a little bit that first time we walked out onto the field. He didn't talk to us in the locker room. [He talked to us about] why we were called up and how we would be used to kind of define our roles. Not that we were going to be mop-ups but that we were going to be used in crucial roles, because they were looking at what we could do under those same situations next season.

That team also had 47 players during the season. I realize that you only got there in September, but do you think that constant state of flux, with players, coaches, and managers coming and going, negatively affected the team?[66]

Well, I think that everybody would have to agree that it does. Stability is very important. Look at the Torre years—everybody knew what to expect, and he let everybody know what their role was. If you know what your role is and what's expected of you, it makes it a lot easier to perform. I don't think anybody would ever argue that.

There were a lot of established pitchers on the team, with Ron Guidry, Righetti, Tommy John, Goose Gossage, Rudy May, Dave LaRoche, and Shane Rawley. Did any of them help you in any way when you got called up?

Pretty much all of them. Great bunch of guys, and not just the pitchers—Roy Smalley, Butch Wyneger, a lot of class people. What you find out from the lower minor leagues as you go up and move toward the major leagues is, everybody is there for the same reason and you're all working toward a common goal—if you don't have the egotistical, self-centered people who are more worried about themselves versus what's best for the team. There were a lot of great people there, like Guidry, Rudy May, and Gossage, and Rawley. They helped me get a couple of hunting guns through Remington and I still have them actually to this day. They invited me to go hunting. Guidry wanted me to come down to Louisiana, and Gossage wanted me to come out to Colorado, and Rudy May stopped here on his way back from California to Kansas City, because he played a couple of years in Kansas City, too. Just great people.

I think everybody knew Piniella would be a manager someday, at least there we did. He was a pretty astute student of the game and he taught a lot with Billy or Clyde or Yogi— Yogi was around a lot.

Did you ever see Dave LaRoche throw the LaLob?[67]

[Laughs] Yes, I did. I actually saw him when his older son, Adam, was playing in a Texas youth league in a tournament here. I got to talking to him and the LaLob actually came up. Everybody remembers the one that he threw Gorman Thomas. Thomas was so mad that he took his helmet off and hit it with the bat. [Laughs]

---

66. The 1982 Yankees, who were the defending AL Champions, went 79–82 and finished in fifth place.
67. The La Lob was an eephus pitch first developed by Rip Sewell in the 1930s. It is a 20-foot-high curve ball thrown on a big arc. LaRoche's was clocked at 28 mph. Only a few pitchers in major league history have thrown it, with LaRoche being the last.

You threw to both Cerone and Wyneger, who were both veteran catchers. Barry Foote was also there your first year. Were they helpful?

Oh, they were both very good to throw to. I don't know if I threw to Barry. Mainly the first year was Rick Cerone and the second year was mostly Wyneger, if I remember correctly. I threw pretty good my first year, because Clyde King came up to me and asked me the next day how I felt and wanted to know how often he could use me.

One thing I remember about Wyneger, throwing to him—I believe we were playing Baltimore—was Billy called a certain pitch and Butch didn't agree with him so he gave me a different pitch. I don't remember who the right-handed hitter was, but Wyneger asked me to throw him a changeup. What I actually threw was like a screwball, where I ran it down and in on the hitter. That's not what Billy called for, I guess. Anyway, the guy got a base hit and Butch immediately called time-out and came out to the mound, and sure enough here comes Billy out of the dugout. Butch just looked at me and said, "The way we do it here is say that we threw the slider and not the screwball." [Laughs] I always thought that was funny. Butch was covering his hind.

You started the 1983 season with Columbus and lit up the International League, leading it with a record 25 saves and going 6–3. That gave you a five-year minor league record of 36–15 with 64 saves. The Yankees called you up again briefly and you appeared in four games. Did Martin tell you anything when you got called up?

No, I don't believe so. I actually got called up earlier twice that year. I got called up on the first of July. I was there for insurance for Guidry, who had hurt his back. He had a doctor's appointment and it wasn't as bad as they thought—he was only going to have to miss a start. When you make a roster move I had to be off for ten days. I couldn't go back and play in Columbus for ten days, so I was up for Dave Righetti's Fourth of July no-hitter. That was pretty neat. I can't be out in the dugout without a uniform, so I watched it on TV in the locker room. What was also neat was I was watching it with Sparky Lyle.[68]

I was throwing the ball awfully well. Probably '83 was the best year of my baseball career. I got called up again in early August and threw against Detroit on Bobby Murcer Day, which was really special. I gave Kirk Gibson the hat trick. I got him three times that day. [Laughs] He was so mad. I wasn't used to throwing five-plus innings and man, I pinched a nerve in my neck. I think that was probably one of the big things that hurt my chances for the next year. Billy didn't put up with stuff like that and I got sent back down for the rest of the year. I actually missed 20 days in AAA from that pinched nerve. It was just kind of a freak thing.

---

68. Lyle was retired at that time and visiting the team.

After the 1983 season did anyone from the organization say anything to you about your future with the organization?

Yeah, directly, indirectly, different people said different things. The more common denominator between everything everybody said was that I had nothing left to prove in the minor leagues. They weren't going to send me back there anymore, and I would have been out of options soon anyway. They needed a backup middle infielder and that's why I was traded to the Angels for Tim Foli.

How surprised were you when that trade happened on December 7?

Not real surprised—it was just a matter of where I was going to go. I kind of wanted to go to the Cubs. Barry Foote was with the Cubs at that point doing some scouting and he saw me in the [AAA] playoffs. I talked to him a little bit and they wanted me.

Did you look at this trade as an opportunity to stick in the majors?

Yeah, but I think I viewed it more as a chance to come into my own. That's why I wanted to go to the Cubs, because they're a National League team and as a reliever you throw more often and shorter, and that's what I was used to. My AAA manager was Johnny Oates, who was just a fabulous manager who knew how to work the bullpen, and that's why I had such a great year.

The problem that I ran into in '84 was that John McNamara was the manager and he wasn't as good with the bullpen. You would throw six days in a row and then you might sit for two weeks! It's hard on you physically and I was hard on myself because I didn't find something to better prepare myself and to keep myself in game shape. Your body likes a routine and it was anything but a routine that year.

I think I threw at one point five out of six days and the last of those games were against the Yankees, back-to-back days. I knew everybody there, so you're trying to throw a little harder. Then we went to Cleveland and I threw again there in relief. I was throwing very well, but I threw a changeup and didn't follow through right. I pulled a muscle in the back of my shoulder and had to get a cortisone shot. They didn't DL me, but I sat for about 15 days and I was fine again. That was the only time I got hurt in '85, but my elbow started to really hurt me in the spring of '85. It was bone chips but the Angels doctors couldn't find anything. They sent me on a rehab assignment to AAA Edmonton and I wound up lying there all year. I would just do certain movements and it would catch and just be so painful.

By the spring of '86 my elbow was shot so they released me. However, they couldn't with an injury so I'm not sure what went on down there, but I went to other doctors besides their own team doctors. I went to Boston to Dr. Pappas, who was the Red Sox doctor, and he was very good. He found it immediately and the problem was, I threw with it for a year and a half. It chewed me up pretty good. I had the surgery but I never came back from it—the top on the gun was '88–'89. I thought it would be good to get away from the game for a little while and reevaluate what I wanted to do.

I'm coaching in high school now. I like working with kids; it's fun.

Have you been back to Yankee Stadium?

No, I haven't. This past season I would have loved to since it's the last season.

Any other Yankee memory?

The strike year of '81. Yogi traveled with us in AA and that was a neat experience. All the Yankee coaches went with different teams and Yogi was with us. I had a lot of different conversations with him and that was very special. He would call me Muscles, I was so skinny. [Laughs]

TOPPS

KAUFMAN, CURT GERARD
Born: July 19, 1957 Omaha, Nebraska
Bats: Right Throws: Right
Height: 6' 2" Weight: 175

Year	Team	G	W-L	SV	GS	CG	IP	SO	W	ERA
1982	YANKEES	7	1-0	0	0	0	8.7	1	6	5.19
1983	YANKEES	4	0-0	0	0	0	8.7	8	4	3.12
1984	Angels	29	2-3	1	1	0	69.0	41	20	4.57
	Total 3 Years	40	3-3	1	1	0	86.3	50	30	4.48

BRACE Photo

JUAN BONILLA
1985, 1987

You were born in Santurce, Puerto Rico. That's a very big baseball town.

Oh yes, that's correct. I came to the U.S. I believe in the fall of 1972 for college.

Were you a Santurce Crabbers fan?

Not really, I was more of a San Juan fan. It was a family thing. My dad played some ball there and one of the coaches from that team was always at my house and always brought me baseballs and things like that. It just stuck with me. Clemente played for [San Juan] too. Cepeda played for the Crabbers and Reggie Jackson did, too—that's when I was growing up. We used to jump the fence in left field to get into the stadium and watch them play, then run back home. [Laughs] We never got caught, luckily.

You must have played a lot of baseball growing up there?

Yes, I did. I was probably hitting a baseball when I was three or four years old. I never did any organized games until I was about twelve years old.

You played in the PONY League and also in the Colt World Series when you were 16.

Yes, we were representing Puerto Rico. The majority of the players were from the San Juan area. We would play other teams from the Caribbean. The Colt World Series was in Lafayette, Indiana, and we went up there to play in the tournament. At a regional tournament in North Carolina the coach approached us there and wound up taking three of us, and two more later [to Florida State University]. We lost the first game there, then won the regional and then went to Lewiston, Idaho, We never lost a game in a double-elimination tournament for the American Legion World Series. The FSU coach first saw us there in North Carolina.

At FSU you became an All-American for the Seminoles. Were you always a second baseman?

No, actually I was a third baseman, but when I got to college I couldn't catch a cold, [Laughs] so they moved me to second. I played three years at second base and was an All-American as a second baseman. Those aluminum bats kind of threw me off a little bit, but it was a learning experience. I have to thank Woody Woodward for moving me to second base. He was the head coach at FSU and also was with the Yankees.

I was picked by the Yankees in either the 18th or 23rd round in the [1979] draft—I don't remember; it was way back when—but they never contacted me so I didn't sign with them.

The following year (1978) the Indians signed you as an amateur free agent as a 23-year-old and you signed.

Yes, it was a good opportunity at the time. I always wanted to play in the big leagues.

Just prior to the 1981 season the Indians traded you to the Padres, where you became their everyday second baseman, replacing former All-Star Dave Cash. That trade worked out pretty good for you.

Yes, it did. I got the opportunity to play with Ozzie at short. I'll tell you one thing, I never saw anybody like him.

Was that a bit overwhelming, coming up from the minors and immediately starting next to Ozzie Smith?

The mentality there was different; I'd have to say that I was ready. I was 24 or 25 years old, so I was a little more mature then. It kind of never hit me, you know, what he stood for at the time: the best shortstop in the game. To me he was just Ozzie the wizard playing right beside me. Now that I have the time to look back I say, "Wow, I played with this guy."

Well, if you were nervous you didn't show it. You wound up fourth in the NL Rookie of the Year voting with a .290 batting average.

Yeah, but again, it was a lot of hard work. Playing with Ozzie you have to work. At the time I thought that we were going to be together for a long time, but he went to the Cardinals the following year. So then we got Gary [Templeton] in and . . . two different shortstops. It was a lot of fun playing with Ozzie though—I had the same way of thinking.

In your sophomore year you broke a wrist in a collision at first base. What happened?

I remember it like it was yesterday. It was a bunt situation. Willie Magee was the batter and it was a slow bunt that had some backspin. The pitcher grabbed it and I went to cover first base. The throw was in the line of the runner and when I went to catch it my hand hit his ribs and I got a compound fracture of the wrist. I felt like he took my hand with him. I still feel the pain [Laughs], mentally, that is. I haven't had any problems since the surgery they did.

In 1983 you had a bounce-back year for the Padres, playing in 150 games at second base, although your average suffered somewhat from the injury. The team let you go after the season. Did you play anywhere in 1984?

No, I didn't. I was just trying to get healthy.

In 1985 the Yankees signed you as a free agent. How did you feel about coming to New York?

Let's put it this way: a dream come true. Never imagined that would happen; then all of a sudden I'm there. I was invited to spring training with the big club and after three-quarters of it, towards the end they sent me back down to the minors, but it lasted only a couple of days. They called me back up and I performed well enough to make the roster. They took me to Boston, where they had the opening day that year. I have a clipping somewhere saying I had a 100,000 to 1 shot to make the club. [Laughs] I wish I would have bet a couple dollars on that!

Great memories, in fact the memories that I keep the most. New York is the melting pot, where you have everybody from everywhere, different nationalities and backgrounds. They know their baseball and they get to know you. The memories are vivid—I get goose bumps. The best fans in the world are in New York and they're at Yankee Stadium. Since the minute I walked in there they treated me very well. You start to get to know the fans because basically they sit on the same side at every game. You wave your hand at them and they say, "Go get 'em, Juan!" "Have a great day," or "We need this one"—that was a favorite. Some of them in Spanish, some of them in English, and some of them in some language that I never understood. [Laughs] Very colorful.

I never lived there because I basically lived out of a suitcase. You never knew what was going to happen with the Columbus shuttle! [Laughs] I stayed at the Hilton. That was a little further out in, I think, Hackensack; that name comes to mind. We never knew what was going to happen next.

After starting the season with the Yankees they sent you down to Columbus [AAA], where you responded by hitting .330 in the International League. You didn't seem to have lost anything from your game.

You're correct. As a matter of fact I won the batting title there.

In 1985 the Yankees had Willie Randolph at second base and Andre Robertson as a utility infielder. Also, at Columbus infielder Rex Hudler played a good number of games at second. Were you discouraged at all by this apparent lack of opportunity for an infielder, specifically a second baseman, on the Yankees at this time?

Not necessarily, no. I was never discouraged. I had a great supporting cast in my family, especially my wife, Jean. She kept saying, "Hey, you'll be there. You'll be there." With her backing I couldn't lose. I played basically every game at second at Columbus.

Had you ever been to Yankee Stadium before?

Never had.

What was it like walking out onto the field at Yankee Stadium for the first time wearing a Yankee uniform?

I couldn't believe that I was there. You know, when you're a baseball player and you know the great ones have been there, Yankee Stadium is filled with ghosts. Walking down that tunnel onto the field, it's like every one of them getting you. The feeling putting on that uniform is, your chest is about five feet wide. It's very hard to explain; hopefully you can make some sense out of what I just said. The only thing that happened is that I couldn't wear number 3.[69] [Laughs] I said to just give me any number and I'll be happy that I'm just on the roster!

You wore number 3 on the Padres and Orioles. Was that number special to you?

Yes, it came from college.

And the Yankees wouldn't let you have number 3?

[Laughs] What can I say?

Yogi Berra was still the manager when you made the team at the beginning of the year, but not for long.

When the Yankees broke spring training, Yogi Berra was the manager. I believe about ten games into the season, maybe a little more, George fired Yogi and called back in Billy Martin.

Were you surprised when that happened? Because they still talk about that in New York.

I can't tell you what goes through the mind of people, but I have to tell you [George Steinbrenner] is one of the greatest men I've ever known. But a great businessman, what can you say? The Yankees since George has been the owner have been topsy-turvy. I can tell you that Yogi was the one that took me, and Billy was the one that sent me down. I don't know the reason for that either. I hadn't been playing much. Willie [Randolph] was the starting second baseman. I would

---

69. Babe Ruth's number, retired in 1948.

have loved to stay in New York, don't get me wrong, but I had an opportunity to play every day [in Columbus].

The Yankees actually had a very good team that year and came in second in the AL East to Toronto by just two games.

Correct. We had an opportunity to beat them too in the next-to-last game of the season. I was there. They called me back up in September at the end of the AAA season.

Were you surprised when the Yankees released you at the end of the season?

[Laughs] Which one?

1985.

Again, people do things for whatever is better for the ball club. Maybe I wasn't part of it, but I had an opportunity when I signed with the Orioles as a free agent the following year.

In 1986 you had a good year in Baltimore.

Yes, I believe I played in 102 games at second base. It was over 100. What I remember about that, of course, was playing with Cal [Ripken]. I'll never forget something Earl Weaver said to me: "Nobody has started over 100 games that wasn't either a shortstop or first baseman," next to Ripken. I don't know how true that is, but I'm in good company then! When he said that it made me feel good; it made me feel welcome there.

In 1986 you became one of 127 infielders to play alongside Cal Ripken.

[Laughs] Yes, I might be a trivia question one day.

In 1987 the Yankees went out and signed you again. How did that come about?

Well, when the Orioles released me it was because they felt Cal's brother, Billy Ripken, was ready. I'm a utility infielder no longer; I was a starting second baseman. I don't know how that works into the picture, but I was grateful that it happened. It gave me an opportunity to get back to where I belonged.

I had surgery on my ankle that winter. I had twisted an ankle getting in shape. I went into spring training and I was with the big club, but they knew about it and took care of all the bills. So they sent me down to AAA to rehab and basically I had no range; I couldn't make sudden moves. They gave me an opportunity to become part of the coaching staff and they sent me to Prince

William, Virginia. I was there maybe half of a season as a player-coach and what happened was that Willie got hurt.

I see the Yankees then called you back up to New York after Randolph's knee surgery. The rest of the games at second base in '87 were split between yourself and Bobby Meacham.

Correct. Coming back to New York gave me an opportunity to be a coach. In '88 I went to Ft. Lauderdale in A ball, where Buck Showalter was the manager and I was the first base coach. Of course I accepted—a job is a job, especially in baseball. I wish I could have stayed [playing] up to today, especially when I see utility players making five or six million dollars a year! [Laughs]

I called it quits after 1989 and started following my son around. He had an opportunity to play professionally for the Orioles in the minor leagues.

On July 27, 1987, the Yankees played the Braves in Cooperstown for the annual Hall of Fame game. New York won 3–0.

Wow. [Laughs] You know who went deep in that game!

You hit what was described as a towering home run to left center.

I got the ball. I got the ball to prove it. A lady came over and said, "This is the home run you hit. Do you want the ball?" I said, "Don't you want it?" and she said, "No, you can have it" and she gave it to me. I hit it off Jose Alvarez, a right-handed pitcher. He was a relief pitcher for the Braves and we were friends at the time too.

I think we flew there because we were coming from somewhere and we took some buses from the airport. I never had an opportunity to go to the Hall of Fame, though.

You and Henry Cotto both went deep and won the game.

Yeah, my roomie. We roomed together on the road.

Lou Piniella was your manager in 1987. How was he to play for?

Very easy. On and off the field he was always talking to you and giving you information. You know, keep your eyes open; this guy does this or that in this situation.

Willie Randolph was a senior player on the Yankees when you were there. Did you get to know your fellow second baseman, or did he help you in any way?

Yes, he did, and as a matter of fact he also became a friend. We knew right from the get-go I'm not here to take his job; I'm just here to work hard and stay. I knew he was the second baseman, and with that understanding he helped in every way. He used to move me left to right on certain batters and tell me to shorten up or back up. He was always thinking about the game.

I have to say, his charisma, the way he presented himself and did things on the field, he was a very smart individual.

Don Mattingly?

The hit man.

You can say that you've played in some good company with Ozzie Smith, Cal Ripken, and now Donnie Baseball.

I'll tell you what, nothing went by, nothing went by. Groundballs that I thought I had, Mattingly was right there even though the glove side was not on that side. Hard working individual. I've never seen anything like it, and with the understanding that he wasn't that good of a player in the minor leagues. When I got to meet him and saw the time he dedicated to the job, it was just phenomenal.

Any other Yankee memory?

I hit a home run on August 1, 1987, at Yankee Stadium off Frank Tanana. My only home run at Yankee Stadium.

And it was in front of 55,103 fans, too.

[Laughs] Well, that's my daughter's birthday and I hit a home run for every club I played for on that date! It was always my dream to play for the Yankees and hit a home run at Yankee Stadium, and I can tell you that I fulfilled my dream.

I'm going to tell you another story. We were in spring training in '86 when I was with the Orioles and we were in, I believe, Ft. Lauderdale.[70] It's been raining all day and George came in and hired helicopters to dry the field. I'm running sprints before the game on the left field line, and we approached and talked a little bit. I said to him, "Thank you for the opportunity that you've given me. Always remember that I'm a Yankee at heart." I don't know if that had anything to do with hiring me back in '87, but I'll remember that for the rest of my life.

---

70. The Yankees' spring training complex.

Have you ever been back to Yankee Stadium since you retired from the game?

No, I haven't, but I look forward to it one day. Hopefully I'll get to the new one before I pass. [Laughs]

TOPPS

BONILLA, JUAN GUILLERMO
Born: February 12, 1955 Santurce, Puerto Rico
Bats: Right Throws: Right
Height: 5' 9" Weight: 170

Year	Team	G	AB	H	2B	3B	HR	AVG	RBI	R
1981	Padres	99	369	107	13	2	1	.290	25	30
1982	Padres	45	182	51	6	2	0	.280	8	21
1983	Padres	152	556	132	17	4	4	.237	45	55
1985	YANKEES	8	16	2	1	0	0	.125	2	0
1986	Orioles	102	284	69	10	1	1	.243	18	33
1987	YANKEES	23	55	14	3	0	1	.255	3	6
	Total 6 Years	429	1462	375	50	9	7	.256	101	145

National Baseball Hall of Fame

PAUL ZUVELLA
1986–87

You were born in San Mateo, California, near San Jose. Were you a Yankee fan or a Giants and A's fan?

Ha! No, a Giants fan growing up, not A's.

The Giants seem to be more popular out there.

You know, probably. Especially on the peninsula and the west side of the bay people are Giants fans. On the East Bay folks are A's fans.

You attended Samuel Ayer High School in Milpitas, California. Were you on their baseball team?

I was. I was MVP of the league my junior year, my first year on varsity. The beginning of senior year I had some professional scouts come up to me. I remember one had asked me if I had to rate on a scale of 0–10, if you would play professional baseball next year if you were drafted, what would you rate it? Being a young, naive guy I said, "Zero. I'm going to go to school." So I totally lost any bargaining power I may have had. I was young for my year—I started college when I was 17. I didn't really have any interest in starting a professional career out of high school. I got an opportunity to go to Stanford, and for anyone that's hard to pass up.

Were you always an infielder?

Yes, ever since I was 12 years old or so.

Did you have a regular position on Stanford University's team?

I did. My freshman year I played a little bit of infield and a little bit of outfield just to get some at bats, and sophomore year I was their third baseman. I was a shortstop in high school and Stanford recruited me as a shortstop. By the time I turned junior [at Stanford] and the shortstop was graduating, we got a junior college transfer named Dave Meier who played with the Twins, and Rangers, and Cubs for a while. They put him at short and moved me to second. Even though I was a shortstop in high school, I never really played it in college, and as soon as I got signed professionally they told me I was a shortstop! [Laughs]

You must have had a pretty good college career, because you drew attention from major league teams.

I did. I had some pretty good years. My senior year I was second-team All-American. In fact the guy who was first-team All-American was Tim Teufel, who played for the Mets for a while.

You were drafted by the Brewers in 1979 but didn't sign.

That's correct. That was after my junior year in college. I had a good year my junior year and the Brewers drafted me in the 10th or 11th round. I just wanted to go back and get my degree. Back then a 10th-round draft choice—they offered me like $10,000, and maybe they were going to pay for my last year of school, but it wasn't enough to pry me away from getting my degree.

The Braves then drafted you the following year, in 1980, in the 15th round and you signed. Were you happy it was the Braves?

Yeah. In fact the guy who signed me was Charlie Silvera, who was a scout with the Braves back then and was a backup for Yogi Berra for a while in New York.

You made your major league debut on September 4, 1982, a little more than two years after signing. Did you ever imagine that you would get to the majors so quickly?

Not really, no. I was pretty lucky. After signing professionally that first year I played high A ball and did pretty well and hit over .300. At that time the Braves needed middle infielders. They just didn't have a lot of middle infielders and they were not a very good organization at the time. I came up with some players that did pretty good. Gerald Perry, the hitting coach for the Cubs now, Brook Jacoby, who is the hitting coach for the Reds, Paul Runge, Albert Hall, Brad Komminsk—we had some good young players who came up through their system. In '81 I played a full year at AA and in '82 I played a full year at AAA, so I moved up pretty quickly.

In 1980 you hit .315 at A ball, followed by .299 AA 1981, .281 AAA 1982, .287 AAA 1983, and .303 AAA 1984. You seemed to have no difficulty hitting at any level in the minors.

Correct, I didn't because I played every day. That was the thing for me: when I got a chance to play in the big leagues it was mostly as a part-time player. I always had a tough time coming off the bench from an offensive standpoint. When I got traded to the Yankees they gave me a chance to play every day. They traded for me to be their everyday shortstop, but it just so happened that I didn't hit the ball very well. They don't have a lot of patience there.

After four up-and-down seasons with the Braves, they trade you on June 3, 1986, to the Yankees with Claudell Washington for Ken Griffey Sr. and Andre Robertson. What did you think about the trade?

By then I had been lobbying them to get traded or something because the Braves had Rafael Ramirez as their shortstop and Glenn Hubbard as their second baseman, and those guys had really good years in '82, when they won the division with Atlanta, which was my first time when

I got called up. Then '83 came along and '84 came along and it became clear that they were going to stick with those guys and I didn't have a chance to play there. In '85 I was the utility guy in Atlanta and I did OK and finally started to acclimate to coming off the bench. Then in '86 I got sent back down. I thought, I need to get out of here, so I welcomed the trade. The only issue was that I had just found out that my wife was pregnant for the first time, so there was a lot going on in our lives. We came to New York and it was a change in leagues. I don't want to say Milpitas was a small town, but it was more suburbia than big city, so it was a bit of an adjustment.

In '86 when I got traded over I think I just stayed in a hotel. They just put me up in a hotel and then when I got sent to Columbus for the last month I stayed in a hotel there. I was up and down a lot that first year. I was up for six weeks and then down for a month, then up for a month. In '87 I was up and down a bunch. I was just set to get an apartment and I got sent down to Columbus. When I got called back up I said, you know what, I'm not even going to try to get an apartment; [Laughs] I'll just stay in a hotel and see what happens. The "Columbus shuttle," and that's exactly what it is. These are real people and real lives. It's not an easy situation to be involved in when you're trying to raise a family, but it's what baseball is. You're thankful for the opportunities, but at the same time you think, I have to perform well so they don't keep bouncing my family around.

You had already been a major leaguer for four years, but what was it like to walk out onto the field at Yankee Stadium wearing a Yankee uniform? Did that have any impact on you?

Yeah, it certainly did, no question. You try and take it all in, but at the same time you have a job to do and you're in a new league trying to acclimate to a new team with new teammates and surroundings. Some of these guys you've been coming up against—I know Don Mattingly; I played against him a bunch in the minors. Now they're your teammates and you want to show that you belong and you want to get off to a hot start. For me it didn't happen that way, and it was in the middle of a pennant race, too. The bases are still 90 feet and you have a job to do.

But did you like the pinstripes better than those powder-blue uniforms?

[Laughs] No question! I certainly enjoyed my time in the Braves organization. I think if you ask any major league player, when they're coming up and really learning how to become a professional baseball player, they have a lot of fond memories of their early years and the people that they knew then.

During your two years with the Yankees the infield was basically Mattingly at first base, Randolph at second, Tolleson at shortstop, and Pagliarulo at third. You just mentioned

the lack of opportunities with the Braves—were you discouraged by the Yankees having a seemingly set infield?

I got an opportunity for all of about three weeks. I struggled and was hitting the ball pretty well, but I didn't get any hits. I had like a 0 for 30 slump. I had never had that in my whole life, but I think I only struck out two or three times during that. I was hitting the ball pretty well, but they didn't find any holes.

Your Yankee career probably didn't start as well as you wanted it to— you went 0–28.

Yeah. Then I started to hit the ball. I started to come out of it. I think I got four hits in three games and then they traded for someone else. I was the kind of player that needed to feel comfortable. Most players do; there's a little bit of adjustment there.

Were you pressing at all?

Yeah, without question, I must have been. The more you think about just trying to relax and play your game, the harder that becomes.

New York fans can be tough. Did they catch on to your slump?

You know, I think they probably did. I thought the fans were great, really. I still remember coming out to a day game and I was in the middle of that slump, I was there maybe a week or ten days, and there was a young guy standing there with a sign that said "Paul Zuvella Fan Club." [Laughs] Yeah, he was over by our dugout.

In 1986 and '87 the Yanks seemed to have a number of utility-type players. Along with you there was Bobby Meacham, Randy Velarde, Dale Berra, Mike Fischlin, and Lenn Sakata. That' a lot of competition.

Correct. I think honestly Yankee fans now look at the shortstop position and say we've been blessed. You look at Derek Jeter—he's the prototypical shortstop and he's been there forever and he's a gamer. You can't say enough about the kind of career he's had and the kind of leader he is and the kind of person he is. During the time that I played there were a lot of us that just kind of filled the position and did the best that we could. We didn't have that continuity, and knowing that if we didn't get three hits that night that we were going to play the next day anyway. It was not easy wondering if you were going to be in the lineup the next day. I think at that time George Steinbrenner demanded a winner and wasn't as patient as he was later on, when they started to have some very good teams. He became a little more patient because they were winning. I was there at a time when we were in the crucible, if you will.

After the '86 season did you think that you would be back with New York?

You know, I didn't. I was surprised that they brought me back—just how quickly they dismissed me and found another shortstop [Tolleson]. Looking back now, they had traded senior [Ken Griffey] for me and Claudell and I guess they wanted to see how I'd do given a fresh start. I was their utility guy in '87. I was there for six weeks and maybe got five at bats.

In spring training of '87 Steinbrenner was disenchanted with the play of Bobby Meacham at shortstop. Do you remember that?

You know, I had heard that. What you try and do in the middle of all that is just say, "Whatever. I'm going to do my job and not pay attention to that stuff." It's a hard enough game as it is for most of the guys in the majors, for all of us actually. It's not an easy game. For most of us who toil in the minors for a quite a while and you're good enough to get to the big leagues, the hard part is staying there and you try and not think about the extra stuff too much.

Did you ever meet George Steinbrenner?

Not personally, I never did. I saw him walking through our clubhouse a few times.

In 1987 you went back to Columbus, where you hit .301, with more walks than strikeouts, which was the norm for your career. Why did the success that you had at AAA seem to elude you in the majors?

Honestly, it really was the lack of steady play. I think I was on five different AAA All-Star teams. When that's the case you can play in the major leagues. Given the right circumstance and opportunity I think I could have been a pretty darn good major league player. A lot of people thought that at the time. The way my career went, I was with an organization that wasn't very patient and wasn't given an opportunity to work through some of those adjustments. When I look back at my career overall, I look at the times when I was an everyday player wherever it was and I was a pretty solid player. I was one of those guys who would help your team win.

An unusual point about your time with the Yankees in that era was that you had the same manager for two consecutive years. How did you find Piniella to play for?

I think at the time Lou was navigating through things too—he had just started managing. He was feeling the pressure and the uncertainty of it all. Some of the decisions that he was making you could see he would wonder what the ramifications would be from ownership. Obviously he's a nice guy, a hard-nosed guy that you had to respect as a player, even though I didn't know him

226

when he played. Anyone who knows the history of the game and the history of the people that came before you had to respect him. But I wasn't myself there—I just didn't play well.

Did you get to know Don Mattingly at all?

Yeah, I had known Don from playing against him before, so we had a little bit of a connection there. Very nice guy. He was a good midwestern guy who really worked hard. I played against him in AA and AAA. He was a spray hitter who hit the ball to left field all the time and went down to winter ball and found out how to pull the ball, and the rest is history. Donnie was always one of the best fielding first basemen I ever played with. He was pretty amazing. Don was the kind of guy that you knew that if you didn't have the most accurate throw, he was still going to figure out how to pick it or come off the bag and make a tag at the same time.

I do remember being in New York when Donnie had his consecutive streak of hitting home runs, which was fun to be around. I thought Don was the kind of guy who led by example: he just went out and worked hard every day and plied his trade and became very good at it.

Willie Randolph had already been with the Yankees for over ten years when you got there. He could be described as an "under-the-radar" guy. Could you have seen him becoming a longtime major league coach and manager?

At the time no. Not in New York with the Mets, but maybe in Cleveland or Kansas City, where you're not in the hot seat all the time. The fact that he handled it so well as a player, it makes sense that he would be able to handle it as a manager. If you really stop and think about it, he had the right approach to the game. He went out there every day and just did his job. That's the kind of guy who makes the perfect manager.

In the two years you were there Pagliarulo hit 32 and 28 home runs. What type of hitter and player was he?

Pags was a good hitter. He was a home run-type hitter. I don't know if he did good average wise. He used that porch in right[71] to his advantage, that's for sure. He was a hard worker—I

---

71. The infield dimensions of a baseball field are strictly controlled, but the size and shape of the rest of the field vary quite a bit, so that each field plays a bit differently. To prevent easy home runs, a rule passed in 1951 established the minimum distance from home plate to the right and left field walls of future stadiums at 325 feet. Fields already in existence, including the old Yankee Stadium, were permitted to keep their dimensions. The new Yankee Stadium was allowed to keep its old dimensions. The right field wall at Yankee Stadium is 314 feet from home plate. This is referred to as a "short porch." For comparison, the longest Major League right field was 370' at Mile High Stadium (Colorado Rockies), and the shortest was 258' at Polo Grounds (New York Giants).

remember he was *always* taking extra batting practice under the tunnel and out on the field in the afternoon before regular BP. He made himself a good hitter.

On October 5, 1987, the Yankees released you. Did that surprise you?

At that point no. I really didn't get that much of an opportunity in '87 to play that much. Again, I would have little spurts here and there where I would start to hit a little bit and then they would put me back on the bench and try someone else. By that time I figured it was time to try somewhere else.

On October 13 the Indians signed you and you wound up on the team for the better part of the year.

Yes. That was a good sign for me because at that time Doc Edwards was the manager there. He had managed against me in AAA and remembered what kind of player I was. They signed me potentially to be an everyday player and at the end of spring training [1988] they sent me down. I wound up having one of the best years of my career at Colorado Springs, and I got called up halfway through. Everything was coming together for me and I was comfortable.

You spent nine years in the major leagues, none of which were full seasons. You showed a lot of heart by never giving up your dream of playing in the big leagues.

Everybody hears about the All-Stars and great players, and with the media today, baseball players are brought into everybody's living rooms all the time. For me the guys who aren't as recognizable and aren't the guys who have the multimillion dollar contracts really have the same amount of stories and heartache in trying to become a major league player as the other guys. Those guys are the backbone of baseball. The guys who you never hear of are the fabric of the game.

Have you ever been back to Yankee Stadium?

You know what we did? We came back and I brought my youngest son, who had never seen me play there. In fact my oldest son was only a baby, so he can't really say he saw me play there either. We saw the Yanks play the Angels in July [2008]. I called Bobby Meacham, who I'm still good friends with, and he told me that it was kind of a zoo the last 20 or 30 home games.

Joe Torre was your first manager with the 1982 Braves. You only had a few brief call-ups under him, but are you surprised that here it is 26 years later and he's managing in the playoffs?

He had a great demeanor to be a manager. At the time I was kind of new to the whole thing and I just went out and tried to play. I had only been a professional player for two to three years. But he was laid back and he knew his baseball. It doesn't surprise me that he's hung in as long as he has and did so well with the Yankees. It's very interesting to see him go to L.A. and now he's in the championship. You have to tip your hat to him.

After retiring as a player in 1991 you continued your baseball career as a coach and manager with a lot of success.

Baseball America named me best managerial prospect. I was on the fast track, you could say. Managing in the minors was something I really enjoyed doing, I had always had pretty good people skills and used to substitute teach in the off-season. I enjoyed that teaching-coaching thing and it was a good fit for me. I managed in AAA for a couple of years and coached in the big leagues for the Rockies for a year. My kids just got to the age where they were hitting middle school. The last year I managed was 1998 and I was gone for seven months. When I added up all the days here and there, I was with my family for all of 60 days. My kids were at an age where they need their dad around. When I retired my farm director's secretary told me, "I admire that. You're giving up something you love for someone you love." That was it in a nutshell.

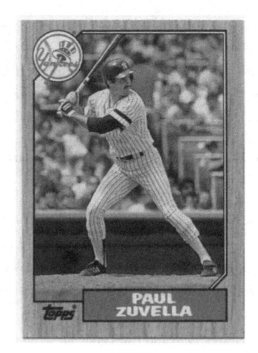

TOPPS

Zuvella, Paul
Born: October 31, 1958 San Mateo, California
Bats: Right Throws: Right
Height: 6' 0" Weight: 178

Year	Team	G	AB	H	2B	3B	HR	AVG	RBI	R
1982	Braves	2	1	0	0	0	0	.000	0	0
1983	Braves	3	5	0	0	0	0	.000	0	0
1984	Braves	11	25	5	1	0	0	.200	1	2
1985	Braves	81	190	48	8	1	0	.253	4	16
1986	YANKEES	21	48	4	1	0	0	.083	2	2
1987	YANKEES	14	34	6	0	0	0	.176	0	2
1988	Indians	51	130	30	5	1	0	.231	7	9
1989	Indians	24	58	16	2	0	2	.276	6	10
1991	Royals	2	0	0	0	0	0	.---	0	0
	Total 9 Years	209	491	109	17	2	2	.222	20	41

National Basebll Hall of Fame

BOB BROWER
1989

231

You were born in Queens, New York, and raised there and on Long Island before eventually moving to Virginia. That's Mets country. Where you a Met fan?

Yes, but I was also a Mickey Mantle fan. I got to meet him through one of my uncles somewhere outside the stadium. I was swayed to be a Mets fan by my cousins, who lived in Brooklyn. Back then Mickey Mantle was the guy and we used to flip the trading cards and lay them out in our spokes. That's why the cards are so high—if we only knew what we know now.

Did you play a lot growing up prior to high school?

You know what? I grew up in a neighborhood where there were a lot of kids and I had two brothers and we just played all the time. Having an older brother helped, trying to keep up with him and his friends. I think the first time I ever played in a game was when his team was short a player and they asked me to play, and I came out of the stands and played.

You attended James Madison High School in Virginia, where you were a four-sport player: baseball, basketball, track, and football.

Yeah. [Laughs] I played that fourth sport my senior year.

That senior year, the only year that you played football, you scored 20 touchdowns!

I had a pretty good year.

Were baseball scouts looking at you by the end of high school?

You know, I was about a .330 hitter but I never worked at baseball, I just played it. I played a lot of basketball in high school and that's pretty much what I did with my free time. I wasn't very serious about baseball back then. There was a guy named Syd Thrift who was from my hometown and was the GM of the Yankees when I played for them. He made a comment in the paper that of all the people from northern Virginia, if I were to sign a pro contract out of high school, he thought I would be in the big leagues in three years.

After high school you moved on to Duke University and played both football and baseball. At some point you gave up football to concentrate on baseball. How did that come about?

I went there on a football scholarship. I had some scholarship [offers] in basketball and some in baseball, not much, but the football really opened up and all of a sudden everybody on the East Coast just rushed in.

Part of the agreement was that if I played football I would be allowed to play baseball. In my sophomore year we had a change in coaching and [the new coach] started leveraging not playing baseball and made it uncomfortable. He actually didn't play me my sophomore year very much and that kind of soured me a little bit on football, that coaching staff. In my junior year I came back [to football] and was the starting tailback, but five games into the season got hurt when I cracked some ribs. In baseball that year I just had a breakout year. I went to Alaska and played with some of the best players in the country on the Nashua Miners [collegiate baseball]. I got to see guys who were the best players in the country and said, you know what? I'm a better athlete than any one of these guys and the only reason that I'm hitting .280 and they're hitting .320 is because this is what they do. I just do it part-time and never work at it.

In 1981 you led the nation in triples with 11.

In '81 it was one of those years—there were four school records that I broke and two [Southeastern Conference] records that I broke. The game just opened up for me, and I could start doing things on a level that I liked. Then I go to Alaska and see there really, really good players, and the only difference between me and them is that they do it all the time. I've got to commit myself all the time.

Did it surprise you when you went undrafted at the end of your college career?

Yes, but the draft wasn't a real big thing back then. My junior year I didn't get drafted, my senior year I didn't get drafted, and yeah, I was down. Especially after giving up football my senior year, I was bummed out. My college coach called my one day and said that I was pouting. I told him yes and he said, "Stop pouting. Do you want to play? Because I'm going to make some phone calls." He came back with one team, the Mets, but then said they have too many athletic outfielders. He called me back again and asked, "How about the Texas Rangers?" I didn't know anything about the Texas Rangers or even what league they were in. I'd never read a box score in my life. He knew somebody that knew somebody and the next thing I know I'm off to Sarasota, Florida. Mr. Tom Grieve, who was a coach back then, picked me up at the airport. I had two big, full duffle bags and I was two weeks late [for spring training] and I get in the car and he's mad. I get in the front of this station wagon and he's mad and starts grunting that he's got 12 outfielders, I'm two and a half weeks late, I'm a senior, and that he doesn't need this. He told me that chances are I'll be back in the car in two days. [Laughs] Actually, it was perfect because that's what you don't tell me. It lit the fire so that instead of being nervous, now I'm pissed.

He brings me back and I'm late and the players are already working out. Paul Raybone, a bald-headed old black man who just shuffled along, gave me this uniform. It was powder-blue pants and a red T-shirt and there's no elastic in my pants. I put it on and go out and tell him, "Mr. Raybone, I can't go out there looking like this." He looks at me and says, "Boy, what the f*** do you think this is? This ain't the big leagues—this is the bush leagues!" Then he says, "Yeah, you're right," and laughs and gets me another pair of pants.

I walked out there and everybody looks at me and is just sizing me up. Tom Grieve threw me into the BP session against the pitching machine. I'd never even picked up a wood bat before. Cecil Brim is hitting before me and never hit a ball out of the cage. So I'm getting a little nervous and go and pick up the biggest bat I see. It's a huge U1 with no handle; it was a big old log. I get in there and say, I'm just going to put the bat head out on the ball. On like the third or forth swing I hit a ball dead out to right center field. No one had hit one out in a while and I ended up hitting two or three balls out and had a good round. Right after that [Grieve] says that we were going to run and he made a race with four or five guys. We raced and I did good. At the end of the day he grabbed me and said, "We're going to sign you." He gave me a contract with no bonus and I said, "No signing bonus?" [Laughs] He goes, "Nope. This is your chance. You either take it or you don't." I started from the bottom.

In 1982 they sent you to the Gulf Coast League. You steadily worked your way up the Rangers minor league system, twice stealing over 50 bases in a season. By 1986 you were playing for Oklahoma City AAA and scored an amazing 130 runs in 140 games. How satisfied were you with your progress?

With me I did it year-round. I played in the Instructional League two years, Mexico a year, in the Dominican Republic a year. Basically for four or five years I played year-round. I could start seeing some progress, definitely. I knew there was nothing else to prove in the minors. In the big leagues, though, you need sponsorship. You need coaches that like you. When I got up there the Rangers had their outfield—[manager] Bobby Valentine had his guys in the outfield—and I wasn't one of them.

After your September call-up in '86 you had a nice season in 1987, hitting .261 with 14 homeruns and 15 stolen bases. On July 21 you became one of the few players in history to hit an inside-the-park grandslam. What can you recall from that game?

Yeah, the pitcher was Eric Plunk and he had walked the bases loaded. What happened was, Pete Incaviglia had left because his daughter was born and I was scratched into the lineup to start. Eric comes out. He throws a hundred miles an hour and here I come thinking, OK, great. He throws me two curve balls and I'm 0–2. He tries to throw me another one and I just hit it to the right center gap. Louie Polonia dove and missed it.

It seemed like you were on your way now, but you didn't have a very good year in 1988.

What happened was, we were in New York and I think it was on July Fourth. I went to break up a double play with Wayne Tolleson and I had to dive to the inside of the bag. The combination of my shoulder hitting the bag and him diving back, he tore my labrum. The Ranger doctors misdiagnosed it and told me it was just tendonitis. They injected me and I made it through the season.

In January Scott Boras called me and I told him that I can't even brush my hair. He said, "What?" and before you know it I'm in [Dr.] Andrews' office. He told me I had a torn labrum. We scoped it in January [1988]. The thing that kind of cut my chord with Bobby Valentine was I had the surgery and didn't call him. It was me, Scott Boras, and Tom Grieve on the phone and we decided to do it right away. When I came back [Valentine] was pissed at me and didn't give me the time of day after that. I just wanted a chance to play and he would find a reason not to play me. After my shoulder got better, during '88 my elbow started hurting from throwing differently because of the shoulder and then I pulled a calf muscle.

On December 5, 1988, the Rangers traded you to New York for Bobby Meacham. How did you feel about coming to the Yankees?

When they traded me I was basically damaged goods. If I had been healthy then we would be talking a different story here. New York is a good place for me and if I had played healthy it would have been great. I basically played in pain until June with a blown elbow, until I checked a swing against Randy Johnson and I just walked back and said to Dallas, "I'm done. I can't pick up a bat anymore."

They took me off the roster and sent me down and told me to just rest, when I really just should have had the surgery right then. I went down to Columbus for ten days and I was just supposed to DH and rest. They put me in the outfield and I said, this is just crazy. I had Tommy John surgery then by Dr. Andrews.

It was a shame because the Yankees told me that I was going to be their center fielder, but deep down in my heart I knew something was the matter with my elbow. The Yankee front office basically told me, "This is yours," and it was killing me because it was like I had a knife in my elbow. Winnie [Winfield] was out that whole year with his back. I made the team that spring [1989], but stayed in extended spring rehabbing along with Wayne Tolleson. I had a slight pull in my groin.

Your first game as a Yankee came on April 16 against the Twins at Yankee Stadium. Even though you had played there as a Ranger, did you have any special feeling putting on a Yankee uniform and walking out onto the field at Yankee Stadium?

Oh, absolutely. When you put on your first major league uniform it's a special feeling, but when you put on a Yankee uniform it is an awesome feeling, and a lot of pride. With me growing up in New York there were other intangibles, like my family that lived in New York. It's very special, and remember my story of coming from nothing and to work your way all the way up. The biggest thing for me was I wanted to play every day and help that team win. I played against Dykstra coming up and we had a very similar game, but I thought my game was more controlled and high energy.

Your second game as a Yankee was played at the old Exhibition Stadium in Toronto. You hit a home run off Cy Young winner Mike Flanagan. New York swept Toronto in that three-game series and you went 5 for 10. That was a nice way to start your pinstripe career.

Yes, and again, it's about playing. It's about getting in there and getting settled in and playing.

How did you find playing for Dallas Green?

I loved Dallas. I'm the kind of guy that likes those hard-core, tough coaches. You always want a pat on the back and I truly looked up to him and wanted to play for him. There was some good and bad with him, I thought. But you know, some of that stuff, like standing on the foul line during infield [practice] with his arms crossed watching us— I don't know if that was an intimidation thing but I thought it was kind of strange or different, especially when your elbow is hurting.

I was in the clubhouse for our first meeting with Dallas Green. There was Tommy John, Righetti, Guidry—you know, a bunch of old guys—and I was excited to be a Yankee. It was spring training and I was ready to go, and then Dallas comes in and basically said, "We're not a very good team, but if you follow me and we do this together we can do this, we have a chance." I remember thinking, yeah, alright, let's go. He had me. Then he left and some of the veterans started calling him Moses—you know, "Follow me." It was liked they poisoned it and from then you knew the season was going to be screwed up because the veterans weren't on the same page as Dallas. I was like, let's go, and the veterans were the opposite. I was shocked by that.

This may have been the only team that you were a member of during your career that you were not the fastest man on the club. The '89 Yankees had Rickey Henderson [77 steals] and Steve Sax [43 steals].

My legs were my gift. I brought my legs every day. I could run. Rickey and I lockered next to each other, but I wasn't there long enough to get to know [my teammates]. I kind of ran with Mattingly a little bit more. He was more of my cup of tea, a little laid back. Donnie wasn't an overpowering guy physically, but his work ethic was very focused. He was very professional about what he did. Although I did sit on Rickey Henderson's glasses one day. Back then most guys had those flip-down glasses, but he just had a pair of Ray-Ban wire-frame designer glasses. I remember everybody teasing him [about them] during the games. Somehow he left them on the bench and I sat on them by accident. Well, I got an earful of "Rickey": "You sat on Rickey's glasses. You broke Rickey's glasses. What's Rickey gonna do without his glasses?" [Laughs] I told him, "You tell Rickey I'm sorry." He was good; we did talk baseball a lot. In spring training he took tape and made a square around his locker and reporters weren't allowed to step inside of it.

The problem with that team—and again, I came in as an outsider—was that we were a terrible team. We ended up with one of the worst records for a Yankee team ever in '89. The other thing I remember about the Yankees was the reporters in the locker room. The reporters outnumbered the players and I thought it was crazy because it wasn't our locker room. It was a public locker room and I thought that wasn't healthy for the team. Everybody used to go back to the trainer's room or the room where they ate and they'd hide back there. They just never let the team be alone.

In 1990 you came back and played 66 games in Columbus. What happened to your career after that?

I was rehabbing and went back to Columbus, but at the end of those 66 games I had surgery again on the same elbow. I had a lot of pain and they opened it up again. They called it a neuroma, which was all the nerves were bundled back in a ball.

I missed all of 1991 and then in '92 I went down to Florida with George Mason University and worked out with the team, coached first base, wore their uniform, and took infield with them. In the mornings I'd drive to all the minor league ballparks and introduce myself to the farm directors and say, "I'm healthy and looking to play again." This is what I had to do to get a job. I went to eight teams and they all said no. The ninth team was Doug Melvin with Baltimore. At first he said no, but I challenged him and he gave me a chance. I told him to get all of his guys out here and I'll run, hit, and throw against them, and if any of them do anything better than me I'll leave. He looked at me and said, "I just love your attitude. I'll give you a locker but you're probably not going to get signed." During spring training the Rangers offered me to be their starting center fielder at AAA for $3000 or more a month. So I went back with the Rangers and played at Oklahoma City in '92. After that, though, it was just time.

After your playing career you stayed in the game in a unique way. You went to work for agent Scott Boras.

Scott represented me when I played. After I finished playing I went to work back at Duke University as an intern in their athletic department for $18,000, then decided that that's not what I wanted to do. He called me and asked me to go look at a player and I did. After that we just kept talking and he asked me if I wanted to come and work with him. I think I was his third employee. He has probably 60–70 now.

You're now his vice president.

I am one of them, yes. I oversee the amateur draft, but I also take care of numerous clients that I brought into the company. I think we have on any given day about 65–70 major leaguers and about 60 minor leaguers. The thing that people hear is the names and they think we're this big, gigantic company. We are not a very big company; it's just that our players are really successful. We had eight guys on the All-Star team [in 2008]. It has its moments. You have your good and your bad.

Have you gotten back to Yankee Stadium since you retired as a player?

Actually, I don't think I've been back to Yankee Stadium. I'm the kind of guy who was never in awe of where I was. When I was with the Yankees it was great but I wasn't in awe of it—I didn't have time to be. I could be sitting there talking to George Brett or Don Mattingly and I was like, OK, this is cool, instead of trying to get pictures taken with those guys. It would be nice to see [new Yankee Stadium] one of these days.

Bowman/TOPPS

BROWER, ROBERT RICHARD
Born: January 10, 1960 Jamaica, New York
Bats: Right Throws: Right
Height: 5' 11" Weight: 185

Year	Team	G	AB	H	2B	3B	HR	AVG	RBI	R
1986	Rangers	21	9	1	1	0	0	.111	0	3
1987	Rangers	127	303	79	10	3	14	.261	46	63
1988	Rangers	82	201	45	7	0	1	.224	11	29
1989	YANKEES	26	69	16	3	0	2	.232	3	9
	Total 4 Years	256	582	141	21	3	17	.242	60	104

National Baseball Hall of Fame

CLAY PARKER
1989–90

You were born in Columbia, Louisiana, and grew up in Pistolthicket. I guess you were not a Yankee fan?

Well, not really. I lived in a very rural area and we had only two channels that we could pick up on TV. New York was a long way from Pistolthicket, Louisiana. I'll tell you what—I did become a Yankees fan however in the mid '70s. Ron Guidry being from Louisiana caught my attention and through the newspaper and *Sports Illustrated* I would keep up with the Yankees and particularly Ron as often as I could.

In high school you were an all-around athlete. All-State in track and football and you won a state javelin championship. You were on the baseball team, too, I suppose.

Yeah, I played high school baseball. As a pitcher and shortstop I had a really good arm. I quarterbacked on the football team, threw the javelin, and pitched on the baseball team. It was during that time that I developed some pretty serious arm problems. For a certain time of the year, mainly early spring, I would go to football practice and throw the football, then go to baseball practice and do whatever, and maybe even play a game, and then I would get a little bit of throwing the javelin in. I just really overworked my arm doing all three. In hindsight that was really a dumb thing to do.

I started having some big-time shoulder problems right before my senior baseball season. Two doctors told me not to pitch ever again because there were some shoulder issues there. I had a third opinion who told me to take a couple of weeks off and then see how it feels and then come back and try [pitching]. I did that and I was clocked as high as 92 miles an hour in my first game back. I thought things were fine and then, being young and invincible, I went back to throwing the football and javelin during baseball season and that was the beginning of my long-term shoulder problems. That led to me favoring my elbow, which eventually led to the career-ending Tommy John surgery.

After attracting a lot of attention you wound up at Louisiana State University on a football scholarship and played in the 1983 Orange Bowl and the 1985 Sugar Bowl for the LSU Tigers.

Yeah, there was never a time in my life that I couldn't punt a football and punt it very well. I knew that I was going to do that in college, and if my arm would allow me to pitch, I was also going to do that as well. The LSU baseball coach was very well aware that I could pitch at that level and I gutted it out, really. I still had arm problems at LSU that would continue throughout my baseball career. I was able to get by for a few short years in the big leagues. It was a situation where I went from having a good arm, where I could throw a football 70 yards or a javelin over 200 feet or a baseball 90-plus miles per hour—at one time I could do that. Again, through my feeling of invincibility at a young age I certainly overdid it. To this day I still have arm problems, but I can go out and have a catch with my kids now. What I had to do for my career was learn how to pitch. I got nowhere near the fastball that I had at 18–19 years old, so if I'm going to have a career in baseball I've got to learn the finer points of pitching. I really became a student of the game and was able to get by with a mediocre at best fastball.

You said that you were a punter at LSU, not a quarterback.

I was a punter at LSU. They did take me as a quarterback. However, after my freshman year it was agreed that I would be the punter and an emergency quarterback. Quarterbacking would have been a year-round job for me, and playing baseball would not allow that. I realized that these guys were better quarterbacks than I was, and I'm not willing to give up baseball just to try and compete with them as long as I could punt and be a part of the team, which I enjoyed tremendously.

Did you prefer baseball over football?

I think so. I felt so much more in control as a pitcher than a punter. Although playing in front of 75–80,000 fans on Saturday nights—that's pretty thrilling, even though I was just the punter.

Upon graduating you were offered a three-year contract with the Dallas Cowboys.

Yes, and that was pretty tough to turn down, but at that time I just felt that I needed to give baseball a shot. I remember sitting in Ruth's Chris Steak House and seeing this contract laid out in front of me. It was contingent on me making the team. In hindsight I'm not sure that it was a smart thing to do, with my arm being in the shape that it was. I don't know if it was something that I needed to prove to myself, but again, I loved baseball more than football and my dream was to play in the major leagues.

In 1984 you were drafted by the Twins in the 21st round but did not sign. Was that to stay in college?

Yes, it was to play my senior year of football. At that time I was still undecided if I wanted to play baseball or football at the next level.

The following year, in 1985, the Mariners took you in the 15th round and you signed.

Yes. There had been some talk that I would go much higher, but I think as the scouts would see the inconsistency in my velocity, that played into it. I certainly don't blame them, because I would come out throwing 90–92 one game; then I'd be 84–85 the next. That was pretty much it for my career, how the arm would come and go.

The Mariners sent you right away to Bellingham, Washington, rookie ball. You pitched in 10 games that first year and went 6–1 with a 1.55 ERA and had 69 strikeouts to just 16 walks.

Yeah, that was pretty easy. At that point I was learning how to use my stuff, how to pitch and set up hitters.

The next two years you progressed quickly through AA and AAA and received a September call-up to the Mariners in '87. Do you remember being told that you were going to the big leagues?

Oh yes. That was a dream come true.

Do you remember who told you?

Yeah, Bill Plumber, who was my manager, and Ross Grimsley, the pitching coach for the Calgary Cannons. I had a very good year at AA and continued to have a good year at AAA. There had been a lot of talk that I'd get called up. I tried to put it out of my mind as much as I could. It was a dream come true. All the hard work since I was eight years old came to a head at that moment.

Were you surprised at how quickly you got up to the majors?

No, I really wasn't. I was disappointed that my arm didn't hold out longer. When I signed out of LSU I knew that I could do it, but it was a matter of having an arm healthy enough to allow me to. Once I got to A ball and then AA, where Dan Warthen was my pitching coach at Chattanooga, I really started turning pitching into a chess match. I would think two or three pitches ahead. It really became fun for me. Now obviously it didn't work out for every pitch and every batter, but I had an idea what I wanted to do every time every batter stepped up to the plate.

Your career in Seattle lasted three games. On December 22, 1987, you were traded to the Yankees with Lee Gueterman and Wade Taylor for Steve Trout and Henry Cotto. How did you feel about coming to New York?

At first I didn't want to leave [Seattle]. I had developed a lot of friendships and thought I could pitch in Seattle and do well. But when it was the Yankees, I thought that this was the opportunity of a lifetime and this doesn't come around too often. So I was very excited to go to the Yankees.

Had you ever been to New York before?

No. The first time I was in New York was as a New York Yankee.

In 1988 the Yankees kept you at Columbus, where you only appeared in ten games. Was that part of the injuries?

Well, I went to winter ball down in Venezuela and on the first road trip, we went to this town where their mound was absolutely horrible. I was the fifth pitcher to come away with an injury on that mound that season, a very short season. It was like pitching off of a three-foot-high mound and your stride was probably six inches longer because of the steepness of the mound. I was told before the game to be careful of this mound because four guys had gotten injuries, and sure enough, in the first inning I blow my right groin. It was a pretty serious pull. That was the winter of '87 and I was still feeling the pull in spring in '89 and would have to get it wrapped up.

The Yankees started me at AAA and I pitched the opening game and I blew my groin out. Then I would try to come back a week or two or three later and I would blow it out again. In June of that year they shut me down and said, "Look, it's just going to take more time than we thought."

You started the 1989 season at Columbus and went 3–0 with a 1.66 ERA before you were recalled in May. What was it like walking out onto the field at Yankee Stadium wearing a Yankees uniform for the first time?

Hard to describe. I'll tell you that I will never forget it, but I don't know if I could describe it. The feeling of "I made it; this is it." Then I quickly realized that I don't want to leave here, that I'm going to bust my tail and do the very best that I can and stay healthy and pitch a long time here, and help this team get back to its winning ways.

Dallas Green was still the manager when you got called up. Did he say anything to you?

I really liked Dallas. I thought Dallas was a very good manager. I thought his departure was premature, but we were struggling during those couple of years during the late '80s and early '90s. I enjoyed playing for Dallas Green. At the time when I got called up, John Candelaria had gone down with an injury. My first day there I was part of the team and Dallas told me, "I'm glad you're here and I know that you'll do well and now let's go out and win some games."

Your first game for the Yankees came on Tuesday night, May 16, at the Oakland Coliseum. You started and went seven innings while picking up your first major league win.

Yeah, it was a good team we played against and the Yankees had been struggling against Oakland, so it came at a pretty good time. The Yankees needed a good outing out of me and I put the ball where I needed to with some pretty decent stuff on it. I think we won 3–2. From there we flew up to Seattle and I had another good game. I pitched a complete game and struck out ten, and things were going pretty well.

You were a member of the Yankees at a strange time. Their 87 and 95 losses in 1988 and '89 were the most for consecutive years since 1912 and '13. What do you think the problem was in the late '80s?

[Laughs] I didn't realize that. I knew we were struggling. If I had been there during the good times maybe I could have pinpointed something. For the most part I just think other teams were better than us. I don't think it was one thing like managing, coaching, or hitting, or pitching.

Don Slaught was the starting catcher and by that time he was a veteran catcher. How was he to throw to as a young pitcher?

Yeah, he was good. Donnie was a good catcher who knew the game. I probably threw as much to Bob Geren, who I'd pitched to at AAA and who was called up at about the same time I was. I think with the familiarity that he had with me initially, he caught the majority of my games.

Amazingly the Yankees only had one pitcher with more than seven wins in '89: Andy Hawkins, who was 15–15 in 208 innings.

That's Andy. He was a very quiet leader that you could count on going out there. I don't think he ever had any arm problems. Every fifth day you could count on the fact that he was going to be out there. Good or bad, he was going to give you some innings. When I came up I pitched very well for my first seven starts for the Yankees and had actually worked my way up to the number two starter behind Andy Hawkins.

The 1989 Yankees had a lot of veteran pitchers who were winding down their careers, including Tommy John, Goose Gossage, Dave LaPoint, Rich Dotson, and John Candelaria. Did you take anything from being around those guys?

Oh, I think there was something to learn from all those guys. Watching Dave LaPoint, who was a left-hander, work the batters as he did. Rich Dotson had a very similar approach to the game as I did, so I tried to pick his brain as much as I could.

Did you get to know the captain at all?

Yeah, it was a pleasure to play on the same team as Don Mattingly. Anytime that I was on the mound and I could look over my left shoulder and see him playing first base, I realized that it was a pretty good thing going here. A tremendous leader. His work ethic and intensity were incredible. Unfortunately, at that time he was starting to develop some lower-back problems and that affected his swing and it affected his play, but he was out there giving it everything he had every single day.

In 1989 and '90 Steve Balboni, who had come up with the Yankees in 1981, was back with the team. Steve was always known as being a classic all-or-nothing swinger.

[Laughs] He was a funny guy. It seemed like more times than most he would come through in the clutch. Yeah, there were times when he would go 0 for 4 with three strikeouts, but when we really needed him to come through he'd put the ball out of the park.

On August 16, 1989, Dallas Green was fired as Yankee manager and replaced by Bucky Dent. Did that surprise you?

Yeah, it did, but there had been talk prior to then that there would be a change, and as a player you realize that so many things are out of your control. You always knew where you stood with Dallas, and I respected him for that—there was no question that Dallas was running the show. I think he would have done a good long-term job with the Yankees, but at that point the upper management decided that a change needed to be made. I knew Bucky from AAA, where he was my manager, so he was a familiar face. All of us as players realize that whoever is manager, you have to go out and give it everything you have.

The Yankees finished in fifth place with a 74–87 record. Did you think that you would be back for 1990?

Oh yeah. After beginning the season as a starter, they moved me to the bullpen, where, after some of the arm problems, I finished strong. I think they were looking at me as one of those guys who could start and long relieve.

If 1989 was a bad year for the Yankees, 1990 was horrific. The team finished in seventh place (last) with a 67–95 record. The team batting average was just .241 and an injured Don Mattingly dropped to .256. Tim Leary finished with a 9–19 record only because the manager sat him down for his last couple of starts in order to avoid the possibility of him losing 20 games. How was Bucky Dent coping with this?

It was just a tough time. [Laughs] It was tough to be a manager, a coach, and a player. When you're losing more games than winning that's not a good thing, especially as a New York Yankee. When things are going bad it's hard not to expect bad things to happen. It's frustrating. You've got to do something to right that ship, and I think that's why Bucky was brought on.

On July 4, 1990, you were traded to the Tigers with Lance McCullers for Matt Nokes. By this time did you see this as your ticket out of New York?

Not really, because I wasn't ready to jump ship. I didn't care how bad things were going; I thought I could help out. Going to the Tigers was not high on my list, but once I got there I was surrounded by wonderful human beings. I had great teammates, with Frank Tanana at the top of that list. Sparky Anderson managed the team. I wasn't there long, but long enough to make some really good friends.

Did you ever meet George Steinbrenner?

Oh, I did. He was in the clubhouse one day that I was the starting pitcher and he came up behind me and put his hand on my shoulder and said, "We really need a good game out of you today." [Laughs]

No pressure!

Yeah. [Laughs]

When Stump Merrill was hired to replace Dent during the 1990 season, it was the 17th managerial change under Steinbrenner since his ownership began in 1973. That's 17 changes in 17 years! Did you get a sense that there may have been too much uncertainty or chaos with all the players, coaches, and managers coming and going constantly, or that maybe Steinbrenner was too involved with the day-to-day operation of the team?

I think that any very successful businessman, when things go bad you become impatient and yes, I would certainly put Mr. George Steinbrenner in that category of being impatient. Looking for results now, and "If you guys can't do the job I'll find somebody else that can."

What happened to your career after 1990?

I went back to the Mariners and I had arm surgery in '92. I had no business playing ball at this time and I had the surgery and I *still* had no business playing ball. I rehabbed for three years. I wanted to be absolutely certain that when I walked away from the game, I had given it all that I could. After not playing in '93 and '94 I tried to come back in '95. That was the lockout year after the strike. I signed a AAA contract with the New Orleans Zephers. I had to prove it to myself that it was done, and that would make it easier to walk away from the game. I couldn't pitch; there was a pain and a numbness every time that I threw the baseball. I have permanent nerve damage in the elbow. I have the mentality that the harder I work the better it's going to get, but with an injury like this it didn't matter. By that time we had two kids—we have four now—so it made it easier to walk away from the game that I loved since I could walk.

Have you ever been back to Yankee Stadium since you retired as a player?

Went back this summer [2008], yes. I took my kids for the very first time. We went back in June. Dave Eiland, who is the pitching coach now, is a former teammate of mine. I talked to Dave and it was good to see him. We watched the Yankees beat the Padres. Pettitte pitched a wonderful game and Mo came in and closed it, and A-Rod and Giambi went deep. My two boys are big baseball and big Yankee fans, and I had fun just watching them take it all in.

Any Yankee story that I may have missed?

I think one of the highlights is Old-Timers' Day, when I've got the same uniform as Joe DiMaggio, Mickey Mantle, Whitey Ford, Catfish Hunter, and all these guys are walking around the same clubhouse. It doesn't get any better than that.

The other one and probably the biggest highlight was having President Nixon actually introduce himself to me. I had pitched the day before and I got to the ballpark really early. Arthur Richman, our P.R. Director, comes in the clubhouse and I just happen to glance up and I give Arthur a wave, Then I noticed someone behind him that just kind of disappeared into Dallas Green's office. I thought, gosh it looked so much like President Nixon. I was the only player there and was about to do some extra running when they came back out and sure enough, it was Arthur Richman and President Nixon. Arthur comes over with the president right behind him and he says, "Mr. President I'd like to introduce you to one of our players." The president holds his hand out and says, "Clay Parker, that was a great game you pitched last night." It was really neat—he had seen me pitch the day before. That's a memory that I'll never forget, obviously.

I would have loved to have played for 10 or 15 years, but I'm very blessed to have played for as long as I did. That's how I sum up my career. Having played for the New York Yankees was absolutely incredible.

TOPPS

PARKER, JAMES CLAYTON
Born: December 19, 1962 Columbia, Louisiana
Bats: Right Throws: Right
Height: 6' 1" Weight: 185

Year	Team	G	W-L	SV	GS	CG	IP	SO	W	ERA
1987	Mariners	3	0-0	0	1	0	7.7	8	4	10.57
1989	YANKEES	22	4-5	0	17	2	120.0	53	31	3.68
1990	YANKEES	5	1-1	0	2	0	22.0	20	7	4.50
1990	Tigers	24	2-2	0	1	0	51.0	20	25	3.18
1992	Mariners	8	0-2	0	6	0	33.3	20	11	7.56
	Total 4 Years	62	7-10	0	27	2	234.0	121	78	4.42

1990s

National Baseball Hall of Fame

JOE AUSANIO
1994–95

You grew up in Kingston, New York. Did that make you a Yankee fan?

I actually grew up a Red Sox fan, believe it or not. There weren't too many in Kingston. I was a big Fred Lynn fan. I loved Fred Lynn.

You were drafted by the Braves in 1984 at 18 years old but did not sign.

That's right. I went to college instead.

You must have had an impressive high school career?

Yeah, I was pretty good. I threw hard and I was a two-position player. I played short and pitched. I was recruited as a pitcher for Jacksonville University. I had a good college career, but I knew that I'd be a better professional pitcher than college pitcher because of the aluminum bats. I used to give up a lot of Texas Leaguers.[72] Those would have been broken bats with wood, but with the aluminum wound up being a flare to left or right, and that would cost me. So I didn't have the most impressive college statistics, but I always threw hard. I always had a lot of strikeouts.

In 1988 you were drafted by the Pirates in the 11th round and signed. Did you think that you had a shot at making the major leagues?

You know, I always felt I had the ability to get there; it was just whether I was going to get the breaks and just have the right opportunity to set myself up to get there. I think I realized that more during my first year of professional baseball, when I was competing against all the top draft picks and was just mowing them down. That's when I really thought that I had a shot.

In your second season you led the Carolina League with 20 saves and were named the Pirates' organization Pitcher of the Year. That must have been a pretty good feeling, to get that honor so quickly.

It was. Getting drafted in the 11th round I wasn't a top, top pick, but my first couple of years in professional baseball I had successful years. I went to Watertown and led the New York-Penn League in saves that year. Then I went down to the Carolina Leagues and just had a dominating season. I just pitched really well for the first couple years of my professional career.

In 1992, then Pirates GM Ted Simmons told you that he did not think that you could pitch at the major league level.

Yes, he did.

---

72. A weak fly ball that lands between the infield and the outfield, for a single. Also called a "flare."

That was some reversal of fortune. Did you think about leaving the game at that point?

It always hurts when someone tells you that you're not good enough to pitch at the next level. I felt that I had done everything that I could to get to the next level. In 1990 I had gone to Venezuela to play winter ball and I was named the Pitcher of the Year and the Reliever of the Year—the first time that the same pitcher had garnered both awards. I was 9–1 with 12 saves and a one point something ERA, and I led the league in strikeouts as a closer. So I had an unbelievable season at Venezuela, but the Pirates were just backlogged. That was in their heyday when they had Bonds, Bonilla, Drabek, and Van Slyke. They were one of the better teams and it was just tough to break into that rotation and that bullpen.

After six years in the minors the Yankees drafted you on December 13, 1993. How did you feel about the move?

Well, I was happy because I happened to be with the Expos that year, in '93. I got Rule 5 drafted[73] by the Yankees. I knew that I would have a fresh opportunity with them. Nardi Contreras was the roving pitching instructor with the Expos. He had gone over to the Yankees and he was the one who basically told them, "We need to draft this guy." He said I was a steal.

In 1994 it all seemed to come together for you. You led Columbus AAA with 13 saves. A teammate of yours named Mariano Rivera had zero saves. Not many guys can say they had more saves than him.

No, that's right. [Laughs] Mariano and I were on the same team and I actually went into the closer role by default. I was one of those guys who had just made the team. I was in the bullpen and I would get my opportunity to pitch every once in a while. They were grooming Mark Hutton, the 6' 8" Australian guy, to be the next closer, but he just wasn't resilient enough. He couldn't pitch back-to-back nights. I stepped into the closer role and I just started closing games one after another.

You got called up in July as a 28-year-old rookie. How did you learn that you were finally going up?

Actually I was home. We were off for the All-Star break and I was cooking dinner and the phone rang. Some of the guys were over at the house because we were about to watch the major league All-Star game.

---

73. The Rule 5 draft occurs every December. The purpose of the draft is to bring young players into the majors and keep them there for at least one year, instead of being stockpiled in the minors. The idea behind the draft is that if a major league team is willing to accept a player, he should be allowed to move up to the majors.

The guys were teasing me saying, "Hey Joe, that's for you. You're going to the major leagues." Sure enough, I picked up the phone and it was Mitch Lukavitch. I'm not sure what his title was with the Yankees, but he said, "Joe, you can pack your bags, son. You're going to New York tomorrow." I just sat there. I couldn't believe it—all those years toiling in the minors to finally get that opportunity.

Had you ever been to New York City or the stadium before this?

Oh yeah, plenty of times. When I got down to New York, because it was the All-Star break, the team wasn't there. They were all gone their separate ways. I did a little workout and then walked into the clubhouse. The equipment manager, Nick Priore, came up to me and said, "You look like Goose Gossage," so he threw me 54! [Laughs] I said, "OK." I was just happy to be there. I'd take whatever they'd give me.

That evening we flew out to Seattle for a West Coast road trip. The plane was probably half full because guys were meeting the team out there coming back from All-Star break vacations.

You got to Seattle and your first game was on Thursday, July 14, 1994, at the Kingdome. Buck Showalter brought you into the game in the eighth inning with the Yankees loosing 7–6. The first batter that you faced, Dan Wilson, lined out but then two future Yankees got on when Alex Rodriguez singled and Tino Martinez walked. The Yanks got out of the inning only giving up one run and then scored seven in the ninth to win 13–8. How memorable was that?

Steve Howe came in after me and Griffey got a hit off of him and the run scored. It was memorable, but I'd say the next night was more memorable, when I got my first major league win. After the game Connors told me, "Good job." The hit that I gave up to Rodriguez was just a miscommunication between Mattingly and Pat Kelly. It was a ground ball and they both stopped and looked at each other. It should have been an out because I was over covering first base. It was just one of those things that happen. Then Martinez walked on a 3–2 pitch that was very close and could have easily gone both ways, but of course he was going to get the call before me. It wasn't a bad outing at all.

I'm going to assume you didn't yell at Don Mattingly.

[Laughs] Ah . . . no.

Your first game at Yankee Stadium came on July 26, against the Red Sox, of all teams, when you came on in relief in the eighth inning in front of about 40,000 fans. What did that feel like, walking out to the mound at the stadium wearing pinstripes?

I didn't walk, I sprinted. All I kept saying was holy ****, holy ****, holy **** as I was running in. I couldn't believe I was there. It was one of those things where I was ready before I warmed up because I was so pumped up. I had an unbelievable first inning. I blew away Otis Nixon, Tim Naehring flew out to right, and I struck out John Valentin to end the inning. It was electric. It was just an electric feeling. There were two busloads of relatives and friends and people walking around with banners. It really was amazing.

The only loss of your career came on August 11, which was the last game before the strike.

That's correct. When we were going on strike, the next day the Yankees sent me to Columbus to keep pitching. They didn't want me sitting around, because they were thinking maybe [the strike] will be a couple of weeks, and since I had options available I could go back and forth as many times as they wanted. The union actually filed a grievance on my behalf saying that the Yankees couldn't do that, and I actually ended up getting all the strike time because of that. I got paid and got all the major league time as well.

It had to be somewhat disappointing to have paid your dues all those years in the minors only to have the season end after your first month.

Yeah, it was tough. It was hard. But it was at the point where the guys were saying, "We're going to go out on strike and I'll see you in a couple of days." I just remember being ecstatic to be there. But I also knew I had to do what those guys were telling me to do. It was just very disheartening when that season got cancelled. I was so disappointed.

You were throwing the ball really well when you came up. I read that you had a fastball that really moved.

I had a good-moving fastball with decent velocity, and I threw a pretty good split-fingered fastball. It was just one of those things where I was in the wrong place at the wrong time. But it was the right place at the right time as well, because I don't regret anything. Just the fact that I had the opportunity—a lot of people can never say that. The fact that I was able to get four major league wins and only one major league loss and a save—even though it was a whirlwind it was still an amazing experience I'll never forget.

Jimmy Key was 17–4 in that strike-shortened season. How impressive was he?[74]

He wasn't impressive—he was just masterful. It wasn't like when you saw him throw you went, "Wow, this guy is unbelievable!" He just knew how to pitch and he knew how to get himself out of jams. He would spot his fastball and he would throw his changeup in any count. He was the epitome of a pitcher. He knew how to pitch. I was a thrower. I would just go out there and try to blow you away, but he would outthink you. He would show you a little something and then freeze you with a fastball.

After the 1994 season did the Yankees tell you anything about their plans for you?

No. The only thing I remember is that I had hurt my knee in the off-season and I had to have surgery. I got myself back into shape before spring training, hoping that there would be a spring training. I was pitching unbelievable in spring training. I was having a great spring training. Then the Yankees made the trade for John Wetteland, and I remember sitting in my locker crying and thinking, I'm in trouble now. I mean, they're bringing this guy in and they have Howe, Wetteland, Wickman, and they don't need me anymore. That's how I felt. Buck Showalter came up to me and said, "Absolutely not. You're in our plans and we're going to bring you to New York with us." So I felt a little bit better, but I felt that it was taken away from me with the strike, and now here's John Wetteland, one of the best closers in the big leagues.

You came back in 1995 and had a good season. By the end of your second season your pitching record stood at 4–1 with one save. Were you surprised when the Yankees granted you free agency on October 15, 1995?

I was, but I wasn't. Because when they fired Showalter I figured that there was going to be a bunch of us who were in trouble—those of us who were so-called fringe players, players who were possibly going to help the team and possibly not going to be there may be gone. Joe Torre was going to bring in guys he wanted and I was resigned to the fact that that was possibly going to happen.

Speaking about that, you were with the Yankees at a strange time. The team, especially the pitching staff, was changing dramatically.

---

74. In 1994 David Cone of the Kansas City Royals was chosen over Jimmy Key for the American League Cy Young Award for best pitcher of the year. Cone had 16 wins and 5 losses to Key's 17 wins and 4 losses.

The 1994 starting staff was Jimmy Key, Jim Abbott, Melido Perez, Terry Mulholland, and Scott Kamieniecki. Steve Howe was the closer, with just 15 saves. By 1996 fans wouldn't recognize the staff.[75] With the changeover in the manager and coaches, you sensed these changes coming, it sounds like.

Well, yeah. Obviously when a new regime comes in they're going to make changes, even though we did pretty well. It just didn't add up for the people who were in charge, is all.

When you signed with the Mets after the 1995 season did you view that as a better opportunity for you?

I had offers from three teams: the Mets, A's, and the Rockies. The A's and the Mets were my two biggest pursuers. The thing with the Mets was, I lived in New York and I had played in New York, so I said to myself, would I rather be in Oakland or New York? I wasn't thinking minor leagues, I was thinking major leagues. So the next best thing would be the New York Mets if I couldn't play for the Yankees. I think I may have had a better opportunity with the A's, but for me it was all about the convenience of being closer to home.

I was unbelievably surprised when they sent me down to Norfolk [AAA], because if you look at the statistics, I didn't give up a run in spring training. I only gave up one hit in nine innings. I was absolutely just mowing people down and I said to myself, "I'm making this team." It sucked because I was pitching really well. Even Dallas Green, when he sent me down, said, "I have to tell you, you surprised a lot of us." At that point, though, I didn't want to hear that, because I knew I gave myself every opportunity to make that team.

You played during Don Mattingly's final two seasons. Did you get to know him at all?

I did. I got to know Donnie and he was always available to give advice. He wouldn't just give it, but if you went and asked he would be there for you. I think leading quietly is a good way to describe him. He was great to me and I'm just really grateful that I had the opportunity to play with him.

Did you live at home during your time with the Yanks?

I actually did, I would go home sometimes. Kingston is only 90 miles from the stadium; it's not that bad of a drive. My sister lived in Rockland County [closer than Kingston], so I would stay with her as well.

---

75. During 1995 the Yankees acquired David Cone and Wetteland and brought up Mariano Rivera and Andy Pettitte. After the '95 season they acquired Jeff Nelson, Kenny Rogers, and Dwight Gooden.

On the road I roomed with either Dave Silvestri, Russ Davis, or Sterling Hitchcock, and Andy Pettitte a couple of times.

Most of the time you threw to Mike Stanley, who was a veteran catcher. How good was he to work with for a new major league pitcher?

He was real good. A lot of times he wouldn't let me shake him off though. That would be frustrating, because you still want to throw what you want to throw, but a lot of times he would have a better idea of some of the major league hitters than I, so I'd just go with what he said.

Dave Eiland is now the Yankee pitching coach. Did he seem like someone who would wind up being in charge of the staff someday?

Dave was also one of my roommates. He was always a very good teacher and just an overall student of the game. He and I would talk strategy. Dave Eiland was a very good pitcher. He was another guy who was very masterful in getting hitters out. He would do it in different ways, with backdoor sliders, and just freeze left-handers. I learned a lot by watching Dave pitch.

You stayed in the game after your retirement, I see.

Yeah, after a couple of years working in the cellular industry I went to work locally for the Hudson Valley Renegades [Class A]. We've been with the Tampa Rays for a number of years now.

Any special Yankee memory?

I think when you talk about Mattingly, one of my most amazing moments in my career was when Mattingly hit the home run against the Seattle Mariners in game 2 of the 1995 AL playoffs. The place—I never heard Yankee Stadium like that ever. I just remember all the fans in right field pouring their beers on the field and soaking Jay Buhner with beer, and Lou Piniella pulled the team off the field. In the same game, Jim Leyritz and I were very close, and I went up to him and said, "Dude, you gotta end this." When he hit that home run I remember hugging him at home plate and saying thank you, because we were tired and we knew that we had to fly to Seattle after the game.[76] It was crazy. I think Donnie batted .400 in that series.

When the team went out to Seattle, do you think that those two long games and all the emotion and then the long flight drained the team at all?

---

76. The game had gone 15 innings in the rain. Leyritz's two-run home run won the game for the Yankees 7–5.

Nah, I don't think that. Seattle was a good team. Obviously Randy Johnson was at the top of his game then and they had some lineup, with Griffey Jr., Edgar Martinez, Jay Buhner. They were a strong team. For those five games they were better than us.

Were you surprised when Mattingly retired after that final game against the Mariners?

A little bit. I think he still had a lot more to accomplish and could have easily had another 500 hits. I didn't think he was at the end of his career. He may have thought that it was just time— only the individual knows that. I was surprised, especially after that series that he had, but then again, he might have said, "I'm going out on top." He couldn't have done any more than he did in that series.

AUSANIO, JOSEPH JOHN
Born: December 9, 1965 Kingston, New York
Bats: Right Throws: Right
Height: 6' 1" Weight: 205 lbs.

Year	Team	G	W-L	SV	GS	CG	IP	SO	W	ERA
1994	YANKEES	13	2-1	0	0	0	15.7	15	6	5.17
1995	YANKEES	28	2-0	1	0	0	37.7	36	23	5.73
	Total 2 Years	41	4-1	1	0	0	53.3	51	29	5.57

National Baseball Hall of Fame

JIM MECIR
1996–97

You were from New York. Were you a Yankees or Mets fan growing up?

To tell you the truth, I loved baseball, so I was kind of both. I watched them both. I was probably more of a Yankee fan, but then in the '80s, when the Yankees weren't so good and the Mets started getting good and everybody jumped on their bandwagon, I started having a little disdain for the Mets and I didn't want them to win. [Laughs] I actually found myself rooting for Boston during the series. I liked the old-time Mets. I liked them in the early '70s. Then after that I didn't like them too much. Always a Yankee fan though.

Were you a standout player as far back as high school?

My senior year, yeah, but before that I was kind of small. I was always one of the better players but I wasn't a standout until my senior year. I was always a pitcher.

After high school you went to Eckerd College in Florida, where you enjoyed a nice career. You were chosen third round in 1991 by the Mariners. Did they come and scout you?

Well, you know, as a player they really don't have much contact with you; they were just there. So I never really knew who was there. Sometimes you'd get a tidbit of information that someone was there, but they usually don't come to you and talk to you too much. I know back in high school that the Milwaukee Brewers were looking at me, but at that point I wasn't very polished. You hear bits of information through your coach but they really don't contact you.

When the Mariners did sign you, did you think you had any chance of making the majors?

You know, I really didn't know. Because for me I was always good, but I was also born with a clubfoot, so that was kind of an issue. You hear things like "We don't know if he'll be able to do it with that affliction." I think the game is different now than then. I played for pure enjoyment and loved the game. I know I was better, but growing up you see these players and think, I can't be on that level. Not until college when I was throwing in the 90s and had some good pitches did I think that there was a chance, a very slim chance, but maybe—who knows?

When did you begin throwing the screwball?

In college. My college coach was actually Rich Folkers, a former major leaguer. I saw him teaching a left-hander how to throw it. I guess based on my mechanics I really didn't have a good curve or slider, so I started fooling around with it and it became my pitch.

That was very unusual, for a right-hander to throw the screwball.

Well, because I was born with a clubfoot my mechanics aren't very good. Usually guys drive forward and have some power behind their legs. I kind of pull my upper body sideways to get some power and that allowed me to open up. So that's what allowed me to throw that pitch.

Your advancement through the minors was pretty quick when you were called up to the Mariners in September 1995 and pitched in two games. Were you satisfied with your progress?

My advancement was actually quick because of the second half of my stint in the minor leagues. The first half they didn't protect my arm very good. When I got there they put me in high A right away. I pitched well, but then I started complaining about my elbow and they told me to pitch through it. Then my shoulder hurt. Then even when my shoulder hurt they sent me to the instructional league that year anyway. Then the next year right in spring training I got hurt and I didn't recover my fastball until 1994. There was a point in spring training in '94 where I thought that I could be released because I hadn't really recovered. Then by the end of the spring I threw a couple of pitches that they said were 94 miles an hour and I thought, OK, my arm's back, and now I really have to see what I can do. The two years previously I could only throw 87–88 miles an hour, with no snap on my pitches, so I knew I wasn't going to be very good. So in spring training of '94 I recovered it and I became a reliever. In '94 I was in AA and '95 I was in AAA, then got called up.

You actually debuted as a Mariner on September 4, 1995, at Yankee Stadium[77] and did great, going 3 ⅔ innings and giving up one unearned run. Was it intimidating walking out to that mound at Yankee Stadium?

You never want to say it was downhill from there, but that was the highlight of my career. I was a Yankee fan and one of my favorite players was Don Mattingly, and that was the final month of his career. Even though I got the World Series ring with the Yankees and was in many playoff games with the A's, that was probably the best.

Did you face Mattingly in that game?

Yeah, he went oh for two. Like I said, I couldn't top that after that. Because at that point it's not really a job yet. It's almost like a fan getting to pitch in a game like that. You still have that feeling of, "Oh my God, this is the big leagues."

---

77. Yankees 13, Mariners 3.

How intimidating was that, even though you were a Mariner, a Yankee fan from New York walking out onto the mound at Yankee Stadium?

Well, the strange thing was, it was intimidating before I ever even pitched. I didn't pitch for like three or four days when I got called up, and I remember I didn't sleep well, I hardly ate. When I was throwing in the bullpen I was throwing balls all over the place. Then as soon as I stepped on the mound I was calm and threw like it was any other game. It was very strange.

Did you have family and friends in attendance?

Yes, everybody was there.

After the season (1995) you were traded with Tino Martinez and Jeff Nelson to the Yankees for Sterling Hitchcock and Russ Davis. How did you feel about that?

It was a double-edged sword. My dream as a kid was to wear the pinstripes, but then you also realize that I'm young and I'm trying to get a job, and being with the New York Yankees is not a great place to start. [Laughs] You've got to be there and a stud and do it right away. So it was a bit of a tough two years. Even when I pitched well I was sent down, because somebody like Strawberry is coming off the DL. Or Hideki Irabu—they were paying him a lot of money, so no matter what he was doing, as long as he was healthy he was going to get a job.

In 1996 you went to the Yankees camp in spring training but started the season in Columbus.

Yes, that's correct. I was called up by May.

You pitched in your first game as a Yankee on May 1 in Baltimore at Camden Yards. You came on to start the 10th inning and pitched through the 12th, not giving up a run in three innings. The Yankees eventually won in the 15th inning. Even though you were away this must have been nerve wracking, to be walking out onto a major league field for the first time as a Yankee.

I think that was more intimidating than the first time I pitched in the big leagues as a Mariner at Yankee Stadium, because I'm pitching in a game that really matters. Before that, as a rookie they bring you into games that are blowouts. It's intimidating just pitching, but my bearing on the game wasn't that great. Now I'm expected to do the job when it's extra innings. I pitched three innings. I can't remember what inning it was, but I had bases loaded with two outs and I went 3–0 on Brady Anderson and I struck him out. So that was definitely a big game.

When you were called up for the first time to the Yankees did Torre or Stottlemyre sit you down and talk to you?

Yeah, they talk to you. They bring you in and congratulate you and try to pump you up a little.

A few days later on May 4 you had your debut as a New York Yankee at the stadium. Even though you had pitched there once already as a Mariner, this must have felt different.

Oh yeah, it's unbelievable. It was a tough two years, but I wouldn't change playing for the Yankees for anything. That's just a dream going out there and seeing myself in the pinstripes. It was just amazing. As a kid I used to imagine myself as different Yankees when I'd bat. I'd say I'm Munson or I'm Chambliss or Roy White. It wasn't even like it was really me out there.

So your first game at Yankee Stadium probably didn't go as well as you would have wanted it. You came on in the eighth with the Yankees already losing 7–4 after Jeff Nelson had already blown the save. You got out of the eighth but loaded the bases in the ninth with no outs.

Was that my first time at Yankee Stadium? [Laughs] I remember the situation; I didn't remember that was my first game. I remember I was starting to struggle and Stottlemyre came out and said, "Alright, just relax right here and throw a nice sinker down and away and let him get himself out." I actually threw the pitch that I wanted, a sinker down and away, and he hit it out to the opposite field for a home run.

After that game did Torre or Stottlemyre talk to you to tell you to shake it off, or something along that line?

They talk to you a little bit but at that point in the majors they expect you to anyway. I think you get a talk like that if you're continually struggling. They'll say something after the game like "Don't worry about it," but they don't really call you in and sit you down.

How did the rest of your season in '96 go? The Yankees actually used you in 26 games but then left you off the postseason roster.

Right. Well, my seasons [with the Yankees] weren't that great. Like I said, I was raw. I really didn't exactly know what I was doing at the big-league level yet. I had some really good games, but I also got sent up and down a bunch of times during those two years. I think I started to put pressure on myself, saying I've got to do the job every time to stay there because it was like, no matter what I did it felt like I was coming and going. I put a little too much pressure on myself. I did a lot of fastballs away and screwballs. I don't think I managed the game right. I relied on catchers, and things like that. I really didn't learn how to pitch in the big leagues until I got to the Devil Rays, where they actually gave me a job and I didn't have to worry about getting outs so much and just worry about getting better.

As far as the World Series, I watched it but I didn't feel that I should have been on the postseason roster. Especially that year, I was just trying to get a job and knew I was the 26th guy—anytime somebody went down with an injury I'd be popping back up. Because when you get to the playoffs you usually don't even use your fifth or sixth guy in the bullpen unless there's a blowout. You usually put one of your starters in the pen, so you usually don't even use your whole bullpen. I didn't think I was going to be there. If they had told me that I was on the roster I would have been shocked.

Did you get a World Series ring?

Yes. But I don't think I was there for the ceremony because I started the season again in Columbus.

Who did you pitch to most of the time on the Yankees?

Girardi. He was good, but it's also hard on the catcher because he can't judge what he thinks I should be throwing at times because of the way my stuff works. It's a learning process.

Did you find it was a little difficult in your career having catchers understand you or communicate with you because you were an unusual type of pitcher?

No, I think what it comes down to is, when I myself figured out what I needed to do I just told them and then we got in sync. When I got to the Devil Rays I had John Flaherty and Mike DiFelice and they both worked awesome with me. There were a lot of times after pitching to them for a month or two where I'm thinking, Ok, I don't want to throw this, or I want to pick something else to throw, but they were on the same page with me so there was never a problem.

The 1996 Yankees had an incredible pitching staff, with Andy Pettitte, Jimmy Key, Kenny Rogers, Dwight Gooden, David Cone, Ramiro Mendoza, John Wetteland, Jeff Nelson, Bob Wickman, and Rivera. Were you able to interact with them and gain any benefit from their experience?

Actually, my throwing partner was Wetteland. I learned a lot from him, although he beat me up a lot. We would actually get down and be 60 feet away from each other and throw to each other at full speed with regular gloves on. So he was a maniac. But they would try to help you, even though there was a lot of hazing, but they also sat you down and tried to help you out.

After the 1997 season you were traded to the Red Sox but then quickly chosen in the expansion draft by the Tampa Bay Devil Rays. Did you see this as an opportunity to pitch regularly?

With the Yankees you have to be a pitcher that they think is going get outs consistently right away, because they're the New York Yankees. When I got traded to the Red Sox I was like, "Oh God, this is the same thing." But thankfully they didn't protect me and the Devil Rays took me. I was very unhappy going to Boston because I'd never get a chance to do the job, and maybe not be able to make some errors and still have a job.

I loved going to the Devil Rays. I was actually on my honeymoon in Aruba and I saw it on TV and was unbelievably excited because I knew there that I was probably going to be on the team. Everybody there was young and I had some experience. When I got to spring training they told me that I had a job and to get ready and figure out what I need to do. I didn't have to try out, so that spring I was doing different things—I was throwing more fastballs inside, seeing if my screwball worked pretty good against righties, and other things and I became the pitcher that I wanted to be.

After your 1998 season Yankee GM Bob Watson probably wished he had kept you. It was your breakout year in the majors, going 7–2 in 68 games.

It was a great feeling and it took a lot of weight off my shoulders, because most guys last just a couple of years in the big leagues and after that you don't make enough money and have to get a job. By that time your college education isn't worth as much because you didn't do anything for seven or eight years. It's either all or nothing.

In 1999 you pitched in just 17 games because you were hurt in a collision with pitcher Rick White. Do you remember what happened there?

I have what is called a nonunion fracture of the olecranon[78] in my right elbow. I noticed it in high school because it would hurt when I'd lean on it. A sharp pain would go up my arm. But it would never hurt any other time, not when I was pitching or anything else. It got to the point where I had to do something about it. They showed me an x-ray of it and there's a triangle gap in my elbow, like a wedge. In that gap is just cartilage, not bone.

When I got to the Devil Rays I was just fooling around, nothing big, but I was on the ground and Rick White, who's not very light, was on my legs. I put pressure on my right elbow and it

---

78. The olecranon is a bony projection on the back of the elbow. "Nonunion" means that the fracture has not healed properly.

just snapped, right where that groove was. This was during batting practice, and I was out the rest of the year.

In 2000 you were having another tremendous year (63 games, 10–3) and were traded to the A's on July 28. You were on some great teams in Oakland, but the A's lost the ALDS four consecutive years (twice to the Yankees). How frustrating was that?

I don't think the frustration is so much for four straight years, but two of those years we were up 2–0 and then lost the next three. To me, I think a couple of those teams were World Series teams, but we couldn't do the little things. We needed a couple more Derek Jeter type players that were not only good, but really understood the game. He's invaluable, especially during playoff time. He has intangibles.

In 2001 the A's jumped out to a 2–0 lead in the Division Series against the Yankees, and then came the famous game 3. The Yankees were down two games to zero in the series and won game 3 1–0 while getting only two hits. Mussina pitched brilliantly.[79] Do you remember the Jeter play going down, with Jeremy Giambi being tagged out at home plate?[80]

Oh yeah, because I have to watch it all the time on replays. I didn't have a good view from the bullpen, but we see it all the time. Obviously if he slid he's safe, but what are you going to do?

You were on a team once again that had a very good pitching staff during your time in Oakland. Did you benefit from other members of that staff?

Well, by that time I was actually pretty senior and knew what I was doing. There were a lot of younger guys on that staff.

In 2005 you signed a one-year contract with the Marlins and pitched in a lot of games again (52). Although in your last two years in the majors your record was a combined 1–9, your ERA both years was a full run under the league average and your strikeout to walk ratio was still 2–1. It seems you could have continued to pitch. Did you simply want to retire at that point?

---

79. As did the A's Barry Zito and Mark Guthrie, but that is lost to history.

80. In the bottom of the seventh inning the A's Terence Long hit a line drive down the right field line with Jerry Giambi on first base. It was picked up by outfielder Shane Spencer. Giambi rounded third base and was waved home by the third-base coach. In the meantime, Spencer overthrew the cut-off men. However, shortstop Derek Jeter rushed in, grabbed the ball on a hop with his hand, and flipped it to catcher Jorge Posada. Unaware of the drama taking place, Giambi calculated that he would make it to home easily and failed to slide. In a controversial call, he was tagged out and the Yankees won the game. This is considered by many to be the best play of Jeter's career.

No, I had to. Actually my last four years I struggled big time with knee injuries and just wasn't the same pitcher. As far as the record, that pretty much doesn't count for a setup guy, because usually I only come in a game when we're winning, so I'd only have a chance to lose and I don't have many chances to get a win. From '98 to 2002 I used to pitch one inning plus. My last two years I could only pitch one inning. I couldn't even go a third, sit, and then go back out because my knees were so bad. I think it was going to be my last year anyway in 2005, because my knees were killing me, but it was putting so much pressure on my arm that I tore my rotator cuff in July. I just tried to pitch through it to finish the season. It was only a partial tear and I think it's pretty much healed now, but it takes a full year or more to get back to where it was.

So are you going to make a comeback?

[Laughs] No, my knees didn't come back. They don't heal. There's no ACL, no meniscus, and no cartilage left. Those will never heal.

Who did you room with on the Yankees?

I remember Dale Polly. I really don't remember who else because I was up and down so much. Everybody else was up and down so I roomed with whoever else was up and down.

Ever meet George Steinbrenner?

Ah, yes. I met him once. I only saw him a couple of times.

Did you stay in the game after you retired?

I give private pitching lessons now.

Your dad retired as a captain in the New York City Fire Department after 9/11. Do you have recollections of him taking you to the firehouse as a kid?

He did take me but I remember more going to Madison Square Garden with him to see the cops and the firemen play hockey and stuff like that. I do remember going to his firehouse, but that wasn't as exciting as watching the hockey and boxing! [Laughs]

National Baseball Hall of Fame

MECIR, JAMES JASON
Born: May 16, 1970 Bayside, New York
Bats: Both Throws: Right
Height: 6' 1" Weight: 195

Year	Team	G	W-L	SV	GS	CG	IP	SO	W	ERA
1995	Mariners	2	0-0	0	0	0	4.7	3	2	0.00
1996	YANKEES	26	1-1	0	0	0	40.3	38	23	5.13
1997	YANKEES	25	0-4	0	0	0	33.7	25	10	5.88
1998	Devil Rays	68	7-2	0	0	0	84.0	77	33	3.11
1999	Devil Rays	17	0-1	0	0	0	20.7	15	14	2.61
2000	Devil Rays	38	7-2	1	0	0	49.7	33	22	3.08
2000	A's	25	3-1	4	0	0	35.3	37	14	2.80
2001	A's	54	2-8	3	0	0	63.0	61	26	3.43
2002	A's	61	6-4	1	0	0	67.7	53	29	4.26
2003	A's	41	2-3	1	0	0	37.0	25	16	5.59
2004	A's	65	0-5	2	0	0	47.7	49	19	3.59
2005	Marlins	52	1-4	0	0	0	43.3	34	17	3.12
	Total 11 Years	474	29-35	12	0	0	527.0	450	225	3.77

Getty images

Mike Buddie
1998–99

You were born in Berea, Ohio, which is a suburb of Cleveland, and grew up in Cleveland. So I guess you were an Indians fan?

Absolutely! I was not a Yankee fan. As a matter of fact, when I got the call that I had been drafted by the Yankees I hung up the phone and my parents said, "Who was it?" I said, "What's the one team that you wouldn't want me to get drafted by?" They both said, "The Yankees." [Laughs] But they learned to adjust quickly. [The Yankees] had a history of knocking out the Cleveland Indians for a long time.

Did you play a lot of baseball growing up in Cleveland?

I did. I played a lot of baseball. I played football in the fall and winter, and then I wrestled in the spring and played baseball in the summer. It was probably equal thirds for me—I wasn't a product of this generation, where you've got to play baseball year-round to keep up with all the travel teams. I definitely started young. I'm the youngest of three boys, so when my oldest brother, who was four years older, started doing anything I just kind of tagged along.

While attending St. Ignatius High School you were a two-time state wrestling champion.

Yes.

Did you break your arm in competition?

Yes, I broke my left arm in a wrestling match. It was just a hairline so I didn't miss much.

St. Ignatius's football team won the State Championship in 1988 and you were a tight end on that team as well. You were an all-around athlete.

Yes. It's pretty interesting. I was very good in wrestling and pretty much had my pick of scholarship offers in wrestling. After my junior year I made it clear that I didn't want to wrestle in college. My middle brother was a college wrestler and I'd watch him come home for Thanksgiving and not be able to eat, so I told the college coaches, "Don't waste your time. I don't want to wrestle. I want to play baseball." It was the same for football coaches. I had a couple of Big Ten schools and some other schools interested in me to play tight end and I told them also that I wasn't interested in playing football in college, that I just wanted to play baseball. Fast-forward to my senior year, and the only schools that were interested in me for baseball were Kent State, Akron, Marietta—small Ohio schools. I had a panic because my oldest brother had gone to Duke and my middle brother was in Stanford, and I started thinking, I can't go to Akron. I called the wrestling coach at Northwestern and said to him, "This doesn't appear to be working out. Are you still interested in me?" He said, "Absolutely. We'll give you a scholarship for wrestling and let you walk on to baseball if you want." So I signed a letter of intent to go to Northwestern. To make a long story short, in mid-June, after I had graduated high school, I was just playing summer ball and a couple of scouts saw me and asked me if I would sign if they drafted me. I told them, "Absolutely not. I'm going to college and I'm actually going to wrestle at Northwestern." They both said, "What are you doing? You're throwing 87–88 mph." I said, "Well, nobody offered me a scholarship." They made a couple of phone calls and the next thing I know Wake Forrest calls me and they offered me a scholarship sight unseen. I had never even seen the campus. The thought of getting to come south and play baseball and not have to deal with snow was it. The guys from Northwestern were great. They released me from my letter of intent and I wound up coming to Wake Forrest.

That seems like the right decision—you had a pretty good career at Wake Forrest University.

I really blossomed in college. Since I stopped wrestling and football and really focused on baseball and had some real coaching, I stepped it up pretty quickly. I went from throwing 86 as a high school senior to 91 as a college freshman. I pitched 100 innings—I think I led the team in innings as a freshman. Wake Forrest didn't have a great baseball program at that point, but I got to pitch against Clemson, and Georgia Tech, and North Carolina, who were all very good. That helped—the scouts came to see guys from Clemson and of course they pay attention and notice the guy pitching for the other team. That led to me ultimately being drafted by the Yankees.

Back in '92, as far as the scouts, it was the same faces at most of the games and I had a pretty good feeling of who was interested. They used to do personality interviews and things like that after games. So I was personally spoken to by about 20 different scouts from 20 different teams, and none of them were Yankees. Most of the scouts, as it got close, would say to me that they turned me in for the eighth to twelfth round, and some would say sixth to tenth round. On draft day I was sitting next to the phone and heard nothing all day. At about dinnertime a scout from the Rockies called me and I asked him if he had drafted me. He said no, that he was calling to find out where I went and I told him that I hadn't heard a word. He said that was weird, because he had turned me in for the eighth round and that they were now in the fourteenth round. About half an hour later another scout from the Reds called and said, "Hey, where'd you go?" [Laughs] I told him that I still hadn't heard anything. As it turns out, every team in major league baseball except the Yankees calls you right when they draft you. They have a guy there like an assistant GM who calls. With the Yankees they wait until the end of the day and then they call everybody.

Were you surprised that you went in the fourth round?

I was. Actually, the Yankees had traded away their second- and third-round picks in 1991 to get Mike Gallego, and so I was actually the second player that the Yankees drafted. Derek Jeter was the first. I had spoken to 20 scouts and they had all said the same thing: eighth, ninth, tenth round. I had never had a conversation with any of the Yankees' scouts. Then they're the ones who draft me, and they draft me four rounds higher than I expected to go. I was rewarded for waiting all day for the phone to ring!

I understand that you were an Indians fan but after being drafted did it sink in—Babe Ruth, Mickey Mantle, Whitey Ford, the tradition?

Oh, absolutely. At the time, in 1992, the Yankees were also in that down period when Mattingly was their one bright spot. I actually thought, there's a chance to advance here. I'm not going to be stuck; they're going to be looking for people to help the team. I signed three or four days after the draft—I didn't hold out at all. I couldn't wait to get started. I went to a minicamp in Tampa right away for about two weeks to get back in shape, and then they shipped me up to Oneonta, New York, in the New York-Penn League. I remember the first day going in there and getting a locker, and they hand you your uniform pants. The uniform pants that I had, I looked on the inseam and it had *Winfield* stitched in it. That was the moment that, when you talk about Babe Ruth, when I looked in these pants and said, "Oh ****, these were Dave Winfield's pants." That was one of those moments that was kind of cool.

The Yankees sent you right away to Oneonta (Low A) in 1992. After that you gradually worked your way up to Greensboro (A), Tampa (High A), and Norwich (AA) as a starter. Was it at that point that they switched you to reliever?

I started all five of those years. If you look at my statistics, I was never horrible and never great. I was 10–12 and 12–6. I was just a .500-type pitcher. I stayed healthy and had 30 starts every year, it seemed like. The beauty of staying with one organization as long as I did was relationships with people like Mark Newman and Rob Thompson—guys that were on the low end of the totem pole when I was drafted in '92, and by 1996 had moved up the ladder to front office positions. So they knew me and were very honest with me, and said there are very few Andy Pettittes of the world who come up through the system and get to New York and become a quality starter.

There are two types of starting pitchers in the minor leagues. One, you just fizzle out and they put you in the bullpen because they need an arm in the bullpen. So they let you pitch that year in the bullpen and then they release you. And then two, there are guys they genuinely feel that are better suited for the bullpen, and they convinced me that I was one of those guys.

After the 1996 season the Yankees sent me to the Arizona Fall League. There was a pitching coach out there named Marty DeMerritt. He was actually a pitching coach with the Chicago Cubs at that time. He was instrumental in me turning the corner. He saw my numbers and sat me down and said, "Obviously you have good stuff and you strike out a lot of people, but you're walking a lot of guys." He said, "Take it or leave it: here's my advice to you. While you're here in the AFL for the next two months don't worry about strikeouts, don't worry about ERA, and don't worry about runs. The only thing I want you to do is make the hitters hit one of the first four pitches. We're going to judge you on whether the hitter gets to see more than four pitches. If he does, you failed. If he hits one of the first four pitches for a double off the wall, or you strike him out on three or four pitches, count that as a positive; that's a success." I looked at him and thought he was absolutely crazy. He told me that I'm far enough along in my career where I don't have to try it, but that I should have that mindset to go after hitters and challenge them and try to get them out on the first four pitches. I bought into it and what I did was stop trying to throw that first pitch on the outside corner and was throwing it at the outside half. I had an unbelievable fall. After that I got invited to the Yankees major league camp for the first time. I think I was there for all of two weeks and never got into a game, but it's a big deal going to major league camp. It's one thing to see these guys on TV and another to be in the locker room sitting next to David Cone and you think, you know what? I'm not that different from these guys.

Apparently Joe Torre thought so also. You made the team at the end of spring training in 1998.

Actually I was the last player cut in spring training in '98. They opened the season on the West Coast and I went with the team from Tampa to San Diego, where we had an exhibition game that I pitched in. They went up to Anaheim to open up the season and they put me on a plane back to Tampa because the minor leagues had two more weeks of spring training. I got back to Tampa and threw a couple innings, and they let us start driving north to Columbus. I drove 12 hours and stopped at a hotel. I got a phone call that Mariano Rivera had pulled his hamstring and to go to the airport in the morning and fly out to Seattle to meet [the team].

Did you get much sleep that night?

[Laughs] Absolutely none. I went from Tampa to San Diego, back to Tampa, drove 12 hours, and wound up getting on an airplane in Charlotte, North Carolina, and flew back to Seattle. I got there in the second inning and wound up pitching the eighth inning. Joe Torre liked to get guys right in there. So that was a whirlwind week for me. I was back up for the fourth game of the season.

Had you ever been to New York City before getting called up to the big leagues?

No. The two years that I was at Norwich, when we would break spring training and go north we would drive right through the city. When we would have a day off in AA we could get tickets and go down and see the Yankees play, but my roommate and I decided that we weren't going to go see a Yankees game until we were in uniform. I remember driving over the bridge, but the only time I was there was when we would drive through [New York].

What was it like finally getting to Yankee Stadium and walking out onto that field wearing a Yankee uniform?

[Laughs] Unlike anything I'd ever done in my life. Especially being a rookie on that '98 team that won more games than any other team in baseball history, I had that feeling of, just don't screw anything up. Joe Torre was great. He was just a great manager to play for because he's honest with you. Some people like having smoke blown at them, but I'd get called up and Joe would call me into his office and say, "Hey, look, Jeff Nelson got a herniated disk and they say he's going to need 30 days of rehab, so you're here for 30 days. Whether you throw 25 scoreless innings or give up 25 runs your first three innings, when Jeff's healthy you're going back to Columbus." That took a little pressure off—I knew my role. I pitched well. I didn't pitch horrible and I didn't pitch great. I pitched in a lot of games that we were either winning 13–1 or loosing 13–1. That has its value. If I come in and we're losing 13–1 after three innings, my job is to pitch six innings and not embarrass the team and allow Joe not to have to use one of his go-to guys in a blowout game. That team, there was Chili Davis and Tim Rains in their 20th and 21st season in the big leagues, and Bernie Williams and Jeter. It was basically 24 All-Stars, current and former All-Stars, and me! It was a who's who of All-Star baseball players on that team. Daryl Strawberry was our fifth outfielder. It was amazing—we didn't know how special at that time. The chemistry of that team was just great.

How did you find the New York fans?

One of the funny things about when I progressed and then the Yankees let me go and I wound up signing with the Brewers was getting spoiled as a New York Yankee. After seven full seasons in the minor leagues I finally get called up to New York. Whether we were in Anaheim, or Detroit, or Cleveland, there were 5–6,000 fans in the stands at three o'clock watching us stretch. With my naïveté I'm thinking, this is great, the fans come early to see us in the major leagues. Then I go to Milwaukee three years later and come out to stretch at three o'clock in Houston, and there's four people there. Then it dawned on me that it's just the Yankees.

Talk about Yankee baseball fans being so knowledgeable. I was shagging flies out at Yankee Stadium with Shane [Spencer]. I'd been up a little bit longer than he'd been. He hadn't had that monster August and September yet. When you're shagging flies out at the warning track you've got 500 fans shouting, "Hey, Paul O'Neil, give me that ball!" I was too nervous to ever throw a ball to anybody because I didn't know if rookies were allowed to do this. I'm not going to give away Yankee property. [Laughs] So here I am, I've been recalled from Columbus for 48 hours and I'm not in the program yet, and they look at me and see number 52 and start yelling, "Mike Buddie! Hey, Mike Buddie!" I don't want to turn around and acknowledge them. When you're standing next to Chad Curtis and Joe Girardi you don't want to act like you're big-timing it and turn around and wave to the fans.

You wound up on the Columbus shuttle in 1998 but still had a great year. Splitting the season you went 5–0 with two saves at AAA and 4–1 with the Yankees. How satisfied were you after the season with your performance?

I think I handled it pretty good. I was hoping to travel with the team in the postseason, but I was an alternate and kept at Tampa to throw and stay in shape in case something happened to someone during the ALDS and ALCS. The win-loss record of 4–1 is a bit misleading. I would come into games we were losing 5–1, get two guys out, and our offense would explode and we'd go up 8–5. Then they'd bring in Mariano and I'd get the win. I thought I could have done better. When I watched the Yankees this year on TV and saw the ERAs of some of the guys in the bullpen I thought, what a shame I'm not there now! I'd have fit right in with these guys. That year, though, Ramiro Mendoza had a 3.10 ERA. Graeme Lloyd, Mike Stanton, Mariano—they were all two or below. Even our starting pitchers, Cone and Wells, had great years. Pettitte was phenomenal that year. You look around and everybody has a 3.50 ERA or below, and here I am with a 5.60 and I kind of feel like the weakest link.

I started a game in Oakland when I hadn't started a game in two full seasons. We had a doubleheader in Oakland and we literally had no arms left. Joe asked me to start that game and I gave up five runs in the bottom of the first and I'm sure that he's thinking, "Good grief, what am I going to do? The one guy who I've got who's healthy just gave up five runs in the first." I ended up throwing five scoreless innings after that and getting us through the sixth inning, and we were still losing 5–0. Kenny Rogers started for Oakland that day and we ended up scoring 10 runs in the top of the ninth and wound up winning. I threw 115 pitches that night, which was by far the most I had thrown in several years. Joe came up to me between games and said, "That was really great and I'm proud of you, but we have to take you off the roster and send you to Columbus so we can activate Mike Jurzembek to start the second game." [Laughs]

You're a part of baseball history, being on the 1998 Yankees, but was it frustrating finally making it to the majors at 27 and being on a team that had Andy Pettitte, David Cone, David Wells, Orlando Hernandez, Mariano Rivera, Mike Stanton, Graeme Lloyd, Jeff Nelson, and Ramiro Mendoza? Did you ever feel that you were never going to make it with this team?

Absolutely. I remember being in the minors in 1995 at Norwich and our backup shortstop was a guy named Roger Burnett. He was our backup shortstop at AA and everybody knew that the Yankees system was loaded at that time. We released our backup shortstop from AA and two days later he was starting in Ottawa [for the Expos] at AAA. There was a "woe is me" feeling in the minors, being stuck behind Bernie Williams, and Hensley Muelens, and Gerald Williams, and meanwhile Montreal has nobody in their outfield. What frustrated me was, you'd start to think that you're getting close to breaking through, and the next day in the paper you'd read that we signed a Cuban guy, "El Duque" somebody, and you think you're bumped back down a peg. Then you read that we signed Hideki Irabu. Absolutely, there are times when you think, what do I have to do to get a chance? I can do what Hideki's doing, and for a lot less money. Looking back on it, though, I say thank God, because I got my shot there and I got my shot at Milwaukee.

Did any of your fellow pitchers jump out at you as the best on the staff?

Well, Mariano—he plays a different sport than the rest of us. I played with him in Greensboro in 1993 and even then he was head and shoulders above the rest of us. I used to joke with him all the time that I was twice the pitcher that he is. I've got an 88-mile-an-hour fastball and a hanging slider, and a decent changeup and a curveball. I'm a pitcher. I've got to get people out with slop. I'd tell him, "You're not a pitcher—you throw one pitch. Whether it's down the middle, or up and in, down and away—it doesn't matter; they're not going to hit it. Try getting guys out with what I'm throwing up there. That's real pitching." He was great. To this day he's one of the nicest guys that I ever played with.

I remember watching David Wells throwing in the bullpen. He never hid the fact that he was out until four in the morning, but he'd get out there and throw his bullpen, and he would just hit location after location. His breaking ball was just so sharp. Talk about a guy who was just created to pitch. I think he let on that he wasn't as smart as he was. He used to say, "I just like to throw it up there, and whatever Girardi puts down, I'll throw," but he had a lot more of an idea than he let on. He was somebody who started pitching when he was five, and was somebody that could just roll out of bed and do things with the baseball that were great—and to be a lefty on top of it.

How helpful was your pitching coach, Mel Stottlemyre?

He was good. Big-league pitching coaches spend most of their time with the starters. Mel treated me good and tried to keep me as fresh as he could. If I hadn't pitched in 13 days he knew that I had to get some pitching in, but also that if I pitch too much that will be the day that they need me to throw five innings of relief. It was tough for him to balance. He was a class act. But most of my preparations were with Tony Cloninger, who was the bullpen coach at the time. He was great. He introduced me to the world of scouting reports, and really watching the game to see who's hitting what in case I have to face them later in the game.

On August 30 you were involved in a little controversy. On a Sunday afternoon in front of over 55,000 fans you were ejected for hitting Mariners right fielder Rob Ducey in the eighth inning. The previous inning Scott Brosius had gotten hit. Ken Griffey Jr. led off with a home run against you before you got two outs and then hit Ducey.

I was a guy who never hit anyone in the minors and I hit two guys in the majors on purpose, Ducey being one of them. It was one of those things where Mike Stanton can't do it, because Mike Stanton can't get suspended for four games.

The first guy that I hit in the majors was Tony Phillips in Toronto. The first night Derek Jeter had gone five for five and we beat the Blue Jays 13–3 or something. The second night Roger Clemens drills Jeter in the first at bat right in the ribs. Pettitte was pitching for us and it was an important series. It was a tight 2–1 game and there was just never a spot for Andy to hit anybody. After Pettitte got into some trouble, Stanton came in and they scored some more runs. It was 5–1 and they brought me in for the eighth inning. I got two quick outs with a runner on second, and I just went ahead and hit Tony Phillips. It was payback for Jeter getting hit.

With Ducey, Brosius had gotten drilled *hard* and for some reason or another nobody had gotten a chance to even the score before I came in. The reason that I got ejected was because the first pitch that I threw at him missed him. That's the worst nightmare as a pitcher, because now you're thinking, they suspect that that might have been on purpose and now if I do it again I'm really going to get thrown out. Scott Brosius is still standing there at third base with a purple rib and thinking, "Well great, he threw at him but he didn't hit him." So I threw at him again and hit him this time. We had an 18-game lead at this point so it wasn't a huge deal, but the umpire had to do his job and throw me out. Jeter, Brosius, Martinez—those guys, the veteran leaders—said something to me in the clubhouse and that was all I needed to hear. The guys in the bullpen knew what happened and why it happened, and Tony Cloninger said to me, "You did the right thing, good job," but Joe [Torre] doesn't get involved in that. It was unfortunate that Griffey hit that home run off me, because some fans probably thought I was frustrated that he had done that.

After going 4–1 for the greatest team ever, you probably wouldn't have believed someone if they told you that you had just one win left in the majors. Did you think that you would be back in New York in '99?

I did. You know, baseball is weird because you never know what day is going to be your last. When you grow up playing this sport, living it, breathing it, when you get to the minors it truly takes over your life. You know at some point that your career is going to be over. Mine ended when I had Tommy John surgery in 2003. What's hardest for me at this point is when I went to spring training in '99 and Darren Holmes is slated for that one spot that I'm going to fight for. Then you had Jason Grimsley and Dan Naulty who came to camp that year, and those are two of the guys that the Mitchell Report[81] singled out. Grimsley makes that team and Dan Naulty makes that team. I had options so they sent me back to the minor leagues. At the time I was thinking that both of them are major league veterans and they both earned those spots and they can't send them to the minor leagues. I was fine with it at the time, but you fast-forward five years and both of those guys admitted they were doing steroids at the time. It makes it tougher to swallow.

One of the things that I'm the most proud of is that every time that I got sent back to AAA, I performed. In AAA you would see guys go up to the major leagues and they'd come back down and they'd pout and mope and go into a slump or not pitch well. As depressing as it was to be in New York for a month and then wake up and you're in Toledo, Ohio, I still managed to pitch well.

I got cut at the end of spring training in '99 but thought it was OK, because that's what happened the year before. I pitched in New York a lot but I didn't pitch well the first half of the year, and lo and behold, nobody got hurt.

You did pretty good at Columbus in '99, going 9–2 with a 2.86 ERA, but made it back to the Yankees for only two games.

Yeah, and I really got lucky to get up there for those two games! Billy Conners, who was the minor league pitching coordinator, really fought for me. He told the club to call me up in September and let me have 30 days major league service time and meal money. He convinced

---

81. Released in December 2007, Senator George Mitchell's investigation into the use of steroids in major league baseball named 89 players alleged to have used steroids or other drugs.

somebody to give me that call-up. They had clinched and were getting ready for the playoffs. I just sat in the back and kept my mouth shut and pitched in a couple of meaningless games.

You started 2000 in Columbus [AAA] again but played just six games before being released on June 9. Did it surprise you when the team let you go?

No, not at all. Having been with that organization since '92, in the spring of 2000 it was obvious that they were going in a different direction. I went to spring training and didn't get to pitch nearly as much as I had in the other springs. They were looking for other guys and pretty much pulled the plug on me at that point. As a courtesy during the last week of spring Mark Newman called me in and said, "Here's the deal: we're going to take you off the 40-man roster because we need to sign an extra outfielder named Lance Johnson from the White Sox. We're going to take you off the roster and give him your spot, but we don't want to send you back to Columbus and have you rot. So what we are going to do is try to trade you." When all the teams broke spring training I stayed in Tampa and they told me it shouldn't be long for me to get traded. That's a courtesy that most franchises wouldn't give the guys, but because of our history they were keeping me in the loop. They said the Chicago White Sox and Montreal were interested. I sat in Tampa but the problem was the Yankees had given me my contract, which was if I was in AAA my salary was $16,000 a month. The Expos had a AAA cap that was $10,000 maybe, and their big hang-up was, "If we get him, we have to pay him the amount you signed him to and we can't afford to do that." I just sat in Tampa until one of our starters in Columbus got hurt and they told me that I might as well go up there and start for them. Once he got healthy they told me that they'll just give me my release and I can just sign with anybody.

You weren't unemployed long. The Brewers signed you on June 12. Did you welcome this as an opportunity to get back to the major leagues and play more?

Correct. The Brewers were really struggling in the bullpen in the majors and so I thought from a career standpoint, let's go there. The rest of that summer [2000] was probably the most fun I ever had in baseball. I went to Indianapolis and pitched my way back into shape. It was a veteran team and I was enjoying every day in AAA and for the first time in five years never thought about pitching in the majors. It was refreshing and fun. I didn't have to think, I've got to get two strikeouts every inning so they'll call me back up. We went to the playoffs and won the International League. After that the manager calls me in and tells me that I'm going to Milwaukee. It had never even entered my mind. I was thinking, they're a small-market team that's 29 games out so they're not just going to call people up. I got to go up and pitch the last three weeks in old County Stadium before they detonated it.

An interesting sidebar to your career is that you appeared in the 1999 Kevin Costner film *For Love of the Game*.

That's partially true. What actually happened was Kevin Costner appeared in the 1999 Mike Buddie film *For Love of the Game*. Universal Studios was making this movie and George Steinbrenner insisted that in order for them to use Yankee Stadium, no actors would wear pinstripes—only current or former Yankee players can wear the uniform. Universal called and asked me if I had a head shot. I told them no, I have a baseball card! [Laughs] They told me to fax that to them and I did, and they called me back and said, "OK, we start filming in two weeks."

Six other Yankee organization players joined you for the filming and you played Jack Spellman, the Yankee pitcher who faced Kevin Costner, I believe.

Yes, and sticking with the theme of my career, I got the loss in that game too. The day that the Yankees swept the Padres [to win the 1998 World Series] they started shooting at Yankee Stadium. They put us up at the Waldorf for six weeks. It was the best off-season job I ever had. We were on set for 13 hours a day and I spent most of it either in the weight room or in the clubhouse playing Playstation until they needed us on the set.

I realize that there was a language barrier, but did you get to know Hideki Irabu during your time with the Yankees?

Yeah, I did. His time in New York was pretty stressful because there were a lot of expectations on him. He was a very laid back guy. He may have had a little bit of a shock with how much scrutiny he was going to be under. He wasn't into the whole workout scene [Laughs[—he liked to sit back and smoke cigarettes and when it was his turn to pitch he was ready. His interpreter hung out in the bullpen so we got to know him a little bit. He was a nice guy who came to New York and didn't get off to a great start, and I don't think he ever recovered from it. Flip-flop that and nobody really knew anything about El Duque or even how old he was. He pitched well on their national team and he came out and was just unbelievable for three or four years.

The pitcher with the lowest ERA on the '98 Yankees may surprise some Yankee fans. It was actually Graeme Lloyd (1.67), who beat out Mariano Rivera (1.91). He was an interesting player, having come from Australia. What did you think of him as a reliever?

Of the relief pitchers he was probably the closest to me. He went out of his way more than anybody, going to lunch on the road and doing some off-season stuff, to help me relax a little bit. He was a real free spirit and low-key guy. Yeah, he was a great pitcher. He knew his role and he had a lot of great insight that helped me, like going from different stadium to different stadium.

Like the mounds, some are high and some are low, and just stuff that the normal person doesn't think about.

Are you surprised to see Mariano, Jeter, Posada, and Pettitte still out there 11 years later?

No. Mariano was in such great physical shape and his mechanics were such that he put minimal stress on his arm. In '98 Girardi was the catcher and Jorge was the backup, and then in '99 they flip-flopped. I'm not surprised any of those guys are still there. Jeter in Greensboro in '93 set the South Atlantic League record for the most errors in a season, but they were almost all on throws; he hadn't harnessed it yet. He was an obvious superstar. I can't believe he's still single, but I can believe he's still in New York.

After your retirement you went back to Wake Forrest and completed your degree 12 years later and stayed on there as a staff member.

Yes, tuition had gone up quite a bit. I'm the Assistant Athletic Director. To be honest, my thought when I signed with the Yankees was to be a coach when my playing days were over. My career lasted a lot longer than I thought it was going to as a player.

My son was born in 2000 and my daughter was born in 2003, and at that point I thought my career was probably done now that I hurt my elbow. I looked and all these coaches that were mentors to me and that I thought I would have a similar career path to and they were divorced. I had asked so much of my wife from the time that I had gotten drafted and realized that it's just a tough lifestyle to raise a family in.

Did you get back to Yankee Stadium this year (2008)?

I did. I'm still in touch with a couple of front-office people who were able to buy some tickets for me. In my roll as a fund-raiser [at Wake Forrest University] I try to get up to the city once or twice in the summer and I'll buy six or eight tickets for a Yankee game and take some of our donors or Wake Forrest alumni. It's a blast getting to see the other side of it. When you're a baseball player you never see what's going on. You never see the people walking up to the stadium in the streets and drinking beer and cheering for the Yankees two hours before the first pitch. I'd love to have been Andy Pettitte, but I have the luxury of being able to take the subway and walk around at Yankee Stadium, and nobody has any idea who I am or that I ever played. I can walk into the memorabilia shops and see the picture of the '98 team and there I am.

I've actually got a great story about the team picture. I'd gotten called up the fourth day of the season and stayed for 20 days, then went back down to AAA for ten days and got called up again and was there for a month, and went back down for three weeks. It was that kind of a season. One time Jeff Nelson had a herniated disk and I was in New York for 40 days. I pitched 21 innings and I think I gave up two or one earned run. I really hit my stride and won two games during that call-up. I was always one of the first people at the park, because when you're a rookie you don't want to be late or appear lazy. I got to the park at about twelve thirty and was working out when I got the dreaded tap on the shoulder from the clubhouse attendant: "Joe needs to talk to you." I went into Joe's office and he said, "Jeff's back and we're sending you back to AAA. You did a good job and I'm sure we'll see you again." At that point it had already happened to me five times that season and I had finally really pitched well and the hope crept in that maybe I'm staying this time. I was frustrated. I went out to my locker and I was still the only guy there. I had a flight that night for Rochester, where the team was. I flung my bag over my shoulder and was headed out and Darryl Strawberry walks in. He and I were at totally different places in our careers but we always went to chapel on Sundays. Darryl says, "What are you doing? Where are you going?" I told him that I'm headed back to AAA for the fifth time this season. He said, "Hold on, today is team picture. Think about this. This is a team picture that you may want to be in. Don't get in a cab, just think about it for a few minutes." I walked back in and went into Joe's office and asked if he would mind if I stuck around for the team picture and he said he hoped that I would. I stayed for the picture and then grabbed my bag and left. At the time I didn't think anything of it at all, but now I'm glad I ran into Darryl Strawberry because as anonymous as I am, I can walk into any mall in the U.S. that has a memorabilia shop and look at the 1998 World Series Championship picture and say, "Hey, there's me." I was feeling so sorry for myself that I almost wasn't in it.

Are you looking forward to visiting the new Yankee Stadium?

Yes, I am. It's funny, when I was there in '98 was when a rafter fell through. I remember coming to the stadium and someone saying, "Hey, the game's cancelled." I'm thinking, what's that about? It's beautiful, 82 degrees and sunny. There was the talk about them putting a new Yankee Stadium in Manhattan. I said, "You guys are crazy. This is Yankee Stadium. They'll never rebuild Yankee Stadium." Now here I am eating my words. I just never thought that stadium would be replaced, but I will definitely be there and check out the new stadium.

BUDDIE, MICHAEL JOSEPH
Born: December 12, 1970 Berea, Ohio
Bats: Right Throws: Right
Height: 6' 3" Weight: 215

Year	Team	G	W-L	SV	GS	CG	IP	SO	W	ERA
1998	YANKEES	24	4-1	0	0	0	41.7	20	13	5.62
1999	YANKEES	2	0-0	0	0	0	2.0	1	0	4.50
2000	Brewers	5	0-0	0	0	0	6.0	5	1	4.50
2001	Brewers	31	0-1	2	0	0	41.7	22	17	3.89
2002	Brewers	25	1-2	0	0	0	39.7	28	21	4.54
	Total 5 Years	87	5-4	2	2	0	131.0	76	52	4.67